Learn to "Make Your Own Medicine"

In this time of transition for ourselves and the planet, the energies of the earth are reawakening in the consciousness of humankind. Now, possibly more than ever before, we are called to deepen our personal Nature connection. Often, we find that the paths we follow are not really our own. We may have spent a great deal of time following the teachings of someone else only to find ourselves misdirected on our journey to Truth. Now is the time to follow the teacher within. Only this inner teacher can truly direct us on our personal paths. When we listen to the wisdom of our inner guide, we are able to stand in the center of our own power. Like the shaman, we can then travel on our own paths, make our personal Earth Walk, follow our highest Spirit Walk.

Presented in what Amber Wolfe calls "cookbook shamanism," *In the Shadow of the Shaman* shares recipes, ingredients, and methods of preparation for experiencing some very ancient wisdoms—wisdoms of Native American and Wiccan traditions, as well as contributions from other philosophies of Nature, as they are used in the shamanic way. Ms. Wolfe encourages us to feel confident and free to use her methods to cook up something new, completely on our own. This blending of ancient formulas and personal methods represents what Ms. Wolfe calls "Aquarian shamanism."

In the Shadow of the Shaman is designed to communicate wisdom and information in the most practical, direct ways possible, so that the wisdom and the energy may be shared for the benefit of all. Whatever your system or tradition, you will find *In the Shadow of the Shaman* a valuable book, a resource, a friend, a gentle guide and support on your journey. Dancing in the shadow of the shaman, you will find new dimensions of Spirit.

About the Author

Amber Wolfe is a psychotherapist in private practice. She combines her twenty years of training in psychology, anthropology, and sociology with a lifetime of attunement to, and study of, the ways of Nature and earth wisdom.

Having lived in the Far East and Polynesia, and having traveled to many other areas of the world, Amber has had the opportunity to learn from many different cultures. Like the shamans of old, she strives to "make her own medicine" by blending the wealth of wisdoms and experiences encountered on her life journey into a workable potion for psychological growth and spiritual development. In her work with clients and workshop participants, she encourages others to find and follow their own paths to wisdom.

Amber is a high priestess in the Celtic traditions of the Craft of the Wise, and she is the creator of some guided imagery tapes designed to evoke and support the quest for spirituality and Nature awareness. She is currently working on several projects exploring the ancient ways of earth wisdom and the psychological benefits of myth.

To Write to the Author

We cannot guarantee that every letter written to the author can be answered, but all will be forwarded. Both the author and the publisher appreciate hearing from readers, learning of your enjoyment and benefit from this book. Llewellyn also publishes a bi-monthly news magazine with news and reviews of practical esoteric studies and articles helpful to the student, and some readers' questions and comments to the author may be answered through this magazine's columns if permission to do is included in the original letter. The author sometimes participates in seminars and workshops, and dates and places are announced in *The Llewellyn New Times*. To write to the author, or to ask a question, write to:

Amber Wolfe
c/o THE LLEWELLYN NEW TIMES
P.O. Box 64383-888, St. Paul, MN 55164-0383, U.S.A.
Please enclose a self-addressed, stamped envelope for reply, or $1.00 to cover costs.

About Llewellyn's New Worlds Spirituality Series

Spirituality may be best defined as the attainment of the highest aspects of human character in relationship to the Divine. In the past, this attainment was most often under the control of fixed doctrines and hierarchical religious structures. Today, however, this quest for spirituality has become more of an individual process. Spirituality has become a process of making a personal connection to the highest, most divine aspects of Self.

One of the strongest concepts, basic to the quest for spirituality in modern times, is the deep recognition of the unity and interrelatedness of all aspects of life. While this concept may have been given lip service in the past, it is being practiced in the present. We are indeed living in a new world of awareness, consciousness, and connectedness.

Ancient wisdom, which predates the teachings of most organized religions, speaks of this same great unity of life. Often this is described as a web, or weaving, of which we are all an active, creative part. Even modern physics has come full circle to meet ancient mysticism with its "new physics" concept of a tissue of events connecting all life. Spirituality has become the domain of each individual in full awareness of his role, and his function in the weaving of life.

As we, too, have come full circle, we have begun to view ancient wisdoms and forms of spirituality with new, and renewed, interest. Many of these ancient spiritual forms carry the message of direct connection to the Divine that we seek today. Moreover, they connect us directly to the web of life by reacquainting us with Nature, with Spirit, and with our most personal, divine Self. Rather than doctrine, these ancient spiritual forms provide direction; rather than dogma, they give us decisive power in our own lives.

In a new world of spirituality, we turn back to ancient forms such as shamanism, Wicca, and earth wisdoms to reclaim sovereignty over our own spiritual lives. We relearn ancient ways so that we can follow our own path and make a direct connection to the most divine aspects of Self, Nature, and Spirit. Our path, we see now, is one active thread in the great weaving of life we call the universe. And our renewed awareness of our function as part of this weaving shows us that we are both the weaving and the weaver. In the new world we share, we find that the quest for spirituality is a personal responsibility— one with positive power and with results to be shared by all.

Other Products by Amber Wolfe

Audio Tapes
Rainflowers
Shamana
Moon Dancing, with music by Kay Gardner

Llewellyn's New Worlds Spirituality Series

IN THE SHADOW OF THE SHAMAN

Connecting with Self, Nature, and Spirit

Written and Illustrated

by

Amber Wolfe

1991
Llewellyn Publications
St. Paul, Minnesota, 55164-0383, U.S.A.

First Edition
Fifth Printing, 1991

International Standard Book Number: 0-87542-888-6
Library of Congress Catalog Number: 88-29388

Cover Painting: Victoria Poyser-Lisi
Illustrations: Amber Wolfe
Book Design: Anne Holm, Brooke Luteyn, and Jack Adair

Library of Congress Cataloging-in-Publication Data
Wolfe, Amber, 1950–
   In the shadow of the shaman: connecting with self, nature, and spirit/ written and illustrated by Amber Wolfe.
   p. cm — (Llewellyn's new worlds spirituality series)
   Bibliography: p.
   ISBN 0-87542-888-6 : $12.95
   1. New Age movement. 2. Shamanism. I. Title. II. Series.
BP605.N48W65 1988
299'.93—dc19   88-29388
                                                                      CIP

Llewellyn Publications
A Division of Llewellyn Worldwide, Ltd.,
P.O. Box 64383, St. Paul, MN 55164-0383

For Danu-Bridget—White Goddess, Mother Muse,
Source of Inspiration and Creativity.
May your sacred fires burn brightly within us.
and
For the Wolf—Trailblazer, Brigand,
Revolutionary Spirit and Teacher of Earth Wisdom.
May you walk in harmony among us.

Acknowledgments

I am grateful for the support, encouragement, and contributions of the following people, without whom *In the Shadow of the Shaman* could not have manifested as it did. Thank you.

I.   For Bruce, my gentle bear in a pack of wild wolves. I love you. Sacred partner.

For Cameron and Caitlin, my children, pagan babies.

For my clan, my Craft circle, my core: Bob Rafferty (Pech Nuada), Kathy Matledge, Joan Oshman, David Fernalld (Aric), and now in spirit—Thomas-John Grieves.

II.   Friends, teachers, fellow travelers:

Cindy Haskett, Shirley Schear (Healing Cloud), Suzy Fernandez, Hilary Karp, Janie Veth, Laura Rutherford Steuhrk, Kathy and Marvin Longshore, Debbie Cates Trahan (Panther Woman), Ted Munger, Carol Alford, Diedra Liberato, Lucia Bettler, Kay Gardner, Chuck Lawrence, Oh Shinnah, Fastwolf, Mary Grimes (Thunder Woman), Lynn Andrews, Frank and Pat Dorey—now in spirit.

And to Timothy Leary for making his Earth Walk now.

III. Special acknowledgment is given to:

Twylah Nitsch—Yehwehnode (She Whose Voice Travels on the Wind), Wolf Clan mother of the Seneca Nation—for wisdom and strength of purpose on many levels. Gentle Earth Woman and Grey Eagle (Elaine and Hal Hubbard), four winds forever. And to the Seneca Wolf Clan. Walk on.

IV.   An ongoing thanks is given to "Clan Llewellyn," who have been blazing trails and sharing wisdom for the entire 20th century—and beyond. Thanks for the opportunity to be a small part of that sharing. It is an honor.

For support and faith above and beyond any author's expectations, I wish to thank Nancy Mostad and David Rogers of Llewellyn. Blessed, blessed be.

V.   Thanks go to Jeanne Tiedemann for her part in the preparation of this manuscript. Here's hoping I didn't "jar your psyche" too often.

Contents

Preface

The path of the shaman is the path of the Self in deepest connection to Nature. Shamanism deals with the purest forms of Nature energies and elements. The shaman stands centered in balance at the core of all energies and all worlds. The relationship that the shaman has to these worlds is the most sacred communion with Nature. It is a most personal connection.

In ancient times, most people were unable to deal directly with the energies of the other worlds. Survival was most difficult, and few others but the shaman could be spared to explore the Nature wisdoms. Today we have evolved in our brains and in our environment to a place of mass communication and technological advances that give us freedom to learn. Now we turn our hearts and minds back to the messages of Nature. We seek once again to journey to the other worlds of Nature—and of our selves. We choose to follow the path of the shaman.

We are mapmakers charting our own path. The path of the shaman leads us in and out of the chaos of pure Nature energies—a collage of elements spinning around us. For a moment in time this collage of chaos crystalizes into a clear vision. We chart our experiences and take our bearings. We travel on, just as the shamans of old.

Some of us travel to learn only for ourselves, and that is enough. We are each wheels spinning within the greater wheels of life. Some of us travel to learn and teach. We grasp at shadows in the darkness, hoping to catch a wisdom to share. Sometimes we are able to do this. Then we share the knowledge sacredly in hopes that others may also be encouraged to learn.

And this we know all too well, what we share is no more or less than our own soul's journey. The shadows we grasp, like the shadows we cast, are none other than our own. When we share our shadowy glimpses of the other worlds, we offer nothing less than a part of our own soul's wisdom. This we do to mark the way for other souls' journeys. The shadow of the shaman is the soul of the shaman. The soul of the xii / In the Shadow of the Shaman

shaman is the soul of Nature.

When we share our journey, as shamans have done throughout the ages, we are sharing sacred wisdom. Like the ancient books of shadows handed down carefully from one person of wisdom to another person of wisdom, we share the knowledge. We cannot share the experience, only tell of it. The experience is yours to find.

In the Shadow of the Shaman follows the ancient tradition of shamans, wizards, wise women, sorcerers, and sorceresses who charted their journeys and shared the wisdom. This book is a manual, a journal, a cookbook of sorts. It is a book of the shadows of one person traveling along the path of the shaman. One person using wisdoms old and new as traveling companions in the journeys to all the worlds of Nature—and beyond.

It is for you to add to this book of shadows or cast it out and make your own. The path of the shaman is the path of the Self. Only you can map the path of your Self. So use the wisdom offered herein to give you strength on your journey. When the reading is done, go out and make your own wisdom in the world. Find the soul of Nature.

In the Shadow of the Shaman is a map of many levels. All worlds are blended, separated, explored, and blended again. All the worlds are shown here with the clarity and the chaos that mark the path of the shaman.

May the shadows cast here encourage your own shamanic journey—journey of the soul.

Amber Wolfe
February 1988
Wolf Moon
Savannah, Georgia

Introduction
Understanding Shamanism

The world of the shaman is constantly moving. Everything in the shaman's world has its own special vibration, unique energy and power. The quest of the shaman is to achieve attunement with these vibrations and familiarity with Spirit. To accomplish this is to attain power. Still, the shaman knows that this cannot be pursued, only received. Power is a gift. That is the first wisdom of shamanism.

The shaman taps directly into the purest forms of Nature's energy. The shaman deals with the elemental forces of Air, Fire, Water, and Earth. All of the energies of all the worlds spin like wheels on the shaman's path. The upper world of the sky journeys, the lower worlds of the earth journeys and the middle world of humankind all connect on the path of the shaman.

All of the worlds of Nature spin like wheels for the shaman. The world of animals, the world of plants, the world of minerals and the world of humans are all spinning wheels on the path of the shaman. All worlds spin and vibrate for the shaman. To deal with these directly, the shaman must know each vibration. He must ride the wheel of each world in order to feel its vibration and direct its power. This is another wisdom of the shaman. The shaman must experience the worlds by riding the wheels of their vibrations. This brings attunement with the deep shamanic energies of Nature.

All the while, the shaman must stay centered and balanced in the midst of the chaos of spinning wheels of energy and vibration. The shaman does this by remaining rooted in personal connection to the earth. From this Earth connection, the shaman is able to reach into Spirit. In this way, the shaman becomes a channel between the energies of the earth and Nature and the energies of Spirit. Like a living tree, the shaman is rooted deep in the earth, reaching and growing into Spirit. The shaman is an Earth connection; the shaman is a connection to Spirit.

In ancient times, the task of the shaman was to be the connection for the people in their dealings with the other worlds. The abilities of the shaman were both feared and revered. To maintain balance in the middle world of humankind while connecting to the other worlds of Nature energies, the shaman often lived apart from others. The path of the shaman was a solitary one. The shaman was the sacred link to the wisdom of Nature and Spirit.

Shamanism has begun to reemerge in the world today. The shaman, revered in antiquity and ridiculed in an age of technology, is being viewed with a new and renewed interest. In the expanded chaos of blended wisdom that we find today, the path of the shaman arises to connect us back to the earth. We seek the balance of the shaman in the midst of rapid change and shifting energies around us.

We expand our consciousness and reach towards Spirit. Still we miss the rooted connection to our Mother Earth. So we seek the ways of the shaman to find balance for ourselves and for the planet. This is shamanic balance for the good of all. We seek the gift of personal power and find it in our love of Nature. We find balance in the wisdom of the earth; we find strength in Spirit.

Like the shamans of old, we may learn to ride the wheels within wheels, which are all the vibrations of the worlds of Nature. We learn to ride the wheels of our Self first and find our own center. From this personal center, we may walk in balance on the path of the shaman. Each aspect of our Self, and each aspect of Nature we come to know, bring us closer to the center of our own power.

As we come to know ourselves and the deep, pure energies of Nature, we develop the consciousness of a shaman. We come to know that Nature has many wisdoms for us all to share and learn. Shamanic consciousness gives us the perception and attunement to understand the wisdoms and the faith to keep us strong on our path. We accept wisdom for the worlds we can see in concrete form. We accept wisdom that comes to us in images and dreams from the worlds of abstract form. We accept wisdom that comes to us purely, without sensation or image, from Spirit—directly into our hearts.

We live in a time of great blending. Most of us are free to choose our own paths and make our own medicine from the many wisdoms offered. All choices are arbitrary, with freedom of mind and consciousness. We make our own maps along our paths. We blend wisdoms from every source to deepen our connection to Self, to Nature, and to Spirit. We come to know that only our experience can bring us shamanic wisdom. Only our own experience can illuminate us, protect us, and initiate us.

We are Aquarian shamans. We came into this Earth Walk ready to reconnect humankind and Nature. We were born with abilities barely dreamed of by the shamans of old. We are here to reawaken the shamanic consciousness of humankind. This consciousness lies deep within us all, sleeping fitfully in the midst of a nightmare of disconnection. It has already awakened in many of us. It will continue to awaken in many more. Each person who awakens his own shamanic consciousness awakens those of others—without a sound, without a fuss. That is still another wisdom of shamanism.

In the wheels within wheels within wheels, which is the universe of the shaman, each new wheel turning is felt. Just by staying centered in our own power and riding the wheels of Self, Spirit, and Nature all alone, we can deepen all of humankind's connection to the shamanic energies. This is an old truth and an old choice of many shamans who chose to live apart from others. This is a choice we have today as we begin to walk on the shamanic path.

We can choose the isolation of the shamans of old, if that is how our inner wisdom guides us. We may also choose the path of the medicine person who dwells in the center of the community she serves. In this time of blending, we may exercise our rights as Aquarians and create our own role on the shamanic path. We may bring the deep inner focus of the shaman together with the shared outward focus of the medicine person. We may create Aquarian shamanism. That is our choice. We live in a time of conscious choice.

The gifts of Nature and Spirit are available to everyone. Resources abound to help you on your own shamanic path. Seek the information and wisdom you need from teachers in all the worlds of Nature. Listen to the wisdom of your inner council. Follow your heart and stay centered in your personal power. That is the way of the shaman. Be the living tree, connected to the earth, reaching for Spirit, channeling the energies of Nature. You are already walking in the shadow of the shaman.

This book has been designed to create a framework from which to make connections with the shamanic energies of Nature, Self, and Spirit. It is based on several very ancient systems using the energies and vibrations of the four cardinal directions and their elements and helpers.

South	Fire	Protectors
West	Water	Initiators
North	Earth	Connectors
East	Air	Illuminators

Know that as you begin your journey you already have at least four sacred helpers from Spirit. You are never alone on your Earth Walk. You are always surrounded with the gift and the power of Love.

Four Winds Wheel

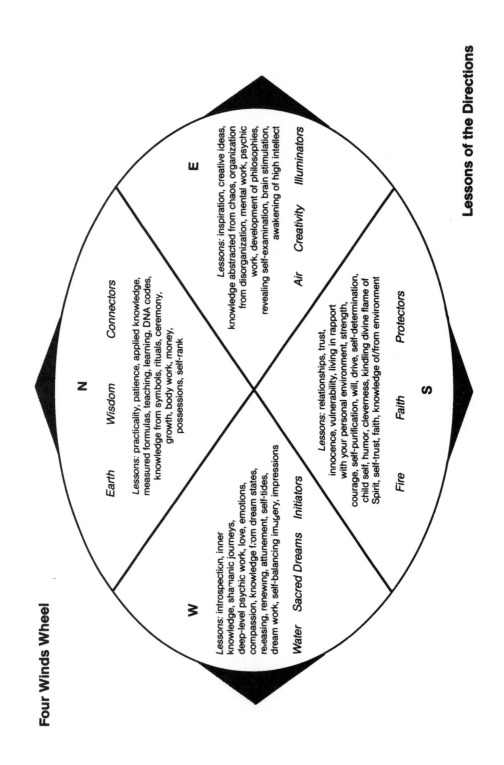

Lessons of the Directions

N — Earth — Wisdom — Connectors

Lessons: practicality, patience, applied knowledge, measured formulas, teaching, learning, DNA codes, knowledge from symbols, rituals, ceremony, growth, body work, money, possessions, self-rank

E — Air — Creativity — Illuminators

Lessons: inspiration, creative ideas, knowledge abstracted from chaos, organization from disorganization, mental work, psychic work, development of philosophies, revealing self-examination, brain stimulation, awakening of high intellect

S — Fire — Faith — Protectors

Lessons: relationships, trust, innocence, vulnerability, living in rapport with your personal environment, strength, courage, self-purification, will, drive, self-determination, child self, humor, cleverness, kindling divine flame of Spirit, self-trust, faith, knowledge of/from environment

W — Water — Sacred Dreams — Initiators

Lessons: introspection, inner knowledge, shamanic journeys, deep-level psychic work, love, emotions, compassion, knowledge from dream states, releasing, renewing, attunement, self-tides, dream work, self-balancing imagery, impressions

Riding The Wheels

Sacred Spinning Woman,
Spin the wheels for me.
For I am on a journey,
Many worlds to see.
I shall ride the wheels of Fire,
Water, Earth, and Air.
Sacred Spinning Woman,
Can you show me where?

Sisters of the Wyrd,
Weave a cloak for me.
For I am on a journey,
Between the worlds to be.
I shall ride the wheels
Of faith and dreams,
Of wisdom and free mind.
Sisters of the Wyrd,
Can you tell me what I'll find?

Witches of the Winds,
Clear the way for me.
For I am on a journey,
The worlds of Self to see.
I shall ride the wheels of life
To Spirit and beyond.
Witches of the Winds,
Send helpers, true and fond.

Grandmother Crystal Woman,
Light the night for me.
For I am on a journey,
In shadow worlds to be.
I shall ride the wheels of vision,
Strength and harmony.
Grandmother Crystal Woman,
Hear me, touch me, heal me.

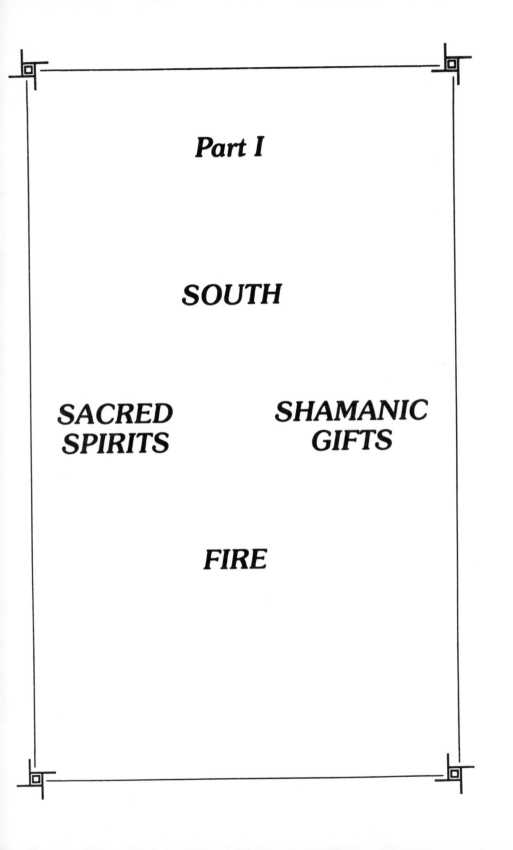

Part I

SOUTH

SACRED
SPIRITS

SHAMANIC
GIFTS

FIRE

ATTRIBUTES OF THE SOUTH

The **Element** of the South is Fire.

The **Wheel of the South** is the wheel of
     Faith and Trust
     Elusiveness
     Innocence
     Vulnerability
     Strength
     Protection
     Relationships—with others, with self, with Nature

The **Energy** or pace of the South is quick, rapid fire.

The **Journey of the South** is the journey of purification.

The **Traditional Colors** of the South are
     Red
     Orange
     Scarlet
     Yellow
     White
     and the Blue of flame

Some **Sacred Spirits** of the South are
     Bridget—goddess of the inner flame of life and
       creation
     Pele—goddess of purification and upheaval
     Vulcan—god of the forge of faith
     Mars—god of strength in conflict
     Hestia—goddess of strength in women
     Michael—archangel of the South, warrior of the
       sacred flames

Djinn—servant of Michael, great Fire giant, for protection

Salamanders—elemental spirits of Fire, ruled by Djinn

Adonai—elemental king of Fire

Some **Animals** of the South are

Porcupine—for protection and to prick you into
action

Badger—for protection in conflict

Coyote—for protection in tricky situations

Fox—for elusiveness and innocence

Hawk—for protection and relationships

Mouse—for vulnerability and elusiveness

Cats—of all sorts, for what Mark Twain called that
"mixture of innocence and sin"

Some **Minerals** of the South are

Pink Carnelian—for kinships and relationships

Red Carnelian—for strength and protection, faith

Gold Amber—for clarity in relationships

Red Amber—for courage, faith

Amber Calcite—for relationships, trust

Blue Amber—for shamanic journeys of purification,
inner flame

Yellow and Gold Fluorite—for personal protection
on journeys

Citrine—for clarity and purification

Fire Opal—for deep inner vision, physical purification
and cleansing

Steel—for strength in trials of life

Iron Ore—for courage, protection

Lava—for purification and upheaval

Some **Plant World Helpers** of the South are

Purification Incenses	*Guardian Incenses*
Sage	Sweetgrass
Juniper	Myrrh
Thyme	Frankincense
Clove	Dragon's Blood Resin
Cinnamon	
Cedar	

Some **Human World Helping Activities** of the South are

Expressive Art	Exercise
Dance	Physical Communication
Drama	Sensuality
Movement	Love

Helping Thoughts for the South:
> In Innocence I am born,
> In Faith do I grow,
> In Strength am I purified,
> In Protection I walk.

Riding the Wheel of the South

We sit in circle, wisps of sage and cedar smoke drifting among us. We begin to steady our breath as the drumming softens and slows to the rhythm of a heatbeat.

"Look for the child within," we are told. "Journey inward, and awaken the sleeping child."

I reach deep into my memories, carefully releasing the cords of adulthood that snag me along the way—analysis, expectation, responsibility. I seek the free child spirit. Then I find myself standing in front of an antique dresser in my grandmother's house. I am eye level with the dresser top, unable to see more than a few strawberry curls of hair in the mirror.

On the dresser is a jewelry box, pale pink with gold flourishes. Standing on my tiptoes, I can just reach it. I take the box down from the dresser and sit on the floor, cradling it in my lap. I unhook the clasp and lift the lid very slowly, hoping to catch the ballerina inside unaware. But she is ready for me, as always, and begins to spin to the music from the jewelry box. I watch her for a few moments. Her gold hair and pink net tutu reflect lights in a mirror inside the lid.

I take my gaze away from the ballerina and examine the treasures inside the box. There, among the pearlized popbeads and an old lipstick tube (Revlon Love That Red!), are other prizes. I find bluejay feathers, a bit of a robin's eggshell, a four-leaf clover, and a variety of special stones, flowers, and twigs. I reach into the pocket of my Dale Evans cowgirl shirt and pull out a small pine cone. It is incredibly tiny, even in my child-sized hands. I carefully nestle it into a bed of dried gardenias from the summer before. I can still catch a bit of their fragrance, deep and sweet, a flower of love.

I hear myself being summoned to return from this journey. The drumbeat is faster now, insistent.

I carefully close the lid of the jewelry box and put it back in its proper place. I stand on the very tips of my toes and shove the box up against the dresser mirror, where I can no longer reach it. I am satisfied that it will be safe in the protective fortress of my grandmother's dresser.

I breathe deeply and return from my journey to the child within. I am complete in the knowledge that the free child still dwells in my heart. She walks beside me on my Nature path. I can see her reflected, like the little ballerina, in all of the Nature treasures that make their home with me now.

The Wheel of the South is the wheel of the child. With the faith, innocence, and trust of a child, we begin our relationships with the sacred objects that Nature brings us.

> But how do we start?
> Where do we go?
> What can we do to find our sacred power objects?

We ask these questions with the excitement and the anticipation of a child. We begin our shamanic path with the eager fire of a child. Now we are ready to receive from ourselves. We are ready to receive from Nature, which is the source of all that we have on earth. Knowing that, we begin.

Of all the objects you have, the most sacred is yourself. Every other object is a reflection of yourself. Every sacred object reflects your strengths, your vulnerabilities, your joys, and your needs. Each object is sacred only in that it provides a symbolic link between your highest Self and the source of all life and wisdom, in Nature and in Spirit.

Power does not reside in an object. Power cannot be bought, sold, or even chosen in a sacred object. Power is. Power abides. Power can flow through a sacred object as it flows through you. Power can flow around you, but you cannot hold it fast. No one can. No object can. Power is a gift that comes as you walk any shamanic or magical path.

Honor power for its gifts to you and do not seek to possess it. It will walk beside you on your journey. The gifts you may bring to power as you ride the Wheel of the South are faith and trust.

Twylah Nitsch, Wolf Clan mother of the Seneca Nation, says that we are always in the South. That way we are able to receive wisdom in faith and trust. Here is a little ceremony to help you on your South journey. Use it as you feel the need.

South Ceremony

Stand facing the North. Consider that when you are facing North you are actually standing in the South. The South is the place of strength, protection, faith, and trust. The South is the place of the Self. Consider the strength of faith and protection. Consider that you are standing in a place of faith in the South as you face wisdom in the North.

Feel the vibration of receiving wisdom from a place of faith in your Self.

Feel the vibration of Self, Nature, and Spirit. Receive these vibrations in trust and faith. Feel the vibrations of strength and protection.

As you stand facing North, you have the West to your left and the East to your right.

Consider the vibrations of the West on your left. These are the vibrations of inner wisdom. Receive these vibrations with faith and trust from your place in the South. Know that you have the strength and protection of the South to help you explore your inner wisdom.

Now consider the vibrations of the East to your right. These are the vibrations of illumination. These are the vibrations of creative flow. Receive these vibrations of illumination and creativity with faith, trust, and strength from your place in the South.

Now consider your relationship with the vibrations of the South. As you stand in the South, you stand in the center of your Self.

Stand in faith—stand in trust—stand in protection—stand in strength.

From the center of your Self, you may journey in harmony and balance. Consider the path you follow and your life journey.

Consider your shamanic path. Go in faith.

Chapter 1

SACRED OBJECTS

One of the most enjoyable aspects of the shamanic path is finding and working with the sacred objects in Nature. Everything has a vibration and an energy that is unique in Nature. As you learn to find and work with objects, you will develop a deeper sensitivity to their vibrations. Even objects that seem very similar, such as two stones of the same kind, will have a slightly different vibration from each other. When you begin to sense this, you have already opened yourself to deep levels of shamanic consciousness.

Truly all objects are sacred objects since they are gifts from Nature. We have many names for these objects:

medicine objects	power objects
sacred helpers	power animals
spirit animals	allies
spirit helpers	totem helpers
talismans	Craft objects
magical tools	ritual items

The list could go on and on. Technically, only those objects with which you have developed a deep, shamanic connection are considered to be your totem objects. These totem objects reflect your own shamanic abilities, or your medicine. Since this book is about learning to walk on the shamanic path, and to develop a shamanic connection to Self, Nature, and Spirit, we can simplify the matter and use the term *totem* to include all sacred objects from the four worlds of Nature, and from Spirit. This will be a good reminder of the kind of

relationship we wish to develop with our totems. A totemic relationship with an object is one in which you work with the vibration and the energy that it represents to you.

The first place to start looking for totems is in your own home. Take some time with all of the treasures from Nature that you already have.

> Consider why you collected them.
> Consider what they represent to you.
> Consider what they reflect in you.

This is the beginning of a totemic relationship.

Another clue to finding totems is to explore the environment around you.

> Where do you choose to live?
> Where do you choose to visit?
> What places in Nature give you the deepest sense
>   of connection?

Answering these questions will direct you to the areas that are already points of connection and places of power for you. You probably already have items from special places in Nature that you can begin a totemic relationship with. Take the time to feel the vibration and energy of some of the items you have collected. This will increase your sensitivity and your shamanic awareness as well.

Part of being on the shamanic path is recognizing, and connecting to, the energies of Nature wherever you may be. Here is an exercise that you can do even in the heart of the city. Remember, shamanic consciousness is not limited by time and place, or to them, as you will see.

This exercise may be as ceremonial or as informal as you choose. Adapt it as need be. You may do it many times, in many places.

Nature Spot Exercise

Explore this place until you find one spot that feels especially comfortable.

This will be your Nature spot. Stand in the middle of that Nature spot.

Take a moment to center yourself, meditate, and connect gently with the energy of that Nature spot.

Stand and face outward from your Nature spot toward whichever direction you choose. (If you know which direction you are facing that is fine, but not necessary for this exercise.) Facing your chosen direction, gaze outward and allow yourself to connect with all that you can see and feel before you. Honor all that is before you by reverently absorbing the energies before you. Imagine a circle surrounding you. Draw it in your mind's eye, beginning in front of you, circling to the right, around yourself and your Nature spot.

When you have done this, turn a quarter turn to the right and face outward in a new direction. Again, gaze outward and connect with all that is before you to see or feel. Reverently honor and absorb the energies of the direction you are facing.

When you have done this, turn a quarter turn to the right again and face outward in a new direction. You have completed half of your circle. Take time to gaze outward and connect with all that you see and feel in this direction. Honor and absorb the energies before you in this Nature spot.

Turn again a quarter turn to the right and face outward in a new direction. You have completed three quarters of your circle. Gaze out before you and connect with what you see and feel in that direction. Reverently honor and absorb the energies of the direction you are facing.

When you have done this, turn a quarter turn to the right one more time and face the direction you started with. You have completed your full circle. Feel the energy of all the directions surrounding you in your complete circle.

From where you stand, at the beginning of your circle, walk forward slowly, no more than twelve paces, and look for an object from Nature. This may be as simple as a leaf or a twig. It may be a feather, a stone, or even a bit of colored glass. When you have walked no more than twelve paces, return slowly, tracing your footsteps back to where you began. You may find something you overlooked the first time. When you have returned to where you started, take a moment to connect with your object from Nature and to give thanks for the gift you have received.

When you are ready, turn a quarter turn to the right and slowly walk forward, no more than twelve paces, to find an object in the next direction. Continue as you began until you have completed your circle of the four directions and have found your objects from Nature.

The key is to find one totem in each direction. If you find four different kinds, that is fine. If you find four similar kinds, that is also fine and may be a clue to the type of energy you need to work with. It's advisable not to concern yourself about what you find as much as how you connect with it. Enjoy yourself.

When you have found each totem, try to leave a little something in return, for thank you.

My adoptive Seneca parents, Grey Eagle and Gentle Earth Woman, carry special pouches of tobacco to give thanks for the gifts they find in Nature. Cornmeal is also good, as are small shells, stones, or herbs. I have often put lots of pennies in my pockets just for this. Copper is a gift from the Earth, too. I also leave small polished stones. I left one in return for a bright red toadstool one day. Later, in the sweat lodge ceremony, I heard someone else tell of finding it. They felt it was a very special totem for them. It sounds funny, but totems travel strange paths.

Totems from Nature will constantly show up in the environment as you follow the shamanic path. You may be concerned that your home will end up as a museum of natural history. That sounds kind of nice unless you get pushed out by the overflow. After you get over the first rush of discovery, you may decide that a totem really isn't yours. At that point, either return it to Nature or share it with someone.

The shaman is a channel of energies and vibrations. Some of the energies and the totems you find are on their way to someone else. It's a special privilege of the shamanic path to carry a totem to another person. Some of your own special totems may come as a gift from (or through) someone else. Try to give and receive totems without expectations about their use or their relationship to the other person. This is not always easy, but it does free the energy to flow through unhampered. There may be a message to deliver with the totem, or a message that comes when you receive a totem. Follow your inner wisdom and relay the message, or not, as you see fit.

One of the most rewarding ways to develop your shamanic consciousness is to collect a variety of totems to work with. You may do this with a set system, let it evolve naturally, or both. There are many systems that chart the attributes of various items from the worlds of Nature.

I have included a number of charts in the appendix at the back, as well as an annotated bibliography, to suggest some ways you can explore various Nature wisdoms. Since the shamanic path involves developing your ability to balance all the wheels of the elements, I suggest that as a guideline to making collections of totems. Here is a sample of an elements system to get you started.

Elements System

Fire
Attribute—Faith, Protection
Animal World—Coyote, Fox
Mineral World—Ruby, Carnelian
Plant World—Cinnamon, Juniper incense
Human World—Physical exercise, Body awareness, Work

Water
Attribute—Inner knowing
Animal World—Dolphin, Bear
Mineral World—Pearl, Coral
Plant World—Chamomile tea
Human World—Dream work, Vision quests

Earth
Attribute—Wisdom
Animal World—Buffalo, Moose
Mineral World—Onyx, Jasper
Plant World—Oak tree (to sit under)
Human World—Ritual, Studying symbols (runes)

Air
Attribute—Creativity
Animal World—Eagle, Hawk
Mineral World—Fluorite
Plant World—Lavender (to burn, or perfume oil)
Human World—Zen meditation, Brainstorming

Using totems as helpers in this manner deepens your connection to the element itself, as well as to the energy of the totem. Explore a variety of systems that you like; then map out your own. Some of the totems you collect to work with will become deeper totems for your own development; some, for your work with others.

You may also use totems to balance your own elements. Elemental astrology provides a useful system to determine your needs. For example, my astrological elements are heavily weighted toward Air,

with Fire and Water coming in second together. The element of Earth is barely represented. To balance things out, I try to work with Earth totems. This may be why so many totems from the Mineral World seem to follow me home. Many times we discover that our higher Self has already begun some of our work for us on the shamanic path.

Another way to find totem items is to buy them. Usually the totems I have bought have turned up at very reasonable prices at places like secondhand stores and charity sales. One person's white elephant is another person's totem, so to speak. This does not mean that a totem cannot show up in an expensive store. Sometimes people need to pay a lot for something in order to appreciate its value. If you expect your totems to be expensive, they certainly will be, whether that cost be monetary or psychological.

A totem, especially one that becomes deeply connected as a medicine totem, is most often found in the environment by you. Sometimes it may be bought, but usually in most unusual circumstances and for an amazing price—virtually a gift.

My totem jaguar rattle came to me in a ratty old curio shop for four dollars. The owner of the shop was actually more surprised than I. Not only did she not remember marking it four dollars, which it was, she didn't remember it at all.

Another time, I found a six-sided smoky quartz crystal in the one-dollar bin at a rock shop. It was a bit cloudy, with a few dings, but I could relate to that. Besides, it packed a pleasant wallop, so I bought it. Soon after, I received a catalog in the mail with crystals and gemstones at outrageous prices. I spotted a smoky quartz identical to mine (minus only the clouds and the dings, that is) for over four hundred dollars.

I read the description in an effort to understand such an amount. I discovered that the smoky quartz had been especially cut in that shape to match the six-sided crystal used by Native American shamans! I like mine cut by Mother Nature.

It's an old wisdom, in the Craft of the Wise, that one never haggles over the price of a magical tool. The same applies to totems. If something attracts you as a totem, and has a fair price that you can pay, don't haggle. If something is priced unreasonably, then the seller is already haggling, and the energy is not right. Nature will provide you with the totems you need. Faith and trust are part of the journey of the shaman.

Among the most delightful totems to find are the totem animals. Strictly speaking, the deep totem animals come most often from the abstract level of form. You connect with these animals through shamanic journeys, which we will explore in the West section.

In the Wheel of the South, totem animals appear in the environment most often. Later, they may also come in dreams and shamanic journeys. But animals of the South wheel are protectors and often share the concrete level of form that you do.

Sometimes totem animals who will appear later in the journeys of the West give hints of their appearance in the South. This was the case with my jaguar rattle. It was one of many hints that came before the earth journey that connected us deeply. My wolf came clearly into the environment long before appearing in dreams and journeys. In this way, she signalled to me her willingness to be a protecting totem.

When you are riding the Wheel of the South, you may begin to connect with your totem animal in several ways. You may watch your environment for hints and clues, or you may also study the various qualities of totem animals that you like. You can tune into them that way. It's a good way to strengthen your shamanic consciousness with the Animal World. If you don't know the traditional qualities of a totem animal, use your own feelings about them. It is your best guideline to a totemic relationship.

Here are a few totem animal qualities:

Wolf—Earth wisdom, protection
Bear—Healing, inner knowing
Fox—Elusiveness, agility, cleverness
Hawk—Perception, focus, protection
Mouse—Innocence, faith, trust
Eagle—High ideals, spiritual philosophy
Dolphin—Psychic abilities, initiators
Heron—Intuition, organization
Horse—Stability, courage
Rabbit—Faith, nurturance
Jaguar—Shamanic wisdom, focused power
Deer—Physical pacing, body awareness
Raven—Inner journeys, dreams
Owl—Symbolic wisdom, shadow work
Mountain Lion—Strength, elusiveness

The qualities you personally see in an animal are the ones that manifest in your totem most often on the Wheel of the South. Later, in the West, the totem animals that come to you in shamanic journeys may represent qualities and energies you were not aware of.

In order to deepen your personal connection to Self, Nature, and Spirit, you may signal your totems with a gentle ceremony. This is effective for all the worlds. It is a good way to begin opening those channels inside your Self and letting the totem energies flow through. It can also be quite effective just before sleeping, for beginning inner journeys and dream work.

For now, you may want to keep this ceremony light. It's often much more effective to let your consciousness evolve and unfold than to jerk it open. After you do this ceremony, pay close attention to your environment for several days. Sometimes the results are dramatic; sometimes subtle. This is best done inside for now.

Totem Ceremony

Set candles in the South—West—North—East.

Set one candle in the center of the four directions.

White candles are good for this, as they represent the trust we bring to our relationship with our totems.

Light the South candle first. Then proceed West, then North, then East; then return to South. This is full circle.

As you light each direction candle, take a moment to honor the gifts and energies of that direction.

South	Fire	Faith
West	Water	Intuition
North	Earth	Wisdom
East	Air	Creativity

You can add other gifts and energies as you feel comfortable.

Return to the South candle when you have finished lighting all except the center candle.

Facing the South candle, look up to honor Spirit above; then look down and honor Mother Earth. As above, so below.

Still standing in the South, turn to face the center candle.

Speaking toward the center candle, say what you hope for in a totem.

Qualities such as patience, courage, determination, wisdom, and so on are good for emphasizing the needs in yourself and the qualities you want strengthened by your relationship with the totem. You can be specific if you want to. For example, you could say "I want to find a totem from the Mineral World to help me make my inner journeys."

However, I advise that you begin with the positive qualities you wish to strengthen in yourself. Then cast them out to the four winds. That way you don't limit what comes to you. Also, they may give you an indication of which world you already have a strong connection to, shamanically.

When you have finished describing what you seek in a totem, light the center candle to signal the way.

Sit for a time and open yourself to your inner visions. You may receive an image or a thought right away.

Also, be very aware of the environment around you.

> What does that shadow remind you of?
> What was that fragrance drifting by?
> What stone was that tumbling off the shelf just then?
> —or in my case, once—
> What was that howling in the back yard? (The dogs whimpered for hours after that.)

Sometimes the results can be pretty quick. Sometimes you have to watch the environment for days. This also depends on the person and the totem. A quiet-spirited person and totem may take a bit longer to connect.

When you are ready to close the ceremony, express your thanks to the totem (even if it hasn't shown up quite yet).

Honor the four directions and all the unseen helpers for their positive contributions.

Blow out each direction candle: South—West—North—East.

Let the center candle burn down if at all possible. A votive candle-holder, on a plate as well, is safest.

Discovering your connection to totem objects can be an enriching experience along the shamanic path. Let your inner counsel advise you and guide you in your choice of totems. With so many vibrations around, it is sometimes difficult to select just the ones you are to dance with. Some totems have a vibration of such depth that you have to consider carefully whether you should connect with them— even when they do call to you.

Totems which have belonged to someone else can be rather tricky, too. Listen to your inner wisdom. Sometimes these totems can be a great gift; other times, something to be avoided completely. Some of these totems may be for someone else, through something you do.

Notes on the Journey

I was at a wonderful gem and mineral show just outside of Houston. One booth had lots of interesting Native American artifacts along with the usual mineral specimens. I was digging through some painted hides when I discovered a very old Plains Indian pipe. When I uncovered it, an indescribable energy jumped at me and hung on tightly.

I very carefully lifted the pipe off of the table and examined it closely. This was clearly not a pipe used for decorative purposes. I have the honor of being a pipe carrier, and I am familiar with the feel of an awakened medicine pipe. The other sensation that I felt in this pipe was a terrific rage.

Here was a sacred medicine pipe—bowl and stem connected, which signals Spirit to enter—tossed on a pile like a curio at a bazaar. I was extremely tempted to buy the pipe just to get it away from where it was. However, my inner wisdom counseled against it. Still, I wondered why I had found it. What was I supposed to do—if anything?

As I mused about this, I found myself gently cradling the bowl of the pipe in my left hand and stroking the stem. I disconnected the pipe, carefully twisting the stem and pulling it away from the bowl. I felt the energy release its hold on me and slowly drain to the ground. I felt intense relief flood through me. That terrific rage subsided with a release of red-brown energy floating skyward.

I knew that eventually someone else would reconnect the pipe. Probably it would be someone who would not realize just what they had in their hands. I went inside myself to that place of inner wisdom. There, on the abstract level, I did a proper pipe ceremony. As I reconnected the pipe on the concrete level, I called from within for the spirit of the pipe to hear me.

I explained the situation the best way I knew how. I said that I would make prayers that the pipe would find a home with someone who knew how sacred it was. I surrounded the pipe with a Turquoise Blue Ray. I set it down gently and walked away, as I knew I must.

Some time later, I happened to glance toward the door. I saw a man carrying the pipe outside. He was holding the pipe very tenderly. On his face was the expression of someone who has just been given a very sacred gift.

Sacred objects travel strange paths. Be open to dance with them when you meet.

Chapter 2

SACRED MESSAGES

Once you have begun to work with totems, you will naturally want to know what they have to communicate to you. Totems bring sacred messages to us from Nature, from Spirit, and from our higher Self. The totems we work with in the South deal primarily with reflections of our higher Self. These reflect our strengths, our vulnerabilities, and our personal shamanic connections to the vibrations of all the worlds.

It's important that we learn to understand the messages of our totems in the South. They form a strong foundation for understanding messages received later in the West from journeys and dream work, in the North from symbol and ritual, and in the East from the chaos of pure creative energy.

The ways in which we receive messages from our totems vary as much as the totems themselves. To simplify things a bit, though, we can divide these ways of receiving messages into three primary categories:

> The first way is through the concrete level of form, or the everyday physical world we inhabit. This is sensory and relates to the physical body.

> The second way is through the abstract level of form, or the worlds of images, journeys, and dreams. This is mental and relates to the mind (not the brain—that's sensory—through the brain). The brain is the organ of the mind.

> The third is from the Spiritual Plane, which is beyond the levels of form, or beyond concrete and abstract.

This is pure, beyond sensory and imagery, and relates
to Spirit.

Messages from the Spiritual Plane are often not recognized until
later, when we have acted on them. Messages from the Spiritual
Plane come without form and communicate as pure thought or ideas.
Rarely are we aware of the process; we simply "know" something.
Many times we have abundantly "spiritual" images to accompany
our totem messages. These are still images.

The energies of totems that deliver messages in imagery inhabit
the level of abstract form. Our imagination creates images that bring
the messages into concrete form. Understanding this doesn't make
the message any less sacred, magical, or "spiritual" in the popular use
of the word. Understanding this makes it easier to get there. Remember,
the shaman is a mapmaker.

Starting with the concrete or physical way to receive messages,
we find totems in our environment. To interpret their messages for us,
we begin by examining them.

What shape is the totem?
What color?
What texture?
What kind of smell or taste does it have?
Does it make a sound?
What are the physical characteristics of the totem?

Be like a new mother who unwraps the baby and counts its
fingers and toes.

Each totem has unique properties and messages for you. Treat
each totem as though you had never experienced anything like it
before. That way you'll open those channels of discovery and shamanic
consciousness that reflect your inquisitive child self.

On the concrete level, you may have specific reactions to the
color, size, shape, texture, smell, or taste of a totem. These reactions
may be a message in themselves. If you aren't certain of your reactions,
but you're certain there is something to the physical characteristics of
a totem, you can use traditional systems to help decode the message.
In this chapter I have included two systems that I find very helpful.

The first, Nature Color Messages, is adapted from several color
systems. I find that a color is very helpful to many people. Perhaps a
color has a strong personal meaning to you that is different from any
meaning you find in a system. As always, please use your personal

reaction as your guide to the message of the totem.

You may also use this color system as a guide to locating totems to help you. For example, if you want to strengthen your intuitive gifts, you can seek blue totems, such as flowers, stones, or even pieces of glass that carry a color energy as well. Use systems to get you started; add to them as you go.

Nature Color Messages

Red	Faith, courage, blood, communication, anger
Yellow	Inspiration, comfort, love, joy
Dark Blue	Intuition, synthesis, rebirth, creation
Dark Green	Growth, abundance, determination, will
Pastel Pink	Love, friendship, work, creativity
White	Purity, service, innocence, wisdom
Violet	Spirituality, gratitude, healing
Orange	Friendship, learning, enthusiasm
Light Blue	Personal honor, self-development, self-knowledge
Light Green	Responsibility, healing, idealism
Rose Pink	Perception, love, prophecy, clarity
Crystal	Magnetism, harmony, wholeness
Black	Goals, achievements, inner wisdom, seeking Light
Grey	Friendship, serenity, loyalty, dreams
Brown	Love of animals, Earth connection, stability
Gold	Action, force, growth, healing
Silver	Receptivity, intuition, self-healing

Sometimes, on the concrete level, the best way to interpret the messages of a totem is to take a closer look. Examine the totem quite closely, using as many of your physical senses as you need to.

For example, a yellow stone may actually have several colors, markings, or even faces in it when examined closely. A lovely pink blossom may actually have a very bitter fragrance or taste. These are messages that you can interpret based on the experiences you have had or are in the midst of. Where, how, and why you found a totem also provide clues to its messages. Pay attention to your senses.

Be aware of changes in the environment—these can be shamanic messages. Be on the lookout for the unusual in Nature. It's good to remember that some things which seem significant may have very ordinary reasons for being. Try to remember the trickster of the South, Coyote Spirit. Don't take everything as being profound or significant. That is a side road on your path. If something unusual happens in your environment, look for its source on the concrete, everyday level first. You'll save your energy that way.

I once had white feathers appear floating in the sky, just out of my reach. I had been doing a solitary pipe ceremony, so I was certain these feathers had some great significance. I knew that feathers meant communication or messages, but I couldn't find out anything beyond that. I realized I had wasted a lot of time and energy chasing my tail when I was told my dog had raided a neighbor's hen house. Guess when? Coyote Spirit will show up to keep you from getting lost in the deep significance of everything—count on it.

One system I use primarily for reading stones comes from Twylah Nitsch. It is a system that she and her mother adapted and shared from Seneca wisdom. I have also found it useful for totems from the Plant World. Although there are many systems that record the attributes of Plant World totems, the Seneca method of examining the shape, textures, and colors has served me well with lots of interesting roots, twigs, and driftwood. I have included a very brief excerpt of this wisdom to get you started.

For more Seneca wisdom, I urge you to contact

> The Seneca Indian Historical Society
> Brant Post Office Box 136
> Brant, New York 14027
> Attention: Wolf Clan Lodge

The Wolf Clan is a teaching clan. They are here to share wisdom and to help us all connect to the Earth. Also, a stamped self-addressed envelope is most gratefully appreciated.

Seneca Stone Wisdom

Textures of Stones

Figures or faces	Spirit helpers; if animals, these have the attributes of the animal
Sparkling	Star rock, charisma, high ideals, charm
Smooth	Willingness to learn and share wisdom as a teacher

Rough	Inclinations to follow one's own methods of learning and sharing wisdom as a teacher, scientific explorer
Light weight, smooth	Gentleness
Heavy, rough	Obstacles, but growth

Shapes of Stones

Round	Flexibility, professional abilities
Oval	Contentment, yet seeking change
Two-sided	Strongly influenced by others
Three-sided	Pyramid shape, intuition, openness to inner wisdom
Four-sided	Nature lovers, self-respect, self-discipline, friendship
Five-sided	Every aspect of creativity, honor for Nature
Six-sided	Fullness of potentials and gifts, decisiveness, trust, sincerity
Seven-sided	Gratitude, a rare stone indicating spiritual leadership
Stone with a hole	Protection stone, reminds us of Spirit

Colors of Stones

Brown	Earthy energy, love of Nature
Grey	Friendly
Black	Seeking Light
Red	Faith
Yellow	Love, communication
Blue	Intuitive gifts
Green	Responsibility, dependability
Pink	Creativity in work
White	Sharing with others
Violet	Gratitude, spiritual enrichment

Now we move a bit more "between the worlds." You may use the physical presence and characteristics of a totem to bring forth messages in the form of images. This is working from the concrete to the abstract and back again. Most shamanic path work and messages occur as links between the concrete and abstract levels. A totem is such a link, and so are you.

Using your sensory channels, examine your totem. Next, go inside your mind and wait for images. I find it most helpful to do this meditatively. You may not think that the images you receive are related to the totem. Stay with it, and let the static clear a bit. You'll learn to know which images relate to that totem as you spend more time relating to the totem itself.

Some images come to us directly from the abstract level without a physical totem being present. This happens a lot with totem animals, whom we see most often in inner vision. The messages are sometimes easier to decode when they arrive in images. As evolved as we may be, we're still a bit clumsy with our physical channels, our soft machine. Images can also be static, though; so take time to fine-tune your awareness.

Another way to use images to receive messages is by the active use of imagery. Create an image in your mind of the totem. This is effectively "calling your totem" and works well with totem animals, as well as with spirit guides from the abstract level. Call in your totem and communicate in images. This is an important step in developing shamanic consciousness. It is also a good prerequisite to shamanic journeys that take you into the abstract level. This we will do in the West. For now, enjoy the active, creative use of images to stretch your gifts and communicate with your totems. Imagination is a shamanic channel. Your brain and your mind do represent the living tree of the shaman. Let them connect and work for you on your journey on the shamanic path.

I close this chapter with an exercise to use for bonding with your totems. You may do this physically on the concrete level; or you may do this exercise completely with imagery. The effect will be the same. The shaman does not make as many arbitrary divisions in consciousness as modern society has taught us to do. Keep that in mind on your journey.

I also include an account, at the end of this chapter, that demonstrates how interwoven the messages, the tasks, and the energies of the totems that come to you can be. We must indeed go beyond the concrete and abstract levels to reach the Spiritual Plane. Sometimes Spirit transcends and moves through all levels. We don't know how— we just know it, and we accept it. Sometimes the Spiritual Plane seems to reach down in sacred, special ways.

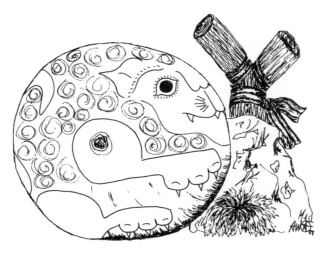

Shamanic Bonding Exercise

Find a quiet place where you can be sure of privacy and protection.

Surround yourself, your totem (or a representation of it) and the area with a golden light.

Use no other sounds, scents, or textures that might distract you, other than the totem itself.

Beginning in the South, offer your totem to the helping spirits and elements of the four directions.

Go South—West—North—East—South.

Offer the totem to Spirit above and Mother Earth below. As above, so below.

Sit quietly, holding your totem in your right hand—either literally or figuratively in image.

Breathe four deep breaths, each time gently releasing your breath on the totem.

Now let your breath flow naturally.

Move the totem to your left hand and rock with it gently.

Make no sound until you begin to feel the vibration of the totem.

Feel the rhythm of the totem.

Rock to its pace.

Know the vibration of the totem.

Stop rocking.

Now re-create the vibration of the totem without a sound, without moving.

Feel it inside your mind.

Feel it in your heart.

Put it in your body memories.

Now take a moment to rest.

Move the totem to your right hand again.

Breathe four deep breaths, each time releasing your breath on the totem. This is called the breath of spirit or intention.

Return to your natural breathing.

Move the totem to your left hand.

Close your eyes and imagine that you and your totem are walking into a dark theater.

On the theater screen is the color red—then orange—then yellow—then green—then blue—then indigo—then violet—then white—and then a blank screen.

Now focus your mind on the blank screen and ask your totem to project pictures onto the screen for you. Just let them flow naturally like your breath. You will remember what you need of what you see.

Stop the pictures and darken the screen to black. Now open your eyes and re-create as much of what you saw in your mind's eye as you can.

You may also find it useful to stare up at the sky or ceiling while you do this. It helps program your pictures. Don't strain to remember. Let what comes back through and leave the rest.

Take a few quiet moments.

When you're ready, put the totem in your right hand (activating hand) and do the four breaths again, as before.

Move the totem to your left hand (receiving hand) and breathe naturally.

With your eyes open, concentrate on one spot or one aspect of the totem.

In imagery, visualize one part, for example, a leaf or one point of a crystal.

Continue to concentrate on one aspect and listen carefully.

Ask your totem to create a sound that you can hear. This is obviously easier with animals.

Ask for one clear note, if possible.

Listen.

Now try to match the sound with your own inner voice.

Listen again.

Now make the sound out loud if you can. If not, again in your inner voice.

Now return to silence, inner and outer.

Take a few moments to rest.

Now put the totem in your right hand once more and do the four breaths.

Return the totem to your left hand and breathe naturally.

With your eyes closed, ask the totem to send a fragrance to you.

When you have received a fragrance, open your eyes and re-create it.

Do the same procedure with a taste.

Now place the totem close to your heart and ask the totem to send an emotion or a feeling to you.

Breathe deeply and experience the emotion of the totem.

Breathe deeply again and return the experience to the totem.

Transmit the feeling to the totem and from the totem.

Place the totem in your right hand and rest.

Now breathe four breaths on the totem and place it against the base of your spine.

Breathing slowly, create an image in your mind's eye of the Ray colors of the chakra or energy points: Red—Orange—Yellow—Green—Blue—Indigo—Violet.

When you have done that, breathe deeply and switch hands while continuing to hold the totem at the base of your spine.

Now, image the colors in reverse: Violet—Indigo—Blue—Green—Yellow—Orange—Red.

Last, take the totem from behind your back, place in both hands, and hold it at arm's length, heart level.

Breathe four breaths on the totem and slowly bring it up to touch your third-eye area.

Hold it for a moment; then gently place the totem a few feet away.

Breathe deeply and express your gratitude.

Honor the directions: South—West—North—East.

Rest and meditate.

This is an exercise. It may be as ceremonial or as informal as you choose. You may add to it or take away. I do advise that you go through it once just as it is to open all the sensory channels. You may also extend the distance between yourself and the totem until you are able to do this without touching at all.

It's also advisable to make notes of your experience. Afterwards, be aware of your environment and your dream states for a few days.

Notes on the Journey

I had spotted a palm-sized piece of dark untumbled amethyst on a stack of papers at a rock shop. It was just the deep violet I vibrate to, and was calling me clearly. The salesperson was unsure of the price and felt she should wait for the owner in case the stone had gem-quality amethyst inside.

I had bought buckets of similar-quality amethysts to tumble and to share. The earthy vibration of the stone was familiar. Gemstone amethyst has an airy element and a higher-pitched vibration. Amethysts are true medicine totems from the Mineral World for me. I was soon to discover once again how deep this shamanic connection between the amethyst and me truly is.

Not wanting to haggle, I told the salesperson I would return later in the week. I knew the stone was mine. It was just a matter of doing the dance to connect with it. The second time I came to inquire about the stone, it had been moved out of sight to a shelf beneath the cash register. Once again, the salesperson had forgotten to inquire about its price, and the owner was not there. Knowing that the soothing quality of the amethyst is a much-needed balance for impatience, I was amused to find it instigating the opposite effect on me. I held the stone for a few quiet moments; then gave it to the salesperson and promised to return soon.

The third time I came to the shop, I had several items to pick up for a workshop I was giving. Neither the salesperson nor my stone was in sight when I came to the cash register with my purchases. Trying to sound casual, I asked the woman at the counter about the stone. I related the story so far while she dug around in boxes and drawers to locate my stone. Finally she found it and placed it in the bag with my other items with a smile. No charge.

I didn't know immediately what had drawn me to that particular stone. But I was soon to find out. Shortly after that, I was to meet Twylah Nitsch for the first time. She made a trip to the Wolf Clan South outside of Houston to set up a teaching lodge and initiate some new clan members.

I had made an appointment to have a stone reading, as well, from her. I got more than I ever dreamed of from that reading. Though I was to study with her intensively later, this was my first introduction to the Seneca methods of reading stones.

When I returned home, it seemed that all of my stones were leaping off the shelves to be read in this way. Once a channel to wisdom is opened, the results can be immediate and dramatic. I spent most of that night using my new-found method of reading the messages in many of my stones.

It wasn't until morning that I remembered the amethyst I had gotten after such a tricky dance. As I pulled it from my purse, I noticed something I had never seen before. One side of the stone was shaped exactly like a wolf: bushy tail curling around her hind legs. I turned the stone over. The other side was shaped, unmistakably, like a bear. As a wolf married to a bear, I felt this was very special. I found later it meant even more than that.

I had been given the privilege of calling the Great Bear and the Great Wolf of the Seneca Nation if the need should ever arise. Doing this calls forth deeper levels than the already powerful vibrations of bear and wolf. This was not something to be taken lightly or used casually. I didn't want to conjecture about how I might ever need this privilege. I just felt honored and filed it in my memories.

Some time later my husband and I returned home, from a much-needed day out together, to find an ambulance parked in the front yard. I shall not attempt to convey the horror of that experience. As it turned out, my daughter, who was barely a year old, had awakened from her nap with a sudden high fever. She had thrown a febrile seizure. Thanks to the calm actions of my babysitter and neighbors, it had not become more complicated.

Still, it was serious enough to warrant a trip to the emergency room and hospitalization. The swamps around Houston are havens for mosquitoes and the like. Meningitis, encephalitis, and other frightful diseases are constant possibilities. What followed were hours of intense discomfort, frustration, and fear.

Finally, my daughter and I were put in a room in Pediatrics. She was in a crib with steel bars. I had a chair that folded out into a cot. Still enraged at what she had had to endure, she fell asleep immediately. I was far from sleep.

I knew that I had to do something to collect my energies, which were scattered everywhere. I reached into my purse for some amethyst to steady my inner hysteria. I pulled out the wolf-bear stone. I hadn't realized it was still in there, but I was so grateful to have it. My husband was home alone with our son.

The hospital was still and quiet. By that time everyone but the night nurses had gone to sleep. I closed the door to our room and turned off all of the lights. Holding the wolf-bear stone in my hand, I opened the curtains. Moonlight flooded the room, and I sat in a circle of it on the floor. I held the stone and rocked myself. Afraid to wake my baby, I cried silent tears. All of the fear and terror came flooding out of me and disappeared in the silver moonlight.

I began the ritual of self-blessing to bring that deepest strength of healing.

"Bless me, Mother, for I am your child."

I spoke to the Mother of all Mothers to keep me calm for whatever was to come. I drew the healing energies of the Moon down into my heart. I felt the nurturance of the true inner mother.

I called for the deepest healing of the Lady to flow to my daughter. I felt it pass through me into the darkened crib and into that tiny little girl. I heard no sound; I saw no movement. I knew that Light had passed through me.

I turned the wolf-bear stone over and over in my hands. I called for the healing energies of the Great Bear and the sacred strength of the Great Wolf of the Seneca. I knew their presence immediately—deeper, stronger, more powerful than I could ever have imagined.

They came without sensation, without form, without even an image in my inner vision to hold on to. They came purely, directly into my heart and soul. I knew their presence.

I had planned to say many things to them, but I had no words. I sat on the floor until the moonlight faded from the room. Then I slept.

The next morning I awoke to find a snarling little daughter. (Bobcat medicine!) There was also an encouraging set of test results and a new diagnosis. A deep inner-ear infection was found in both ears—not serious, but tricky to detect. The febrile seizure necessitated a few days of observation. So we camped out in Pediatrics for four days, me and my bobcat daughter.

On some level the Great Bear and Wolf never left, even when the danger had passed. The room contained a serenity so strong that the nurses would come in from time to time just to rest. To the Bear and the Wolf and the Lady of Silver Lights I am most grateful.

Chapter 3

SACRED CARE

Before you can learn to nurture and take care of your totems, you must learn to do the same for yourself. It is an occupational hazard of people who care for others to overlook their own needs. An added benefit of having the shamanic relationship with totems is the mutual nurturance that develops. But you can't really do an effective job with totems unless you are clear yourself. More than once I've been chided by my medicine teachers about this, so I pass it on to you.

Get strong and stay strong. The strength you develop will deepen your shamanic abilities and increase the connections that your totems have with Self, Nature, and Spirit. You are the living tree. The totems are fruits of that tree. Stay centered and keep up your strength at all times.

A method that I use to do this comes from Wiccan traditions. I mentioned it briefly in the wolf-bear stone story, and I'll share it with you now. It has many different versions and can be adapted to suit your personal preference and needs.

It is traditionally done at the time of the full moon, but I find it to be effective regardless of the time it is used. Besides, the high energy of the full moon period can fool us into thinking we have more strength than we do. Listen to your inner wisdom and to the rhythms of your body; you'll know when you need a strengthening ritual.

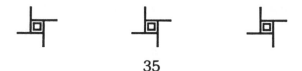

Ritual of Self-Blessing

You will need

> a small votive candle and holder (white is always
> good, but use a color if you feel called to do that)
> an incense stick, cone, or herbs (such as sage or thyme)
> to burn
> a small container of water
> a small container of salt

I find that a sugar and creamer set works very well for this. These can be purchased quite reasonably and set aside just for this use.

This is a ritual which connects you to the deepest levels of healing. It also connects you to the four elements and their energies. In this way it is most helpful for dealing with the shamanic elemental energies of Nature.

The candle represents the element of Fire.

The incense or herbs represent Air.

The container of water is Water.

The container of salt is Earth.

Beyond that, these elements reflect your own needs.

The element of Fire reflects your relationships, protection, ideas, and achievements.

The element of Air reflects your creativity, spirituality, inspiration, and philosophies.

The element of Water reflects your emotions, intuition, dream states, psychic gifts, and healing balance.

The element of Earth reflects your practicality, knowledge, sacred wisdom, and growth.

Find a quiet time and place where you will not be disturbed. You may make this as ceremonial or as informal as you choose.

Light the incense and take a few moments to consider the element of Air.

Consider the gifts that Air reflects in you.

Light the candle and take a few moments to consider the element of Fire.

Consider the gifts that Fire reflects in you.

Take a few moments to consider the element of Water and how it reflects in you.

Take a few moments to consider the element of Earth and how it reflects in you.

Very gently, pour the water into the container of salt. If you are using herbs as an incense, you may sprinkle a few in the water and salt mixture.

Stir the salt and water with your fingers. Consider the blending of elements that creates life itself. Consider the balance of elements and their attributes in your life. Take a few moments to do this.

Facing the candle, dip your fingers in the water mixture and touch your forehead (third-eye area).

Say "Bless me, Mother, for I am your child." (You may substitute other names for sacred deities here, if you choose. You may also say "Spirit," which is quite useful to the spiritual self-blessing.)

Now, dip your fingers in the water mixture and touch the area around your eyes carefully.

Say "Bless my eyes that I may see you."

Dip again and touch your nose.

Say "Bless my nose that I may breathe your essence."

Dip again and touch your ears.

Say "Bless my ears that I may hear your wisdom."

Dip again and touch your mouth.

Say "Bless my mouth that I may speak your name."

Dip again and touch your heart.

Say "Bless my heart that I may feel your love."

Dip again and touch your lower abdomen.

Say "Bless my cauldron center that I may create harmony."

Dip again and touch your feet.

Say "Bless my feet that I may walk in balance."

Dip again and rub your hands together.

Say "Bless my hands that I may share your healing in my work."

Take all the time you need to concentrate on the elements before you. Focus your attention on the candle and visualize healing light flowing into you. Feel strength emerging from deep inside yourself. Breathe deeply and capture that moment. Connect with the source of strength and healing.

When you feel you are finished, blow out the candle. I often save these candles just for this ritual of self-blessing. If I am extremely pressed for time, I simply light the candle and take a few moments to connect with the energy of the ritual.

It is good to leave the incense burning if you can. Air is a communicating element, and smoke is transformation. The incense carries the messages of healing and strength to Spirit. If you have used herbs, it is good to return the ashes to Nature. In this way, you are grounding the energy, bringing the message and the transformation to earth. Make sure the ashes are cold; then place them at the roots of a tree or bush if possible. If not, place them in soil or sand.

The salt and water mixture can be used very effectively in several ways. You may wash your gemstones or other stones in this. Crystals love this, since their energy is so personally connected to yours.

You may save the mixture and dab a little on your third-eye area every day for a few days, as a reminder. You may pour the mixture into your bath for a gentle energizer. When the bathwater drains, visualize a connection between yourself and the energies of Mother Ocean. You may return the mixture to the earth by pouring it on soil or sand. Remember, plants don't thrive in salt; so keep the mixture clear of plants. You may sprinkle the mixture throughout your house to seal in positive energies and protection.

Having taken the time to nurture yourself, you are better able to do the same for your totems. It's always good to be aware that what you feel your totems need is actually what you need. If you feel that your stones or feathers could use a good airing out in the sun, then get out there with them yourself. Whenever possible, share the cleansings and nurturings for your mutual benefit.

There are two basic kinds of cleansing to consider with objects that are to be totems for you. The first is the cleansing that you do when you first obtain a totem object. Often when these totems come directly from Nature, they are not in need of anything but a light ceremony to cleanse any residue you may not be aware of. The best way to do this is to burn sage leaves or thyme in a large shell, ceramic bowl, or iron pot. Pass your hands through the smoke first; then pass the totem through the smoke several times. This is called smudging or, since sage is used so frequently, saging.

Smudging is useful for clearing your own energies, cleansing your aura, and purifying your shamanic channels. It is useful for you and for your totems at any time. Smudging is an effective way to keep energies clear and focused. I have experienced sage's bringing energies together in a room when nothing else had been effective.

Some of my colleagues in biochemical psychology are quite certain that sage has very real effects on the psyche. I'm sure many a Native American medicine elder would be amused at the experiments being done with sage! Thyme is also quite effective for this, and is currently burned in hospitals throughout Europe.

Bundles of sage, called smudge sticks (some with cedar, sweetgrass, or lavender), are available and are very convenient to use. Sometimes these are not easily extinguished. I keep a cup of salt or soil, half full, nearby when I use a smudge stick. When I am finished smudging, I place the smudge stick, lit end down, in the salt or soil. As always, it's good to return the ashes to earth when you can.

Sage is such a good all-purpose herb that I often light sage first and later sprinkle other herb mixtures on top of the burning sage. In much the same way that quartz crystals amplify the energies of other Mineral World totems (as well as our own), sage amplifies the energies of Plant World totems.

Other totems found in Nature require a more concrete-level kind of cleansing. This is particularly true of Animal World totems, such as feathers or talons. While it is doubtful that a bird by the side of the road died of disease, it is only good sense to be aware of health risks to yourself. Sometimes a simple solution of mild soap and saltwater can be used to cleanse a totem. Other times, the organic residue is such that it requires drying or preserving.

One possibility is to hang the totem in a closed but airy place. I find it more effective to preserve these types of totems in a mixture of salt, cinnamon, and cloves. Salt, cinnamon, and cloves are all ideal preservatives. You may add other herbs, such as sage, to the mixture if you choose, but I don't advise the use of strongly scented perfumes or oils. Ground cinnamon and cloves are somewhat expensive in quantity, so make your primary ingredient salt. The salt acts as a drying agent, as well as a preserving one.

It's best to place the totem on a layer of salt, cinnamon, and cloves; then cover it with more of the mixture. This is particularly necessary for totems with lots of organic residue. For totems such as single feathers, I find it sufficient to place them quill end down in a bowl or glass of the mixture. The totems that require being buried in the mixture should be placed in a warm dry place. A high shelf above the clothes dryer is most effective. Incidentally, it is also a wonderful place to dry flowers or herbs on a tray.

Expect the drying time for a totem to take anywhere from six weeks to several months, depending on your climate. After a month or so, you may begin checking to see how it's progressing. Try not to be too anxious. If it doesn't dry sufficiently, you will only have to do it all over again later. The container you use depends on the totem's size. One very large wing I had required the bottom drawer of a dresser, lined with a plastic sack. You may want to cover the container for a few weeks to help the salt work effectively. Again, this has more to do with your climate than anything else. You will have to experiment a bit.

Not all of the Animal World totems that show up in our environment are meant to be preserved. Sometimes it's best just to place them deeper in Nature with a few thoughts about the natural balance of life. Sometimes they seem to require more ceremony. Did you ever bury a baby bird that had fallen from its nest? That same tenderness is quite good with animal totems and can often deepen a shamanic connection between you and the totem itself. Sometimes, animal totems present themselves in our environment for very complicated reasons. Then we must follow our hearts to know what to do.

Notes on the Journey

My husband and I were visiting the Mayan ruins in the Yucatan. We had stopped for the night at a small hotel in the heart of the jungle. When we got to our room, I caught the scent of something strange and disturbing. It passed quickly, so I thought it could have been insecticide or something used to clean the room. Even after the scent was gone, however, I continued to feel uneasy.

We showered and changed to go downstairs to the bar. As we entered the little sitting room next to the bar, I caught the scent again. This time it was quite strong and created a deep sense of uneasiness and fear inside me. The room seemed to be vibrating at a very unpleasant rate, but I couldn't figure out the source. I looked up to find skins of some jungle cats stretched out on hoops hanging high on the walls. I had seen far too many of these already in the market-places, so I couldn't understand why these had such a strong effect. By this time, I was becoming quite dizzy. I left the room so that I could think clearly.

My husband had not picked up on the scent, but he had felt the discomfort of the vibrations in the room. Something clearly had to be done. I asked the bartender about the skins. With a genial smile he told me they were baby jaguars. With that information, the wheels deep within me began spinning wildly.

The area around the bar had begun to clear out as the hotel guests went in to dinner. I realized that after dinner they would most probably convene at the bar once more. I had to act fast to deal with the energies in that room.

I went upstairs to get the only totem helpers I had brought on the trip: a quartz crystal and a piece of black jade. While I was rummaging in my bag to find these, I experienced a most unusual pull of energy from the jungle outside my window. I could see nothing in the pitch black darkness, but what I felt filled me with resolve.

Carrying my stones, I went back downstairs to the bar, ordered a drink, and, while my husband kept the bartender busy, went into the little sitting room. Not exactly sure what to do, I let my higher Self guide me. I put the crystal in my left hand to pull clear energy through. I put the black jade in my right hand to channel negative energies into. I sat staring at the skins and waiting for guidance.

Suddenly, I felt myself being swept into the dark jungle surrounding the hotel. I could feel the damp ground under my feet and the vines catching me as I rushed through the dense foliage. I seemed to be running on four paws. Ahead of me I saw another tiny jaguar running with all the speed it could manage. Behind me I heard the crashing footsteps of man. I was being hunted.

I held tightly to my crystal and my jade on the concrete level while the terror I was experiencing on the abstract level closed in around me. I became tangled in some vines at the base of a huge tree. As I struggled in vain to free myself, I felt a sharp, quick pain burn into my heart. Then nothing was left but the sensation of fear.

Along with that fear, a scent was left, strange and disturbing, the same one that had been in my room and in the room beside the bar. Concentrating on that scent, I gathered it up and pulled the energy through the crystal into the black jade. When I had rested a bit, I pulled healing light and energy through the crystal, into my heart, and out into the black jade. I opened my eyes to find that only a few short minutes had passed on the clock.

The vibration of the room felt calmer and quieter. The only sound was my heart still racing from the exertion. I took a few more moments to slow my own pace. When I could, I called for my husband to check the vibration. He felt a definite change in the room. I felt a definite change in myself.

That night my dreams were filled with scenes of being hunted. Again and again I felt that sharp, burning pain. Again and again I felt myself connect deeper, stronger, to the heart of the jaguar. I awoke just as it was beginning to get light. I had the distinct feeling that I was being watched. The sensations creeping up my spine to raise the hair on the back of my neck indicated much more than a dream. I sat at the window, watching shadows slip through the jungle and through my inner vision until the sun rose.

The next day we made a special trip to Chichen Itza to visit the Temple of Jaguars. Tourists were swarming around the place when we arrived. We had become spoiled at the other ruins, several of which we had seen alone. We focused on the Temple of Jaguars and ignored the rest. After a short time, the great temple was empty. I spent quite a long time there, completely undisturbed.

I was trying to puzzle out the events of the evening before. I was trying to understand this dance that I seemed to be doing with the jaguar. I had found my jaguar rattle shortly before this trip and had felt its deep significance then. Still, I was very resistant. I feared that this connection came from the current popularity of jaguar medicine and the writings about it.

I had shown my jaguar rattle to a medicine teacher I work with just before we left for the Yucatan. She had been very clear that it was a true gift—a gift from the jaguar. I felt that too, but somehow I couldn't trust it. After all, what was a Wiccan, Druidic type doing with a jaguar? I could understand the wolf and several others, but a jaguar didn't seem to fit in my codes.

Something was going on, but I couldn't figure it out. Not even after I had experienced the jaguar, not even as I sat in the Temple of Jaguars, could I understand it. I sat for a long time in that ancient temple. I ran my hands over the weathered carvings and watched the clouds drift by. I decided that regardless of my uncertainty about the jaguar, it had already given me one gift and one extremely sacred experience. I pulled a tiny crystal cluster out of a pouch of stones I had brought to share. I put my love and gratitude into the crystal and placed it behind a stone carving inside the temple.

That night my dreams were filled with jaguars again. This time, they were large and sleek. There was no fear. They rolled and snarled and played like huge kittens. I awoke feeling that I had tapped into something quite deep. Indeed, I had. As with many connections on the path of the shaman, though, I had to wait for it to develop to understand it fully.

It is sometimes easier to begin relating to Animal World totems or power animals as babies. This is especially true of the predators. For one thing, viewing them as babies is a reminder of the developmental nature of the relationship with the totem animal. For another, it's a bit of an ego trip when these powerful spirit animals begin making themselves at home with you. On this shamanic path, as with any spiritual or magical path, it is wise to remember that the ego is a good servant—not a master.

When wolves began appearing in my life, on both the concrete and abstract levels, I was somewhat confused about how to begin relating to them. In a shop one day, I found a small ceramic wolf with big eyes and an expression that seemed to say, "I'm a what?" It was very helpful to dance with that aspect of the wolf first. Later, the stronger aspects developed; and, still later, the dark or shadow aspects.

By beginning with the little-wolf aspect, I was building a foundation and a connection most essential to a true totemic relationship with a power animal. Several years after the wolf and I had begun our dance together, I found another tiny wolf. This one was pewter with a very fierce face. It was in a booth at a department store during

Christmas. It was sitting there along with an assortment of angels, Santas, and Nativity figures. When I asked the salesclerk the price of the little wolf, she assured me that she had no such item. But, of course, she did.

I carry that pewter wolf in my pipe bag as a reminder of the strength and the ferocious energy of that power animal. Dancing with some power animals is a lot like having a tiger by the tail. Better to start out with a cub and grow up together. Believe me, it happens fast enough. You won't have to wait long.

When you have begun a shamanic connection with a totem from any of the worlds, you may want to ceremonially formalize the relationship. You can do this by adopting the totem as your own. This is done with totems that have shown up consistently in your life, in one form or another, on one level or another. It deepens your connection and declares your dedication to your path and to the totem itself.

I find it most effective for Mineral World totems and Animal World totems. Totems from the Plant World seem to require less formal care and ceremony. Perhaps that is because they are so closely connected to the nurturance of Mother Earth. Still, you may use this ceremony to connect with Plant World totems that you carry for protection, such as St. John's wort or buckeye and the like. You may also use this with Plant World totems whose vibrations are so intense that they essentially bridge the worlds. Mandrake is a good example of this. Amber is another.

Human World totems may take the form of little statues or paintings of deities you relate to. Some examples of this would be little Buddhas, happy gods, or many of the beautiful Goddess figures available now. A spirit guide is not a totem, strictly speaking; but if one is showing up in your life, it's nice to honor the relationship ceremonially. Once you've started on the shamanic path, you will be continually amazed at what comes to you and to your life on all levels. A balanced blend of honor and humor will serve you well in all of your shamanic relationships.

Totem Adoption Ceremony

As always, this ceremony may be as elaborate or as simple as you choose.

Find a quiet time and place.

Light sage or incense to clear and focus the energies. If you use sage or herbs, you may want to use the Wolf Clan method of lighting these.

Place your sage or other herbs, such as thyme, cedar, or dragon's blood resin, in the container you are going to burn it in. This is your smudge pot.

Take five matches and lay them out beside the matchbox.

Take the first match; strike it and light the herbs from the direction of the South.

Say "I light the flame of love in the South, which is the place of faith." (You may also add other attributes of the directions as you become familiar with them.)

Strike the next match and light the herbs from the West.

Say "I light the flame of love in the West, which is the place of inner vision."

Strike the third match and light the herbs from the North.

Say "I light the flame of love in the North, which is the place of sacred wisdom."

Strike the fourth match and light the herbs from the East.

Say "I light the flame of love in the East, which is the place of illumination."

Strike the fifth match and light the herbs from the center.

Say "I light the flame of love in the center, which is the vibral core of life."

This ritual is often done by beginning to light the herbs in the East. Since this adoption ceremony has to do with the relationship between you and your totem, I feel it is more closely attuned to the Wheel of the South. So I begin this adoption ceremony in the South.

After you have lit the herbs or the incense, take a few moments to smudge yourself.

Do this by cupping your hands over the smoke and brushing across your face and head as though you were splashing yourself with water. Holding the smudge pot, slowly lower it in front of your body, letting the smoke rise. Next, hold the bowl behind you. Beginning at your feet, raise the bowl to the base of your spine and let the smoke drift up your back to clear your chakra or energy points.

This is not as tricky as it sounds; you will improve with practice. If you are using a feather to fan the flames, be sure to pass the feather through the smoke several times before you begin smudging yourself. Smudge sticks are very useful for this, so long as you watch for stray sparks.

Take the totem, or a representation of the totem if need be, and pass it through the smoke several times.

Holding the totem, surround yourself and it with clear green light to symbolize the heartfelt connection.

Next, cast golden light around to symbolize the active higher energies you wish to bring to this relationship.

Beginning in the South, face each of the four directions. Go South—West—North—East—and back to South. Complete the circle.

In the South, state your intention to kindle the fires of trust that will bond your relationship to this totem. May you bond in true faith, et cetera. (Add your own sentiments to strengthen this ceremony.)

In the West, state your intention to let love flow between you and the totem, which will nourish your inner needs.

In the North, state your intention to let love be felt in your heart with this totem, and to let wisdom guide your purpose together.

In the East, state your intention to let the winds of illumination and creativity blow freely between you so that you may grow together.

Return to face the South and hold the totem up. To Spirit, state your intention to let the highest good be served by your relationship to this totem.

Touch the totem to the ground or floor. To Mother Earth, state your intention to let healing energy flow through you and through this totem.

Meditate for a while on your path and on the relationship you have to this totem, as well as to Self, Nature, and Spirit.

Close the ceremony by honoring all of the elements, spirit keepers, and rulers of the directions, unseen but felt as helpers on your shamanic path.

This ceremony may be deepened to call in the energies of the directions, and also to serve as an initiation for you and your totem. It may also be adapted to charge a totem with a particular energy or purpose.

Initially, however, it is best to begin a totemic relationships with the energy inherent in the totem. This way you develop the channel that totem represents. Later you may want to add to that channel and focus specific energy through it. To begin with, enjoy the relationship with the totem as it basically is.

Finally, a few suggestions about regular cleansing and maintenance of totems. It's important to recognize that overnurturance and overinvolvement with your totems can be a drain on your energies. Usually this indicates that you are being drained of energy elsewhere, probably in your relationships with others. If you find that you are becoming stuck with the idea of constant maintenance of your totems, take a good look at the people you are in relationship with. Your over-care of totems may be a sign of your own needs.

The path of the shaman is a solitary one; yet it is filled with others who will pull on the energies they find in you. Sometimes these people are all too apparent. Sometimes they are quite subtle. When you feel that you are being influenced by someone else, take a long look at the effect that is having. Be certain that you have chosen to be influenced and that you choose what you accept. The shaman must walk clear of the opinions and influences of others to stay centered amidst the direct energies of the shamanic path.

If totem use is exerting too great an influence in your life, then it, too, must be carefully examined. I have found that energies cease to flow properly when I overuse any totem. Actually, a bit of benign neglect is preferable to obsessive involvement.

As you work with your totems, you will learn to sense the needs of each totem—and your needs reflected by each totem. Usually you will sense that the vibration is weakening. Sometimes it seems as though totems hide for a while to get a rest. This is particularly true with crystals, which are so sensitive and reflect directly. When a crystal of mine goes into hiding, I take it as a sign to have some R and R for myself. I also take it as a sign to cleanse other totems I have used frequently.

A gentle bath of water and salt is quite effective for many Mineral World totems. Smudging is always good, as is placing totems in sunlight or moonlight. If a totem is being used a great deal, it must have rest, or the channel to that energy will block. The schedule I use to cleanse, maintain energy, and recharge totems is based on the lunar cycles. I also use the solar or Pagan festivals as a schedule to keep my totems aligned with the cycles of Nature.

Besides, it's fun to attune with as many levels of Nature as possible at these times. I have included a totem-care chart for you in the appendix. This chart includes both solar and lunar schedules and suggestions for totem care at these times. The lunar schedule is easier to follow in regard to regular care and maintenance of your totems. Basically, when the moon is waxing, or getting fuller, it is time to energize or charge yourself and your totems with vitality and positive vibration. When the moon is waning, or decreasing in size, it is time to release any negative buildup that may have gathered around you and your totems.

However, if you need to, you can adapt the energy for use regardless of the cycle of the moon or sun. For example, if the moon is waning when you need to energize your totems and yourself, then concentrate on removing obstacles to that energy or purpose.

If the moon is waxing full when you need to cleanse away some energy, then attract the positive energies that will clear out what you need to remove. This is extremely useful to attune to and utilize the energy of Nature's rhythms. Just be creative about how you do it— not bound by arbitrary or fixed ideas. Nature is constantly changing and accommodating, as you will find riding the shamanic wheels.

Chapter 4

SHAMANIC MEDICINE

Living shamanically involves the use of totems in everyday situations as well as in times of crisis. The old saying about an apple a day keeping the doctor away can be restated in shamanic terms. A totem a day keeps disharmony away. That may seem simplistic, but the point is clear. Shamanic medicine is not just reserved for dramatic ceremonies and healings. Shamanic medicine is a consistent, ongoing attunement with the elements of Nature, Spirit, and Self. One of the most practical and pleasant ways to maintain the state of harmony and attunement is through the use of totems. The shaman utilizes the energies and vibrations of the worlds of Animal, Plant, Mineral, and Human to keep centered in personal power and connected to Spirit.

In ancient times, it was quite acceptable to carry signs, symbols, and actual items relating to your totems with you at all times. In modern society we learn to adapt these while still maintaining the integrity of the totems. Although the person on the shamanic path does not wish to be influenced by the opinions of others, there is no point in creating disharmony. A spirit of independence and self-expression is a valuable asset for the person on the shamanic path. The spirit of rebellion for its own sake is not.

If you choose to expose your totems to people or environments that aren't ready to accept them, it may only succeed in draining energy from you and your totem. As my dear friend T. J. Grieves was fond of saying, why "cast pearls before swine"? It is admirable that your connection to your totem inspires you to carry it with you in your everyday world of career and social interaction. Be creative, and find a way to do this that keeps the energy close and not exposed to the negativity of misunderstanding.

For example, I have a totem made from the talon of an owl holding a crystal geode. It is trimmed in rabbit fur and has owl feathers and a citrine crystal set in it. This is a very sacred totem to me, but is hardly suitable for what I would call public viewing. If I wish to carry an aspect of that special totem, I may do several things. I may place a small crystal under the geode for a time to absorb that energy and carry just the little crystal as a link. I may also carry a small pouch with a scrap of rabbit fur, a small citrine crystal, and a tiny owl feather. The vibration is not as intense as the owl talon totem, which was created ceremonially. However, the effect is more than sufficient for my everyday use. This is not to even mention the convenience. Let's face it: if we allowed ourselves to do it, more than one of us would carry around a wheelbarrow filled with all the special totems we have begun to dance with on the shamanic path. Of course, if we did that, we would find ourselves being swamped by our totems, instead of supported by them.

There are many ways to stay attuned to our totem energies in a very practical, livable way. There are ways more appropriate for our life in the outside world of business, social life, and education. Rest assured, I'm not suggesting conformity. I'm suggesting convenience, and maybe a little compromise. When you are with others who follow shamanic or magical paths, I heartily recommend that you exhibit your totems and your shamanic attunements as much as you choose to. When you are with others who do not, or who seem not to be open to these shamanic ways, I suggest a more subtle display.

You don't want to close off communication with someone who may need you to be a catalyst for his own journey. Your natural spirit will attract many newcomers to the shamanic path. These people will often be quite tender about their abilities and their desires to begin attuning to the deep levels of Nature. It is probably a great deal easier for them to begin a conversation with someone who has a little carved figure of a bear on his desk, rather than with someone wearing a necklace of bear claws, fur still attached.

It is one of the great joys of being on the shamanic path that one has the opportunities to connect with others of similar interests. Sometimes these people are just beginning to open to the wonders and mysteries of shamanism. Other times, there are those whose level of skill and attunement humbles you greatly.

It has been said of witches that they are recognizable only by their own kind. What this really means is that a person on a magical or shamanic path carries a vibration that can only be read or understood by someone else on a similar path. This is not an elitist selection process. It is a deep affirmation of the many, many others quietly following the ways of Nature.

As my Wolf Clan mother said, "There are more of us than there are of them."

I believe it. Be open to encounters with others on shamanic paths. Be aware that any totem you carry serves only to reflect the shamanic energies you are connected to.

Notes on the Journey

I was in a jewelry supply store in New Mexico, looking for small carved birds and animal figures to make a fetish necklace. I was busily exploring the bargain bin where I had discovered lots of treasures before, when the saleswoman approached me and asked if she could help. While she helped gather my order together, we chatted pleasantly. Still, I noted that her manner was a little hesitant. She seemed to want to ask me something but was obviously undecided.

I told her how much I appreciated her help and relayed a few stories of special treasures I had found in the bargain bin during previous visits. This amused her, and she relaxed visibly. We continued to chat as we counted out silver balls for the necklace I was planning to make.

Finally, she looked at me directly and pointed to the pendant I was wearing. It was a single claw, set in silver and surrounded by turquoise.

"That is not a bear claw, is it?" she asked. It was more of a statement than a question.

"No," I replied. "It is wolf."

She looked at me very directly this time. She was a lovely Native American woman about my age, with deep brown eyes and black hair down her back. I thought we must look a sight: grey-eyed, red-haired Celt and brown-eyed, black-haired Native American, eyeball to eyeball, with energy jumping between us. I waited for her next question.

"Do you feel different when you wear that?" she asked, almost testing me.

I thought of all the amazingly wyrd things that have happened to me since the coming of the wolf. In spite of the seriousness of her intention, I had to laugh. Then I looked at her directly. "Oh yes," I told her, "I feel quite different. Why do you ask?"

She pondered the situation for a while, then replied, "I thought you must feel the medicine of the wolf. So many others come in wearing bear claws and other animal totems who do not even know what they are doing." Sadness reflected in her eyes and her words.

I nodded my head in agreement. "But, you know," I said, "perhaps on some level those people do know. Perhaps they are just waking up to the ways of the animal powers and the ways of Nature—at least some of them, if not all of them."

She thought about that quite seriously for a long time. "We must be patient," she said. "It gives me hope to see someone like you who knows what they are doing."

"How did you know about me?" I asked, unable to resist my curiosity (cat medicine).

She looked a little surprised and amused. "Why, the wolves walked in with you when you came in. I saw them clearly."

"Well, we're going to the mountains for a few days," I told her quite seriously. "No doubt they couldn't pass up the chance to come along."

We spent an hour or so sharing lots of information and making contact. She was encouraged to find that so many were earnestly making their way on the path of the shaman, the path of Nature ways. Finally, it was time to leave. We had strengthened each other's faith and opened another channel to share wisdom.

"Keep up your strength," she called to me as I opened the door to leave.

"And you, too," I called back. I purposely held the door wide open for the wolves. We both laughed and the dance was finished.

After you have traveled a shamanic or magical path for a time, you will certainly develop your own methods for determining what totem or magical items to take along on a day-to-day basis. A good friend of mine used to open a drawer filled with a collection of stones, each set in a pendant holder, and say, "Okay, who comes with me today?" Knowing his particular attunement with the Mineral World, I

wouldn't be surprised to hear that the stone for that day practically leaped out of the drawer, ready to go. My friend would either wear one on a chain around his neck or carry a few in the pocket of his conservative three-piece suit. In that way, he managed to maintain his attunement to the Nature energies he required in the midst of a very busy city where the vibrations of Nature were sometimes hard to feel.

If you are just beginning to work with your totems on a daily basis, it's good to start with a simple collection that is easy to carry. You can keep this collection in a small drawstring pouch or a soft leather key case, if you want to. Although the totems are simple, each serves as a representative of the world that it comes from. Together, they form a pretty, solid little package that you can rightfully call a medicine bag. Here are the basics for this collection. You may add to this as you choose to, or you may decide to keep this little collection just as you first put it together.

It is often good to have reminders of the beginning of your journey on the shamanic path. As we go along, we find more and more that we're always at the beginning, on some level, of our journey. I still have the first medicine bag I put together many years ago. I call it my tenderfoot pouch. So, I'll call this collection the same in honor of the dances I've had with that little pouch of totems.

Tenderfoot Pouch
(Use at least one totem from each world.)

Mineral World	A stone, any kind you feel drawn to except a crystal or gemstone
Animal World	A small feather, bit of fur, claw, whiskers, rabbit tails, wings of butterflies, snake skin
Plant World	Dried flowers, leaves, herbs, interesting twigs or roots
Human World	Personal charms, buttons, hair, chains, locket, tiny figures, such as miniatures for games and models

Add a seed or a nut for growth

Add a crystal or gemstone for Spirit

Add a colored marble, bead, or ribbon for your special color

I have seen this collection made up of very tiny totems from each world and worn in a small pouch around the neck or carried in a pocket. Because it represents a whole world of vibrations, it always serves to remind me that everything we connect with is significant. The smallest bit of fluff is as important as the finest wing feather. The tiniest wildflower is as powerful a connector to the Plant World as the rarest blossom.

The tenderfoot pouch can be a good teacher. As you make other collections for medicine pouches, the tenderfoot pouch can serve as a guideline for balancing the energies. Later you may decide to make up just stone pouches or herb pouches. But the tenderfoot pouch is a good reminder that we need all the elements in balance on the shamanic path.

The tenderfoot pouch is also good to give as a special gift to someone you know rather well. You can add a Human World totem of your own as a symbol of your connection to that person, or you can suggest they add their own.

As I was leaving Houston, a very dear friend presented me with a tiny Oriental pouch that she had found at the import store. In it were some of the dearest totems that symbolized our work together over the past several years. Sharing and receiving such totems is a privilege of the shamanic path. When the energy is clear, the gift becomes a channel of strength in and of itself.

The first place to begin your everyday attunement to the shamanic medicine of totems is in your personal environment, your home. There will be some totems and ceremonial objects for special purposes that you choose to keep separate and out of sight. However, there will most likely be many more with which you form daily relationships. The best way to get those relationships usefully rolling is to bring out your totems. Make them a part of your everyday life.

This is not using them for decoration; this is living with them. I know that some people feel the need to keep all their totems wrapped up, boxed up, and hidden from view. This is understandable for some private totems or ceremonial ones, but not for all. The shamanic path is one of living to the fullest with the energies of Nature. Nature totems cannot be hoarded or stored without losing their energy. So go ahead and pull out those totems you don't feel strongly about keeping separate for personal reasons.

Fill bowls with stones and feathers. Start gathering bunches of dried herbs and flowers. Go on and display that rather strange mask you found at a local bazaar. So what if your house looks like a medicine person lives there? Let it be. Live with your totems around you and deepen your connection. Admittedly, this is easier when you live with someone who is at least a lover of Nature. But most people really are, when they remember it. Remind them.

It's also good to shift your totems around from time to time. Usually this occurs naturally when we get in the habit of taking them out in the room, carrying them with us, or using them for specific purposes. It's really interesting to find what sorts of groupings occur with these totems, often without much conscious planning. When you realize how much shamanic medicine you practice without structuring it, you may be pleasantly surprised.

Every action we take with focus and intent is a form of magick. Every time we arrange a few stones and feathers together with awareness, we are using shamanic medicine. Take a close look at some of the totems you put together. You may find you have collected totems to serve a very specific purpose without even realizing it. Later, as you become more familiar with the totem attributes, you will consciously place these together. Even then, you'll find that a surprise or two always seems to sneak in to give more support to your work on the shamanic path.

In the appendix, I have included a chart on totem medicine. It is made up of totems that I use for the usual journeys and wheels of the four directions. There are many other wheels within the wheels I have included in this chart. The ones I have given you can serve as a foundation for your own journey experiences. I do suggest that you begin to keep track of the effect of various totems on your journeys or wheels.

Sometimes these totems follow very traditional attributes, and you may tap into that energy easily. Sometimes totems have very personal reactions to you or to the specifics of riding the wheel you're on. Keeping notes can be valuable. After all, wheels do keep spinning around and around. You may find yourself right back where you started, doing the same things again. This time, though, you have the greatest totem helper of all—personal experience. Pair experience with some useful information about which totems specifically helped in particular situations—you may not have to keep riding that same wheel.

"Pocket power" is a term I use to describe the ongoing specific use of totems for daily shamanic medicine or energy connections. The totems of the Plant and Mineral Worlds naturally lend themselves to this pocket power more easily than Human, Animal, or Spirit World totems. I'm going to give you a variety of specific applications for Plant and Mineral World totems that you may use on a daily basis for what we call in psychology "problems in everyday living."

Before I discuss the Plant and Mineral Worlds, I want to share a few ways that make it possible to utilize Human and Animal World totems easily on a daily basis. Spirit World totems, such as sacred ceremonial items, or totems of extremely high vibration, are probably best left to special use instead of daily application.

A good example of such a high-vibration totem is the Herkimer diamond. Its effect is very intense on most people carrying it as a pocket power, or even in a medicine bag close to the body. Unless a person is very earthy in their aspects—very earthy—the Herkimer diamond has a strong sedative effect.

The Herkimer diamond is a powerful dream and shamanic-journey stone. While it may sound pleasant to be in a state between the worlds of concrete and abstract form, it could have dangerous results. It could also cause some serious psychic fatigue and real-world exhaustion. Save the high-vibration totems for ceremony and occasions separate from the everyday world.

The Human World totems most useful to everyday living are the philosophies of various cultures. We can tap into those philosophies and utilize the ones most effective for the wheel we are riding. Generally speaking, there are four main types of human philosophies: Western, Eastern, Oriental, and Nature. We correlate these with holistic wellness by pairing Western with body, Eastern with spirit, Oriental with mind, and Nature with heart.

Of course, each of these philosophies contains aspects of all the others, but here is a guideline: In order to tap into the attributes of these philosophies, I use the colors and vibrational Rays most closely related to the energy created by that philosophy.

Western	Body	Red, Orange, Electric Blue
Eastern	Spirit	Purple, Indigo, Black
Oriental	Mind	White, Light Blue, Yellow
Nature	Heart	Rust Brown, Green, Turquoise Blue

By doing this, I can use a color as a totem when I need the attributes of a particular philosophy. For example:

> If I need to remember to let energy flow unstructured or to tap into that deep healing void of Eastern meditative philosophy, I carry or wear something indigo, purple, or black.

> If I need the detached focus and objective mindfulness of Oriental philosophy, I carry or wear something light blue, white, or yellow.

> If I need to feel that deep Earth connection of the Nature philosophies, I carry or wear the earth colors of rust brown, green, or turquoise blue.

> When I need the physical-body awareness and linear philosophies of the Western type, I carry or wear red, orange, or electric blue.

Several people I know have made little medicine pouches in various colors just for this purpose. I like cotton scarves and bandanas, which are available in wonderful colors. Sometimes I wear them; sometimes I put herbs and stones in them, tie a knot, and put them in my pocket. We will examine the vibrational color Rays later in more detail. For now it is useful to consider them as a totemic link to the benefits of Human World philosophies.

One way to use Animal World totems on a daily basis is to carry little carvings or fetishes of animals. Another is to carry physical totems of animals, such as feathers or fur. The first way can be rather expensive, and the second way is not always appropriate for everyday use. As we will discover more in the West section, the totemic link between you and your power animals is one of abstract form more than concrete form. The benefit of this is that you are able to connect most effectively to your power animals through the use of images.

The best way to carry the totem attributes of a power animal on a daily basis is to keep them in your imagination. If you're in a situation where you need the strength and high ideals of an eagle, then be the eagle. When you feel your energy and ideals being drained, take a few moments and focus on an image of an eagle flying majestically, higher than any other bird. The effect will be the same, particularly for your everyday use.

If you need to feel shielded and protected, or if you just want to be left alone, call up an image of a porcupine. The link between you and your power animals is an important relationship that develops primarily through shamanic consciousness and the communication of images. The images are the key to the vibrations of the totems. So, go ahead and be like Merlin wearing Archimedes on his shoulder. Image that. Imagination is a shamanic connector, a shamanic channel, a shamanic ally.

The following are some useful Plant and Mineral World totems that you may use as personal shamanic medicine. Carrying these totems or interacting with their energies can help you maintain that balance and centeredness so needed on the path of the shaman.

To strengthen friendships and relationships:

Minerals	*Plants*
Rose Quartz	Lemon Balm
Coral	Daffodil
Topaz	Thyme
Green Jade	Rosemary
Tiger-Eye	Gardenia
Carnelian	Violet

To increase prosperity and career improvement:

Minerals	*Plants*
Malachite	Almond
Aventurine	Mandrake
Sapphire	Nutmeg
Diamond	Honeysuckle
Crystal Geodes	Ferns
Shells	High John the Conqueror root

To increase personal confidence and power:

Minerals	*Plants*
Tourmaline	Ginger
Rutilated Quartz	Ash
Rhodonite	Oak
Garnet	Cinnamon
Amazonite	Clover
Azurite	Carnation

To strengthen intuition and social awareness:

Minerals	*Plants*
Fluorite	Mugwort
Moonstone	Rose
Lapis Lazuli	Citron
Crystals	Marigold
Amethyst	Peppermint
Turquoise	Pine

To increase communication abilities:

Minerals	*Plants*
Amber	Spearmint
Citrine Quartz	Vervain
Topaz	Bay
Sodalite	Iris
Chrysocolla	Sage
Emerald	Sweetgrass

To uplift emotions and increase energy:

Minerals	*Plants*
Petrified Wood	Heather
Agates	Rose
Abalone	Holly
Red Coral	Lavender
Jade	Cedar
Jasper	Morning Glory

Many of these Mineral and Plant World totems may be used effectively for different applications. I have selected these because they are fairly easy to obtain and use daily. Again, it's how you vibrate and connect with a totem that is most important.

For example, if you are a slow-paced, earthy person, you may need a higher vibration, airy stone like the gemstone amethyst to lift your spirits instead of the fiery, earthy energy of the minerals I selected. Experiment to find your personal blend.

If you are an airy person, you may find that mugwort gives you too much intuitive insight for everyday use. Sometimes too much input clouds the issue as much as too little. If you're already pretty intuitive, you might use pine instead for emotional clarity, or sage for communication. The application of specific totem vibrations to your everyday life is similar to ingesting medicine or chemicals. Their action and reaction depend on your individual makeup.

There are countless sources to use in determining the traditional vibrations of Plant and Mineral World totems. I have listed several in the annotated bibliography. You will find points of agreement and disagreement about the various attributes of these totems. Nature wisdom is an aboriginal science, not an exact one. Of course, human nature is neither static nor exact; so feel free to experiment. Make your own medicine.

Many people I have worked with have created such wonderful ways to incorporate their own blends of totems and shamanic medicine in their everyday life. One woman I know keeps a lovely basket of herbs on her desk, which are nicely scented with perfumed oils made from her special Plant World totems. To her office coworkers, the basket seems like another batch of potpourri. Several of her coworkers have begun bringing their own little baskets and jars of potpourri. Potpourri may not be a totem, but it's a beginning of awareness for some.

Another friend of mine is fond of putting lovely feathers in the plant on her desk, and sometimes small stones in the potting soil. For her, the feathers are a direct connection to clearer communication and perception. The stones, which she changes from time to time, reflect her need to bring practical results into her life and specific actions. An unexpected benefit of this is that her clients and coworkers have begun bringing her stones and feathers they have found in Nature. This truly is a step toward Nature awareness.

When shamanic medicine becomes a part of the daily life of the traveler on the shamanic path, it has many fine benefits that spread throughout the environment. The totems often communicate their vibrations without much help from us.

I have been asked at times which Plant and Mineral World totems I would choose if I had to select only a very few. I always reply that it's fortunate I don't have to do this; Nature has an amazingly abundant variety. However, if I did, here is what I would choose and why I would choose them on an everyday basis.

Mineral World

Fluorite to represent the element of Air. Fluorite is a very good connector for all energies. It is a gentle, effective helper for consciousness work from meditative states to shamanic journeys.

Malachite to represent the element of Earth. Malachite is an all-purpose stone for balancing energies of everyday stresses, for overall grounding, healing, and good fortune as well.

Abalone to represent the element of Water. Abalone has the added benefit of rainbow energies from all of the colors it contains. It serves as a great supporter for dealing with emotions and psychological growth. It's also a good connector to the energies of Mother Ocean.

Carnelian to represent the element of Fire. Carnelian inspires, energizes, and protects all at once. It is a great source of strength for all relationships, and our relationship to life and work.

Clear Quartz Crystal to represent Spirit. Even a tiny crystal can amplify our spiritual connections in an extremely effective way. We can program crystals for any kind of purpose merely by breathing the energy of a specific intention into them. The simple clear quartz crystal may well be Mother Earth's birthday present to us all in this New Age.

To this collection I would have to add my special Mineral World totems: **Amber,** for its clarity and ability to bridge the worlds; **Amethyst,** for its spiritual energies; **Aquamarine,** for its serenity and stability. I would advise that each individual choose his own special Mineral World totems. It is almost impossible for anyone else to do this for you.

If I were pressed to choose just one stone (which would be extremely difficult, as you can no doubt tell), it would be the **Turquoise** because turquoise contains the vibrations of all the worlds of Nature and Spirit. Rough or tumbled, set in silver or gold, or unset, it is a stone of universal energies. It enhances growth, personal confidence, strength, and protection. It is a superb connector to the pure, direct energies of Nature and to the gifts of Spirit. Turquoise is a true stone for the shamanic path.

As I wrote this section, I felt extremely pulled by the many wonderful totems of the Mineral World. It is only fair to say that some of my most shamanic work has been done with a very simple *rock*. The vibrations of specific totems are most useful to us all; but a simple stone can also connect us to the Mineral World energies and vibrations— even if we do have to work a little harder.

Having risked alienating most of the Mineral World by choosing a select few, I will do the same with the Plant World. The Plant World totems I have chosen are primarily herbs, which may be carried in pouches, burned as incense, or mixed together as a kind of shamanic potpourri. I find that these herbal blends are wonderful homes for crystals, stones, roots, feathers, shells, and other Nature treasures.

Plant World

Lavender to represent the element of Air. Lavender is a wonderfully pleasant herb to smell, feel, and see. Lavender creates an overall effect of harmony and peace wherever it is used. The energy of lavender can also be concentrated to summon spirits and for divination.

Sage to represent the element of Earth. Strictly speaking, sagebrush is different from garden sage, but both are good overall purifiers and stabilizers of energy. Sage also serves as a strengthener and foundational support for other Plant World totems. It is a good connector to Earth vibrations on the shamanic path.

Thyme to represent the element of Water. Thyme is an excellent clarifier of energy. It is helpful in dispelling negative emotions and vibrations in the environment. Thyme is useful for healings, for overall good feelings, and can encourage intuitive growth.

Frankincense to represent the element of Fire. Frankincense is a superb herb for protection and to seal in personal aura vibrations. It signals a deep spiritual connection to positive purifying energies. Frankincense may be used on an everyday basis, as well as for high ritual and ceremony.

Jasmine to represent the element of Spirit. Jasmine is a powerful connector to the highest vibrations of Love. It also awakens the energy of love and harmony in everyday relationships. Burning jasmine may create a temple atmosphere wherever it is used.

To this collection I would have to add my special Plant World totems: **Spearmint,** for its soothing energies and creative strengths; and **Dragon's Blood Resin,** for its gifts of power and protection.

If I were pressed to choose just one herb from the Plant World (again, a difficult task), it would be **Mugwort,** because mugwort retains an earthy vibration while encouraging psychic work, consciousness expansion, and spiritual healing. Like the living tree of the shaman, mugwort connects Earth and Spirit energies.

Again, it is important for me to qualify my Plant World choices by pointing out that the simplest herb can connect us to the Plant World energies and to the healing vibrations of Nature. Just think how the smell of fresh-mown grass refreshes and inspires us. We don't have to use exotic herbs and complicated mixtures to connect with the energies of Nature.

I will not even consider choosing a few Animal World totems. I would much rather live in a zoo full of animals than do that. I will say that I find any pure white feather to be a wonderful, all-purpose communicator to use for whatever the need may be. Human World totems are best used as the rainbow of energies they are becoming. Like friends, we spend time with each totem when we need its special energy. Still, nothing can compare to the vibrations they create together in our lives.

The shaman stands at the center of all the worlds, balanced with the gifts of power, in harmony with the energy and vibrations of Nature, Self, and Spirit.

I close the Wheel of the South section with the sacred ceremony of the Flowering Tree. It can be a source of great strength and direction for the traveler on the path of the shaman.

Flowering Tree Ceremony

You will need tobacco or cornmeal and a small rock (not crystal) that has significance for you.

Pick a special time and select a tree in Nature that has significance for you.

Honor the directions in the order of South—West—North—East. Be sure to stop at East.

Then sit with your back against the tree, facing South. With your left hand, hold the stone against your heart and ask the stone to ask the tree questions such as "Who am I?" "How do I feel about myself?" South questions relate to emotion.

This way of asking questions connects the worlds, so be especially aware of your environment. It will give you insights and answers.

Now sit so that you are facing West. Hold the stone against your heart, in your left hand, and have the stone ask questions such as "What do I need to know about my body?" West questions relate to body.

Move to the North and use questions like "What do I need to know about my mind?" North questions correspond to mind.

Move to the East and use questions like "What am I here for?" "What is my path?" East questions correspond to spirit.

You may write down or record your impressions as you move through the directions.

When you are done in the East, hug the tree from the East (Indian hug) and leave the tobacco or cornmeal by the tree, as an offering.

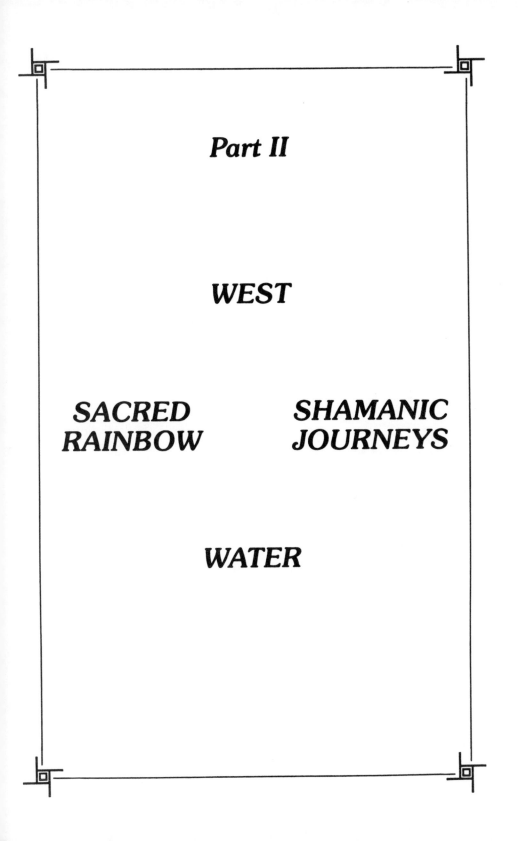

Part II

WEST

*SACRED
RAINBOW*

*SHAMANIC
JOURNEYS*

WATER

ATTRIBUTES OF THE WEST

The **Element** of the West is Water.

The **Wheel of the West** is the wheel of
Inner Knowing
Dreams
Emotions
Feelings
Introspection
Shamanic Journeys
Healing
Balancing active male and receptive female energies

The **Energy** of the West is tidal—it ebbs and flows, but never floods.

The **Journey of the West** is the journey to inner vision.

The **Traditional Colors** of the West are
Blue-Green
Aqua
Grey
Blue-Grey
Black
Indigo
and the White of sea foam in the moonlight

Some **Sacred Spirits** of the West are
Poseidon—god of oceanic consciousness
Neptune—god of psychic flow
Isis—goddess of the rivers of life
Arianrhod—Celtic goddess of the Moon and Earth
Diana—goddess of the New Moon
Selene—goddess of the Full Moon

Hecate—goddess of the Dark Moon
Gabriel—archangel of the West, angel of the Moon
and inner vision
Niksa—servant of Gabriel, fluid shape-changer of the
inner worlds
Undines—elemental spirits of Water, ruled by Niksa
Eheieh—elemental king of Water

Some **Animals** of the West are
Sea Mammals—for psychic communication
Sea Birds—for uplifted emotions
Heron—for intuition and organization
Jaguar—for shamanic journeys
Raven—for dreams and inner knowing
Bear—for introspection and especially for healing
Elk—for feelings and emotions
Fish—of all types, for swimming in the tides of life's
emotions

Some **Minerals** of the West are
Aquamarine—for inner journeys, serenity
Water-Colored Crystals—for psychic flow
River Stones—for emotions
Ocean Rocks—for healing and emotion
Silver—for intuition
Amethyst—for inner journeys, soothing emotions
Mercury—for changeable emotions
White Coral—for flexibility
Rainbow Crystals—for shamanic journeys
Blue Fluorite—for shamanic journeys and dreams
Double-Terminated Crystals—for healing energies

Some **Plant World Helpers** of the West:

Journey Incenses	*Dream Teas*
Lotus	Chamomile
Sandalwood	Jasmine
Mugwort	Raspberry
Camphor	Catnip
Vanilla	Cherry
Violet	Hibiscus

Some **Human World Helping Activities** of the West are

Dream Work	Eastern Void Meditations
Shamanic Consciousness Work	Healing Circles
	Self-Healing
Earth Journeys	Love

Helping Thoughts for the West:

> Feelings are but tiny trickles,
> and emotions gentle brooks
> leading to the great rivers
> of Inner Knowing and Dreams.
> All are pulled to the Deep Ocean Mother
> by the Lady of the Healing Lights.

Riding the Wheel of the West

Mother Ocean

I have sought the refuge of my private island, isolated
    in the ocean of my consciousness.
I stand barefoot on the beach.
The warmth of the sand beneath my feet moves slowly
    up my body.
White-hot sunlight cascades down upon me, caressing
    my head and shoulders.
I breathe in the healing warmth and light.
I am surrounded with a radiant glow of being.
The warmth of the sand and the sun meet in my heart.
I feel the edges of emotion and stress soften and slip
    away in the breeze from the shore.
I feel the trickle of sea foam as the waves sweep up
    the beach to tease me.
Each tiny wave carries me gently into the sea.

Little by little, I merge with the waters of Mother
    Ocean.
I see the sunbeams streaming into the aquamarine
    serenity of the shallows.
Cooler currents coax me ever deeper.
Sunlight fades as I move into the cobalt depths.
Overhead, waves sweep by, gently rocking me.
Below me, still white sand, first rippled, then smooth.
Cobalt becomes indigo as I am at one with the ocean.
The waves pass unnoticed; the ocean bottom vanishes.
No thoughts, no senses, no sounds, as I float in the heal-
    ing void—within the Silence, within the Source.
Deep in the womb of Mother Ocean
I am awaiting rebirth, renewal.

I am stirred within the depths by warm streams of
    water pulling me higher.

Sunlight beckons once again, reaching through the
    cool shadows to wake me.
Waves come rushing at me now, insistently carrying me
    in to the shore.
Clouds of sand and foam tumble around me as the
    crest of my wave breaks, casting me onto the
    beach once more.

I lie face down in the sand, drowsing in the sunlight.
A tiny crab comes to investigate,
    for I am new here once again.
Slowly, I regain my form.
Arms, legs, muscle and bone move in harmony and
    lift me from the sand.

I walk along the beach, unsteadily at first,
    but soon with a stride of purpose.
I see myself reflecting the green of the trees and the
    blue of the sky and the sea.
I am the silvery cast of moonlight on a lavender
    lagoon.
I am cool, flowing energy. I receive; I renew.

Waiting for me on the beach is a man—myself as a
    man, mirroring myself as woman.
Around him fly sparks of sunlight yellow and the fiery
    orange of a sunset sky.
Beneath his feet lava, long cooled, glows red again—
    molten heat.
He is warm, thrusting energy. He activates; he creates.
He is me; and I am he.
She is I; and I am she.

We meet—we merge—we are one.
Auras blend in rainbow hues,
    aligning, balancing, harmonizing.
Vibrations meld into pure white light, blending into
    silver and gold.
I feel myself lifted higher, beyond form.
A fountain of energy flows upward and spills back onto

the earth—creating me anew.

I return from my private island, kept safe in the ocean
   of my consciousness.
I am in balance. I am complete.
I am myself.

The Wheel of the West is the wheel of healing balance from inner vision. In the West, we journey into our higher Self. We travel between the worlds of concrete and abstract form. There we meet our truest teacher, our intuition. Our intuition is our inner teacher. Whatever form we give our inner teacher, we are both student and sage ourselves. We teach ourselves in the West with dreams, with psychic impressions, and with deep self-examination. In the West, we learn the gift of introspection.

We do not merely look inside ourselves—we go inside. We travel into the abstract level of images, dreams, and shamanic journeys. We step into the healing void, and we enter into the Silence.

In the West we merge with the oceanic energies that give us birth and rebirth. We find our balance in the currents of life that flow around us. We find the sacred partner that is our Self. If we are male, we find our female. If we are female, we find our male.

The Oriental symbol of yin-yang balance is also a wheel, ever spinning. In the West we ride that wheel. We ride the wheels of personal balance, healing, and harmony. We ride the wheel of inner visions, dreams, and deep mind. We learn to flow. In the West, we reach the levels of self-initiation. There can be no other kind for the traveler on the path of the shaman.

A totem animal for the West is the bear. It is wise to follow the example of the bear when riding the Wheel of the West. The work of the West requires the solitude and slower energies of hibernation. The healing balance of the West calls for quiet introspection. In the West, we are making maps to inner vision.

Here is a ceremony to help you on the Wheel of the West. You may use it, as you feel the need, to focus your energies and center your power.

West Ceremony

Stand in the South, facing North.

Take a moment to recall the lessons and strengths of the South wheel you have ridden.

Turn to face the South.

Give honor and thanks for the growth you have received. Honor the faith, the trust, the protection.

Now turn to face the West.

Feel the vibrations of the West flow toward you.

When you are ready, step into the West.

Stand in the West, facing East and illumination.

On your left is the wisdom of the North.

On your right is the faith of the South.

Stand in the West.

Feel the energies ebb and flow through you.

Now go into that quiet place of your inner vision.

Imagine yourself as a warrior of Spirit—conquering with the power of love and healing.

In you are the gifts of a true quest knight.

In you are the gifts of a true spiritual priestess.

In you is the balance of the Sacred Path.

In your right hand you hold the Sword of Faith.

Within you, the Grail of Inner Vision.

To your right, the Pentagram Shield of Wisdom.

In front, the blooming Staff of Creativity.

Stand in balance. Center yourself among these energies.

When you are ready, turn to face the West.

Call on the helping spirits and the elements of the West to aid you in your quests between the worlds.

Go in balance.

Chapter 5

SACRED ENERGIES

When we learn to identify Nature color messages from the totems we have found in our environment, we have just begun to tap into the vibrations of color. In the West, we begin to focus our work with color in a more specific manner. The focused energies of colors are quite useful for balancing, healing, and attuning to the abstract levels of consciousness, intuition, and dream work.

The difference in the Nature color energies and the focused energies is a matter of the degree of vibration. Focused color energy is much more intense and powerful. We call these focused color energies *Rays*. These Rays harmonize with the colors in Nature, yet go beyond these in a distilled, concentrated form. Because of their powerful aspects, these Rays are a valuable tool for the shamanic path. They are direct, pure energies.

Consider that the energy of a cut gemstone can be like that of a laser beam. The energy of an uncut natural gemstone is more like that of an aura or glow. The difference of energy vibration between Rays and Nature colors is similar to that. Rays are quite specific in effect. Colors affect more generally. Simply speaking, Rays vibrate and colors radiate. It may seem like splitting hairs to make this difference clear. Yet, the use of Rays in shamanic methods can create very intense reactions, so it is good to be aware of the differences involved.

There are many different systems of color and Ray wisdoms. Some of these differ somewhat concerning the attributes of Ray energies. For the most part, though, there is agreement about the power and the effect of these Ray energies. Some systems stress that these Rays are powers in and of themselves. Other systems stress the importance of the chakras, or human energy points, in relation to the Ray energies. Regardless of the system, the recognition of the significant, direct energies of Rays is universal.

The systematic use of Ray energies has been a shamanic method throughout the ages. This is a method we can adapt for our own use on the shamanic path. Rays can be very real shamanic totems. They can be used on their own, or with other totems—very effectively. In addition, a familiarity with Ray energies deepens our connection to the totems we have.

Ray energies transcend all levels. Because they do this, we are able to use them as pathways to deep shamanic consciousness work. This work includes dream states, inner visions, shamanic journeys, healing, and the balancing of our deep-mind self. We learn to work with Rays by experiencing their energies for ourselves. One of the best ways to experience Ray energies is through the use of images. We begin by exploring these Rays, by actively imaging them. This way, we also become familiar with working in our own inner visions. Later, the Rays will emerge in inner vision, unbidden, giving us valuable insight and information.

The following exercise is adapted from a guided imagery created by a friend, teacher, and Craft brother, now in spirit: Thomas-John Grieves. It is a simple method that I use often to attune to the Ray energies of the basic spectrum and chakra system. Once you have worked with it for a while, you will find it very effective as a doorway to inner vision, as well as to healing balance for yourself.

Crystal Cave

Begin by taking a long, slow, deep breath.

Hold it a moment; then gently release.

Continue to do this for several more times until you feel your body relax and your pace begin to slow and steady.

Stretch your right arm out as far as you can.

Wiggle your fingers; visualize sparks of tension flying away. Relax your arm.

Now do the same with your left arm.

Next, stretch out your right leg as far as you can.

Wiggle your toes and feel the energy release.

Relax your leg and breathe deeply.

Now do the same with your left leg.

Relax, and breathe deeply once more; then let your breathing find its natural rhythm.

In your inner vision, imagine that you are climbing a twisting, steep mountain path.

Take your time. Allow yourself to reach the top of the mountain.

As you come to the top, you find that the path ends at the mouth of a large cave.

Even as you stand at the entrance to the cave, you feel the vibrations from inside.

These vibrations energize you and beckon for you to come inside the cave.

You step inside the cave and find that it glows from an unseen source of light.

You notice that the walls of the cave are covered with beautiful clear crystals.

As you step carefully, you find that the floor of the cave is also studded with crystals.

Above you, the ceiling glitters with still more cystals.

Breathe deeply and absorb the energy of all these crystals.

As you move deeper into the cave, you find that the crystals begin to glow a strong, rich red.

Experience the energy of this Red Ray.

When you have done that, move on deeper into the crystal cave.

As you do so, the crystals around you begin to glow a vibrant orange.

Experience the energy of this Orange Ray.

When you have done that, move on deeper into the crystal cave.

Now the crystals begin to glow a bright, warm yellow.

Experience the energy of this Yellow Ray.

When you have done that, move on deeper into the crystal cave.

Now you feel the vibrations shift to another pace as the crystals around you glow a soothing, healing green.

Experience the energy of this Green Ray.

When you have done that, move on deeper into the crystal cave.

As you do so, the crystals around you begin to glow a cool, gentle blue.

Experience the energy of this Blue Ray.

When you have done so, move on deeper into the crystal cave.

Now the crystals begin to glow a serene indigo.

Experience the energy of this Indigo Ray.

When you have done so, move on deeper into the crystal cave.

As you do so, you notice the crystals around you begin to glow a deep violet.

Experience the energy of this Violet Ray.

When you have done so, move on deeper into the crystal cave.

As you do so, you enter a chamber filled with crystals of all colors.

Rich reds, vibrant oranges, warm yellows, soothing greens, gentle blues, serene indigos, and deep violets.

Experience the Ray energies of these crystals.

Breathe deeply; absorb these energies.

As you do so, you notice that the crystals around you are clear once more.

Only a sparkle of color remains, twinkling inside each crystal. All of the energies remain, deep inside of you.

Experience the balance and energy of all these crystals. Take all the time you need.

When you have done this, move on, once more, inside the crystal cave.

Now you find that you have come full circle on your path.

You see the entrance of the crystal cave just ahead.

The light of the clear crystal around you marks the way. Breathe deeply.

Step out of the crystal cave, onto the mountain path.

See yourself energized by the crystal-cave journey.

Experience the balance of your energies.

Take all the time you need to return down the mountain and back to the present time and place.

Take a long, slow deep breath; hold, stretch, and slowly release your breath.

Experience yourself in balance.

Now you are cleared to continue your journey as you choose to do so.

Another version, which is quite effective, is to image yourself in a large egg-shaped chamber made of crystal. In the chamber is a control panel with buttons of all the colors. As you push each button, the energy of the color surrounds you and vibrates through you. Still another is to image yourself climbing crystal stairs. These change from clear crystal to colors as you walk slowly up the stairs. You can experiment with your own images until you find what works best for you.

Chanting specific sounds to tap Ray energies can have deep-level balancing effects. The systems of harmonics use sound to attune to the Rays for healing, for deep-level meditation, and for journey work. I find that imagery combined with specific sounds creates intense and direct results.

Notes on the Journey

I had felt myself pulled in several directions by the work of many months. Somehow, I no longer fit in my body. Indeed, I had found myself walking down the hall one day as though I were in at least two parts, probably more. The experience was so strong that I knew some rebalancing was needed immediately. The demands of a new baby had left me without the time and energy to accomplish this alone. I sought the help of a woman whose work and energy I knew and trusted completely.

She worked on my physical body first, carefully adjusting the tensions and unknotting the muscles. When she had finished, she guided me meditatively into the healing void. After floating in that darkness for a time, I was asked to experience myself from within that realm of consciousness. I immediately saw a silhouette of myself. It was a dark form on a dark background. I could make out no details, but I knew it was my own shape, my own shadow.

Holding her hands on the soles of my feet, she began chanting soft vowel sounds. Though each one sent an energy current up my spine in my physical body, my shadow image remained unchanged. She reached the sound of *om* and chanted it several times, each one with greater intensity.

Suddenly, my image created many outlines, silhouetted shapes— all of me—all in the bright colors of the spectrum. Like neon colors on a black background, they flashed and reflected my shape. As she chanted the final *om*, all of the colored outlines slammed into the dark shadowy shape that was me.

I felt energy rush into me from just outside my body. I felt more energy rush up my spine to blend with the incoming energy. The colors in my image vibrated intensely; then blackness descended. In a moment my silhouette appeared once more, this time surrounded by an aura of white, blue-violet, and indigo. It was the aura I see when my energies are in balance, one I had not seen for too long.

I felt the welcome vibration of harmony. My images had given me the privilege of watching the Ray energies do their work. The harmonics of sound had created the proper vibration to tap the Rays and to realign my own energies. My aura had shown me the result. I was more than convinced of the systematic use of sound with Rays.

The systems of harmonics are quite ancient and quite powerful. A lifetime (or two) could be spent developing the skills of intonation and vibration. I have found, though, that by chanting the suggested sound and imaging the color of the vibrational Ray, very useful and effective results are created. Harmonics can also be used to focus energies and to charge totem objects with specific Rays to help in our journey. More than any other use I have found, harmonics give an excellent system for self-healing and balancing.

The following is a simple exercise designed primarily for personal healing. It can also be deepened ceremonially and can be used as a pathway to shamanic consciousness. After you have experimented with it, you will have a better sense of its adaptability for your own work.

In the exercise, I included the newer blended Rays with which my colleagues in harmonics have been recently working. It seems only appropriate that a New Age of blended wisdom would also reflect new blended-energy Rays. After you have worked with the energies and aspects of these Rays, you will find them to be a valuable tool. As always, create your own blends and make your own medicine. This exercise is only to get you started.

Aquarian Energies

Imagine yourself sitting in the middle of three circles, each one encircling the next—concentric rings like ripples on the water.

You are the center.

In each circle are crystals.

The circle closest to you has three crystals: red—yellow—blue.

The next circle has three crystals: orange—green—violet.

The outside ring has six crystals: peach—scarlet—rose—turquoise—lime green—indigo.

Twelve crystals—twelve energies.

And you are the center crystal.

Begin with the first circle.

Call upon the energy of the red crystal.

Make the sound of a long *e*.

Visualize the Red Ray vibration lifting from the red crystal and flowing into you—you are the center crystal.

Absorb all that you need of the Red Ray and send it back to the red crystal.

Continue this process until you have completed each circle, and each crystal. Continue until you have absorbed all that you need of the Ray represented in each crystal.

Here are the sounds and colors you use to call for the energies of the Rays.

Rays and Vibrational Sounds

Primary Rays (1st circle, inner)

Red	Sound of long *e*, as in *she*
Yellow	Sound of short *a*, as in *ah*
Blue	Sound of long *o*, as in *boat*

Secondary Rays (2nd circle, middle)

Orange	Sound of short *e*, as in *bet*
Green	Sound of long *a*, as in *say*
Violet	Sound of short *u*, as in *sun*

Blended Rays (new, 3rd circle, outside)

Peach	Sound of short *a*, as in *hat*
Scarlet	Sound of long *i*, as in *ice*
Rose	Sound of *y*, as in *why*
Turquoise	Sound of *aw*, as in *draw*
Lime Green	Sound of short *i*, as in *sit*
Indigo	Sound of *om*, as in *foam*

The energies of Rays can have positive effects when they flow in balance. When they are blocked in their flow, the effects can be negative. Recognizing the symptoms of these effects can be useful in determining which Ray to tap to balance the flow of energies.

Generally speaking, a correct attunement with the Ray energy will realign the proper balance or flow. In the appendix, I have included a chart on the attributes of Ray energies. It will give more information about the positive and negative qualities that manifest from Ray energies. Here is a sample.

Attributes of Ray Energies

Color	Positive	Negative
Red	Strength	Violence
Yellow	Joy	Contempt
Blue	Security	Depression
Orange	Creativity	Ignorance
Green	Sharing	Greed
Violet	Devotion	Obsession
Peach	Peace	Strife
Scarlet	Rapport	Egocentrism
Rose	Serenity	Moroseness
Turquoise	Zeal	Egoism
Lime Green	Openness	Delusion
Indigo	Unity	Pride

It is easy to see how keeping these energies aligned is an important part of shamanic self-healing and balance. I suggest that you begin with the primary and secondary Rays; then later move into working with the newer blended Rays. A very effective result can also be achieved by concentrating on the primary Rays of Red, Yellow, and Blue; then finishing with Indigo, which is the synthesis of these primary Rays.

I find that my Mineral World totems are extremely effective for helping me balance these Ray energies etherically, and for helping me appreciate the aesthetic benefits of Nature colors. In the appendix there is a chart, called Rainbow Stone Energies, that gives guidelines for selecting Mineral World totems that harmonize with Rays and Nature colors. Here is a small sample.

Rainbow Energies	Mineral World Totems
Red (includes Rose and Scarlet)	Jasper
Orange (includes Peach)	Rhodochrosite
Yellow (includes Lime Green)	Peridot
Green	Malachite
Blue (includes Turquoise)	Chrysocolla
Indigo	Azurite
Violet	Sugalite (Royal Azule)
White	Moonstone
Crystal	Selenite
Brown	Sandstone
Black	Onyx
Grey	Hematite
Rainbow	Abalone
Gold	Pyrite
Silver	Mercury

Mineral World totems are convenient to use in working with Ray energies. The natural colors of Mineral World totems harmonize so well with, and give good support to, the energies. Totems from the other worlds of Nature are not so readily harmonized with Ray energies. It's a matter of having to dance with the energies of the totems to determine how you use them in your work with Rays. Often these totems are quite flexible and can be adapted for use with several Ray energies.

For example, the hawk is a powerful predator, quite fiery in his element, and still very precise in his perceptive abilities. If we were to attempt to match these qualities to Ray energies, we would have to start with at least three: Red, for the predatory energy; Orange, for the fiery element; and Yellow, for the perceptive awareness.

I use a hawk totem ceremonially as a messenger who can bring spiritual wisdom down to earth. In this way, the hawk is reflecting the energies of Green and Indigo Rays.

Animal World totems are clearly very complex. It is only through our own dances with them that we can decide how to attune with the Rays they reflect.

Some of the Tibetan-based philosophies have attributed Ray energies to Human World philosophies: Red is attributed to Western philosophies; Blue, to Eastern philosophies; and Yellow, to Oriental philosophies. Tibetan is correlated to the Indigo Ray, as a synthesis of Red, Yellow, and Blue.

My reaction to this is to point out the importance of Nature or aboriginal philosophies. I feel that the Green Ray best reflects the Nature philosophies.

The Green Ray holds the awareness and mindfulness of Yellow, as well as the spirituality and devotion of Blue. Green also carries energies of growth, expansiveness, and renewal, which are vital to the Nature philosophies. If pressed, I would also add a touch of Red to this Green Ray. This would make it a somewhat darker, earthy green color, unlike the green of the rainbow. Also, green is the color of the heart chakra or energy point. Nature philosophies are heartfelt, so I feel this is also appropriate. This is a system I have developed in my own work. I offer it for your consideration.

I use the following exercise to balance the Ray energies of Human World philosophies. We are in an age of blended, shared wisdom. I find it important to stay centered in the chaos that can occur when philosophic energies merge. I use Mineral World totems for this most often. I find that colored beads, glass, and cloth are also very effective for attuning to the Ray energies—so are clear crystals that have been charged with a specific Ray beforehand. Adapt this exercise to suit your own needs and preferences.

Rainbow Philosophies

If you use stones for this, you may wish to refer to the Rainbow Stone Energies chart in the appendix, for suggested harmonizers.

Place a Blue Ray item in the West.

Place a Green Ray item in the North.

Place a Yellow Ray item in the East.

Place a Red Ray item in the South.

Place an Indigo Ray item in the center.

Sit behind the Indigo Ray item in the center of the circle. Take time to feel the energy and vibration of each Ray. Center your own energies and breathe slowly.

Beginning with the Blue Ray, absorb the energies of Eastern spiritual philosophies.

Feel how the energy flows. In your inner vision, allow images of Eastern spiritualities to emerge. Allow the sensation of the Ray energy and the message of your own images to blend. Take a moment to absorb that philosophic blend. Memorize its energy, to recall as needed. Feel the deep connection open between yourself and the Ray energy of this philosophy.

When you feel complete, move to the Green Ray.

Continue this process until you have absorbed and attuned to all of the Ray energies around you. As always, allow your own reactions and your own medicine to create your special connection to the Rays of human philosophies. This is the way of the shaman.

Guidelines for Human World Philosophic Ray Energies

Blue Ray	Eastern spirituality	Flowing energy
Green Ray	Nature consciousness	Heartbeat energy
Yellow Ray	Oriental mindfulness	Uplifting energy
Red Ray	Western physical	Static energy
Indigo Ray	Tibetan synthesis	Centering energy

This exercise is easily done with the use of active imagery. The benefit of using totems is that they become charged with the Ray energies of the philosophies they represent. One man I know liked this so well, he gathered five crystals just for this purpose. Each crystal has its own wrapping cloth in the color of the Ray for the philosophy it represents. Since this man is a teacher of esoteric philosophies, he is able to use this exercise quite often in his own work.

I have a crystal cluster with many points that I use as a collector of direct Ray energies. Geodes are also very good for this as long as they have actual crystal points emerging from inside. One geode I have is affectionately known as "the little people's crystal cave." Because I have used it so many times when I was doing the Crystal Cave exercise, I can simply hold it meditatively for a few moments, and achieve a good sense of healing balance. It is not always necessary to specifically charge totems that you use in your work on the shamanic path. Sometimes all that is needed is to let them share in the journey.

If you do wish to charge a totem object with a specific Ray energy—as my friend did with his crystals—here is a suggestion: Spend time with the totem to determine if the Ray energy you wish to charge it with will harmonize with its own energy.

For example: a carnelian simply will not harmonize with a Violet Ray; a coyote will not fare well with a Blue devotional Ray (though he may trick you into thinking he will); and mugwort cannot be used very effectively with a Red Ray.

After you have considered the compatibility of a totem to a specific Ray energy and feel that it will harmonize well, take time to clean or clear the totem. Do this with imagery, sage smoke, or clear water.

For example, you have decided that the otter will be most helpful in attuning to the Green Ray energies. Take time in your images or inner visions to let the otter swim in crystal-clear water, dry in the sun, and roll in the rich green grass. In this way, you have already begun charging the totem with the Ray energy.

After you have cleansed the totem in preparation to charge it with a specific Ray energy, take time to be very certain of the attributes you wish to tap into. Be sure to balance these correctly.

For example, that little silver charm in the shape of an eagle may be an excellent choice for the Indigo Ray of devotion and idealism. However, if you aren't clear with yourself when you charge the totem, you may end up with a very egotistical eagle!

Be clear about your own needs for specific Ray energies, and be aware of imbalances when they emerge.

Every Ray has positive and negative aspects. Keeping yourself in balance is the most effective connection to the positive aspects of Ray energies. Finally, allow totems that have been charged with specific Ray energies to rest once in a while. Too much use of a direct energy can also block it and cause negative attributes to emerge.

Riding the wheels of Ray energies requires a lot of practice, skill, and self-balance. Sometimes it makes me feel like the original shaman surfer. Surf's up!

I close this chapter with some very brief images designed to help you attune to the Ray energies as they occur in Nature. So often the blend of energies in a Nature setting makes it almost impossible to pick out single Ray energies. Of course, that is one of the special skills of Nature. She makes her own medicine and keeps the blend of ingredients to herself. Mother Nature is the original wise woman.

However, there are times in Nature when pure, direct Ray energies can be experienced quite clearly. These are magic moments. Let these brief images become journey totems to the energies and to inner vision.

Rainbow Ray Images

Red Ray. A fiery sunset reflects in the glass towers of a great urban city. Later, taillights flash in the darkness of city streets. Neon signs beckon the city dweller to partake of the joys and entertainment of the night. The sounds of car horns and a thousand stereos fill the air.

Yellow Ray. Gentle morning sunlight beams down on the sandy shoreline of a winding river. Every grain of sand glistens precisely like a tiny crystal of light. A canoe moves through the water silently. Each ripple carefully reflects its own beam of sunlight. Each drop of water from the canoe paddle pauses for a moment, sparkling in the sunlight, then drops back into the river.

Blue Ray. A sailboat glides through deep ocean waters. A fresh breeze heels the boat as it slices through tall waves, crested with foam. With no land in sight, only a few stray clouds mark the line of the horizon, where the sky meets the sea. A seagull circles overhead in the vast unbroken clarity of the sky.

Orange Ray. Friends gather on a beach at sunset, collecting wood for a bonfire. Laughing with the ease of familiarity, they light the fire and dance joyfully around it. As the evening grows cold, they huddle closer to the flickering flames and glowing embers. For hours into the night, they share their hopes, their goals, and their dreams.

Green Ray. A late afternoon thundershower has swept the air clean. The full growth of midsummer droops, relaxed, under the weight of the raindrops. Tall trees sway gently and reflect in the cool mirror of a fishpond. Evening breezes arrive early to dry the leaves. Each plant, each tree, each blade of grass glows vibrantly as the twilight sky comes to fade the day.

Violet Ray. The baked clay earth of the desert cools as night begins its approach. Sagebrush whispers as the night wind sweeps by. Evening clouds gather behind the distant mountains that rise sharply out of the broad, flat landscape. Tiny creatures scurry in the shadows, searching for sustenance and awaiting the security of nightfall.

Indigo Ray. Lovers make their way through the vast darkness of a forest. The light of a small lantern guides their footsteps on the soft, cool ground. They follow the sound of water running over rocks smoothed by time. They come to a gentle creek, seen only in the small halo of the lantern light. They spread a blanket on the bank of the creek, blow out the lantern flame, and count the stars twinkling down through the trees.

Peach Ray. Small children rush out onto a beach to coax the sun into rising. Soft lights of a new day reflect in the fluffy clouds on the horizon. The morning stars fade in the warm promise of a clear sky. The children wade in gently lapping waves. Each tiny shell they find is greeted as a gift from the sea.

Turquoise Ray. Rocks carved by a thousand winds stand etched against the sky. Like obelisks of stone, they cast visions skyward. The great sweep of sky surrounds and protects all that it covers. Wind-carved monuments stand in tribute to the marriage of land and sky. Great billowing clouds pass in procession—each one smoothly in step with the next.

Scarlet Ray. Snow falls softly, blanketing the land. Trees and bushes covered with ice and snow seem to be ghosts of themselves. A heavy-hanging sky promises more snow and oblivion. Among the ghostly trees a camellia bush struggles to open its winter blossoms. A small pile of snow slips from the leaves of the bush. A flash of color reveals the vibrant camellia blossom, completely undaunted by the silence of winter.

Lime Green Ray. The sun of Incas, Mayans, and Aztecs hangs over the steaming jungle. Vines creep perceptibly among the roots of twisted, tropical trees. Butterflies, like sunlight, flutter among the foliage, stopping to rest on broad, shiny leaves. A tree trunk seems to undulate with a shifting pattern of caterpillars waiting for the release of metamorphosis—and flight.

Rose Ray. The drone of huge bumblebees breaks the nursery stillness of a mountain meadow. Tiny drifts of snow remain in the shadows of great rocks and trees. Dotted across the frosty grasses of the meadow, wildflowers and crocuses announce their arrival. Deep in the stony crags of peaks returning to earth, mountain flowers reveal their hardy lineage.

Chapter 6

SHAMANIC IMAGES

Within the realms of consciousness, the shaman creates a garden of images that he nurtures, and that in turn nurture him. Images are the pathways to inner vision. Images are the language of the abstract level. Images focus and connect the shaman to direct energies. Images are the shaman's key into the worlds of Nature, Spirit, and Self. The use of images gives the follower of the shamanic path the balance needed to ride the wheels within wheels, which is the universe.

With imagery, the shaman can communicate and interpret the messages of all the worlds. Images give form to that which cannot be spoken in words, and birth to ideas otherwise unreachable. Experiential imagery is the way of the shaman, who lives between the worlds of concrete and abstract form. Imagery is a shamanic path.

In order to learn the active shamanic use of imagery, we must first understand a little more about imagery and consciousness work. We have been discussing various Human World philosophies, their vibrational Rays, and their effects on our lives. Now we approach these philosophies in reference to their consciousness work. In doing this, we will see how the active shamanic use of images is a blended method incorporating many approaches to consciousness.

All cultures have aboriginal roots and aboriginal consciousness. The shaman, having direct Nature connections, weaves these consciousness roots together to make a deeper connection to universal consciousness. Grey Eagle uses the image of a pyramid to demonstrate how these philosophies or consciousnesses blend. At the base of the pyramid are different sides, each representing different cultures or philosophies. All of these reach up into Spirit and form the top of the pyramid together.

When we examine one separate philosophy, type of conscious-ness work, or culture, we are making arbitrary divisions. We do this in order to understand all the parts that make up the whole. Shamanic consciousness regards all levels, all forms, as significant. Divisions are made only as is appropriate to function in society. As long as we are making our Earth Walk, we must also make these arbitrary divisions.

I have often thought that it would be far easier at times to be transcendental, in Spirit realms. The shamanic use of images allows us to tap the transcendental levels while we are still very much a part of the earth. The active use of images is a transcendent function that we may use freely for our own journey on the shamanic path. A transcendent function is one that results from the merging of all aspects of self to create a higher synthesis of self.

Carl Jung, the great psychoanalyst and Western mystic, describes this transcendent function as the blending of psychological aspects into a balanced system of self-definition and self-awareness. These psychological aspects, which Jung calls *functions,* are *sensation,* which is sensory and physical; *feeling,* which relates to heartfelt reactions; *intuition,* which arises from inner experiences; and *thinking,* which is intellectual and mental.

When these psychological aspects are in balance, a merged awareness or self-synthesis occurs. This creates holistic growth for the individual. It's like the shaman's staying centered in personal power, balancing abilities or gifts to create a dynamic synthesis. Dynamic synthesis of self is a catalyst for psychological growth and for greater levels of awareness.

This process of blending, synthesizing, and catalysting growth is central to any magical or shamanic path. You are also a wheel, con-stantly moving and changing. Understanding your own abilities to deepen awareness and using them effectively are special gifts.

When you are using shamanic images, you are using all of the aspects or functions that Jung described. Active, or shamanic, images incorporate sensory, emotional, intuitive, and intellectual abilities. Blending these is one of the reasons that shamanic images have such a personal, experiential quality.

In addition to this, each of the four functions described by Jung taps into at least one of the four basic types of Human World philosophies and consciousness work. The function of sensation, being sensory, relates to Western, physical, linear consciousness. The function of feeling, being heartfelt, relates to Nature, earth consciousness. The function of intuition, being inner experience, relates to Eastern, spiritual consciousness. The function of thinking, being intellectual, relates to Oriental, mindfulness consciousness.

Each of these Human World philosophies has its own Ray, as mentioned before. Western consciousness work corresponds to the Red Ray energy; Nature, to the Green Ray; Eastern, to the Blue Ray; and Oriental, to the Yellow Ray.

Shamanic imaging combines all of these Rays, psychological functions, and Human World consciousnesses together. This combination becomes a dynamic synthesis. This dynamic synthesis actively catalysts deeper levels of consciousness, increased psychological functions, and further attunement to the Ray energies.

Considering this, it becomes more understandable why shamanic imaging is such a powerful experience and tool. Shamanic imaging takes transcendent functioning out of the realm of psychological development into the limitless realms of abstract consciousness.

Now, if all this information about consciousness seems a bit much to handle, let's approach it another way. Start with a situation in your everyday life. This can be a relationship or a personal puzzle you are working on. That may be redundant, since relationships often are personal puzzles, but you get the idea. Let's call the situation the puzzle.

To begin with, how did you know you had a puzzle? Did you get that feeling in the pit of your stomach? That's sensation. Did you react to something that happened in regard to the puzzle? That's feeling. Did that little inner voice let you know that you had a puzzle? That's intuition. Did you "put 2 and 2 together" and become aware that you had a puzzle? That's thinking. Did you do all of these only to decide that the puzzle would have to change because you were in a good place with yourself? That's transcendent.

Now, let's take this puzzling situation a little bit further out (or in, as the case may be). Begin by focusing on the puzzle. If other thoughts or images arise, detach and let them pass through your mind. Stay tuned to the puzzle, as though it were the only puzzle in your life—the only puzzle in the world.

Continue to sharpen your focus and concentrate until you have pinpointed one clear aspect of the puzzle. Hold your focus and breathe deeply. Now begin to let yourself detach, even from the one-point aspect you have focused on. Let it slip away. Observe its passing without involvement.

Breathe deeply and find a quiet place inside yourself. Just let all thoughts, sensations, and emotions go. Let your mind float freely until even that has lost definition. Allow yourself to float in the void. Take all the time you need. Your higher Self will know when to return you to the present time and place.

When you feel yourself returning from the void, allow an image to emerge in your consciousness. Trust yourself to not structure it. Allow the image to emerge freely. When you have returned from the void, consider the image you have received.

How does it affect you?
What sensations does it produce in you?

When you have done this, consider how you could use this image to change the puzzling situation. Experiment by changing the image to suit the outcome you want in the puzzling situation.

When you have done so, consider how the new, adjusted image affects you. Consider how it affects the puzzle.

Having done that, allow your image to deepen. Involve yourself in the image, rather than observing it with detachment. Let the image move from your mind to your heart.

How do you feel about the image?
How does the image connect you, emotionally, to the puzzle?
How does this image connect you to the deep-level energies of the puzzle?

Breathe deeply and let other images come forth. Perhaps these images will come as symbols, or as totems from the worlds of Nature. Let these emerge and experience your own reaction to them. Experience your feelings as energies. Allow them to come in colors and shapes; they will connect you to a deeper understanding of the puzzle in your life—and in the life of all worlds.

Connect with the pure energies of the puzzle and with the energies of the images. Experience the situation.

Do you want to change the situation?
Should the puzzle be solved by you?

Do you want to tap into the energies of this puzzle
deeply?

Do you see the puzzle as a small knot in the flow of
energies that you can untie?

Do you see that this puzzle will take care of itself
without you?

Do you see that you are to be involved in this puzzle?

If so, can you shift the energies of the puzzling situation to let the natural flow continue in your life—in
the world?

Can you do this with heartfelt compassion, for the
good of all?

Can you take the awareness, the sensations, the
emerging images, and the heartfelt emotion and
synthesize them to catalyst a change?

If so, then you are balanced, in the center of all the gifts of consciousness. The synthesis you create by riding these wheels of consciousness is a transcendent pathway to Self, Nature, and Spirit. This
ability to synthesize consciousness gives you access to the deepest
levels of healing and inner vision, as well as tools for using your
experiences.

All too often in our shamanic studies, we want to jump into the
deep levels of consciousness rather than follow a balanced path to
reach the same places. This can be like diving into dark water. If you
take time to balance and center yourself in consciousness, the experience and the results will be far more valuable.

Here are four steps, or wheels, to guide you. After you have done
this for a while, it will become automatic. Some practice early on is
helpful. Let your totems help you on this as well.

Four Wheels to Shamanic Imaging

Thinking	Focus your awareness sharply (hawk medicine)
Intuition	Go inside to your inner source (bear medicine)
Sensation	Sense the images and activate (wolf medicine)
Feeling	Check your heartfelt connection (buffalo medicine)

When these are merged, in balance, you will be on the true path to shamanic consciousness. Taking the time and effort to do this is a mark of high ideals for yourself, for Nature, and for Spirit. This is eagle medicine. Fly like the eagle, higher than all others, with the four winds to support you.

Fly Like An Eagle
Fly So High
Circle round the Universe
On Wings of Pure Light.
   —*Native American Chant*

One of the journeys of the West is riding the wheel of self-balance. In order to stay centered in our own power, we must have our energies in balance. Basically, we have two main types of energies, *active* and *receptive*. These are also called *male* and *female energies*, which can make them easier to relate to in human terms. This is fine as long as we don't put limits or expectations on them. Let's not confuse energies with sexuality—or sexuality with spirituality. It could limit us to do so. Here is an exercise in using shamanic images to help balance the active and receptive energies.

Sacred Partners • Balancing Imagery

For this exercise, please image yourself as you are, male or female, and your partner as the opposite sex. After you have worked with shamanic imagery for a while, you can let these emerge unstructured. For now, it's important to work with the specific energies.

Breathe deeply and find that quiet place inside yourself. Go to the place of inner vision.

Imagine that you are walking through a beautiful forest. The trees and underbrush are fresh and full with summer growth.

You walk through the forest for a time, feeling at one with Nature and at peace with yourself. Take all the time you need to do this.

You come to a clearing in the forest. It is a sunlit meadow, beautifully colored with wildflowers and grasses.

Walk to the center of the meadow and sit on a large rock, warm from the sun. You have come to this meadow to meet your sacred partner, the balance of your Self.

When you are ready, look back at the place where you entered this clearing.

There you see your sacred partner coming out of the forest into the meadow.

As your sacred partner walks toward you, take time to note your own reactions.

Take note also of all the details about your sacred partner: physical type, coloring, expression, movement, manner, and period of dress. Absorb these details into your heart, for this sacred partner is a part of you.

When your sacred partner reaches the rock on which you are sitting, greet each other as you feel most comfortable doing.

Let your sacred partner speak to you about the energies you need.

These are the energies of your sacred partner. These are also energies within you—which your sacred partner strengthens and balances. Listen to the wisdom your sacred partner brings to you—from you.

When you have taken all the time you need to absorb the wisdom and energy of your sacred partner, stand face to face as though you were dancing. Hold on to each other's hands and feel yourself spinning around faster and faster. Feel the energies swirl around, while you stay centered, in balance with your sacred partner.

When you stop spinning, you will see that you are looking at yourself through the eyes of your sacred partner.

What do you see?

Do you see yourself differently than when you first imaged yourself walking through the forest?

Take all the time you need to relate to yourself as sacred partner.

Feel the energies you bring in this form. Feel the energies you are, in balance.

When you have taken all of the time you need to know yourself through the eyes of your sacred partner, join hands once again.

This time, allow yourself to spin gently out of your image into the present time and place.

You bring with you the energies of your sacred partner. Energies that you need for balance. Feel the balance.

The Sacred Partners imagery can be embellished and adapted to work on many levels. It can be an exercise in abstract-level communication between you and an Earth Walk partner. Just be certain this person is a true partner, one who is as giving of energies as he is taking. Sacred Partners can also be used to communicate with spirit guides whom you already know. It can also be used with people who have recently gone into Spirit. This can be used to help you and the person in spirit release your Earth Walk connections and begin new ones, if you both wish it.

I have also used Sacred Partners as a way to connect with my totem animals. This is a little bit of experimental reverse anthropomorphism, but can be very interesting. I did this once with a power animal wolf. Imagine my delight when he showed up as Robin Hood. Of course, I knew that Robin and his Sherwood cronies were known historically as "Wolves Heads." Also, Robin Hood images have often been connected shamanically with my active male images. However, this was an interesting, informative way to relate to a balancing of myself.

If you do try creative versions of Sacred Partners, just remember that if what emerges upsets you or frightens you in any way, you can come out of the image immediately. You probably would do it anyway, but it's good to remember that you are able to. If you wish to explore the image that came up, do it on the concrete level. Frightening images are a lot like children's nightmares, which fade in the light of day. Frightening images may just be static from the abstract level, which will clear up, or lose all form, on the concrete level of every day.

If, however, a frightening image continues to emerge in imagery, I suggest that you approach it through the Four Wheels to Shamanic Imaging approach. More often than not, this will take care of the situation for you. It is a very, very rare event when frightening images are more than shadows of our own fears, in spite of what Hollywood sells us.

It is also quite normal to have resistances about dealing with the shamanic levels of consciousness, and the images that arise. After all, we are programmed to stay in our bodies on the concrete level. When we start exploring consciousness, we do have that scary sense of being unprotected—out of our realm—and out of control. Sometimes these fears manifest as images to keep us grounded, more or less. If this happens, spend more time on the Wheel of the South developing your sense of protection and connecting with your protective totems. When you feel ready to explore your inner visions, take a totem with you, either in image, on the concrete level, or both.

In one shamanic image I was very startled by a shadowy animal lurking in a beautiful forest in my inner vision. The way this one was sneaking about disturbed me greatly. Just when I was about to return from my image to consider this, I heard a ferocious growl. A huge brown bear came lumbering up behind me and chased the shadowy varmint away. I was very glad to see him, but puzzled, too. I didn't know I had a bear. In fact, I thought he might have been my husband's bear. That sort of thing happens sometimes. After a few moments, the bear returned, stretched out on the grass beside me, and fell asleep, snoring loudly. I thought then that it must be my husband's bear. Later I was to find that we do, indeed, share that particular bear.

Shamanic imaging is a wonderful way to connect with the energies needed for balance. It is very like the Oriental tradition of dialectical meditation, which encourages you to garden in your own consciousness. Grow and nurture your shamanic images, and they will nurture your own growth.

Another aspect to consider is that active and receptive energies are connectors to self-nurturance. In Western society, we often forget to receive or input energy in balance with the amount of energy we activate or output. It doesn't take very long to get to an energy-depleted state. Shamanic images can be very helpful to the Western mind, which loves to act on images.

A balanced blend of meditative and active consciousness work has the added benefit of personal blending by you. If you have been extremely active, use a more receptive method of consciousness work. Use images to travel into the healing void and connect with your healer self.

If you have been spending too much time with receptive meditative consciousness, take time out to activate your images; apply what you have learned from inner vision. Call up your spiritual-warrior images, whatever works for you. The emerging images of receptive consciousness work and the self-directed images of active consciousness are a magical blend.

Totems are perfect companions for shamanic imaging. Everyone is familiar with all the trappings of magick and shamanism. These trappings of totems are there to focus the energy. The way they work is through the use of shamanic imaging. The shaman communicates with his totems on the magick, or shamanic, levels of consciousness where images arise. Often the shaman's tools have been especially charged or initiated to work with specific energies. This is especially true of sacred power objects, such as staffs, wands, bowls, pipes, and rattles. Natural objects, such as hawk feathers, amethyst, thyme, and sage, have significant energies of their own. But a clay bowl or a stick of wood may be more receptive to being charged with a specific vibration or meaning.

Technically speaking, very few objects actually hold a physical energy charge for long on the concrete level. They do, however, hold one on the abstract level of form and images. Images are such powerful connectors to direct energies that they don't even require form, other than the ones we think of for them. In this way, we create thought-forms as totems.

At times, it is useful to pair a concrete world totem with an abstract world thought-form to help focus the energy. For example, you may have a special image of yourself as a spiritual warrior. This is a thought-form of yourself, so it is already a strong totem. Perhaps you need to be reminded of this on a more concrete level. If so, find a totem object that you feel reflects this spiritual-warrior self. Using shamanic imagery, focus on your thought-form and see—hear—feel—imagine that thought-form entering your totem object. When you do this, it is important to continue using that totem for that thought-form; otherwise, the energies can be too chaotic.

Of course, some totems can be programmed with temporary thought-forms for healing, balance, and magical purposes. But if the thought-form and totem represent something deeply personal concerning your medicine or your self-healing, let the totem be used only for that. If ever you have completed a journey with a deeply personal totem that you had charged with a shamanic image, be certain you know where the totem goes.

Sometimes it's best to retire these totems, but keep them as reminders. The supportive energy they gave you once can still be valuable in your personal environment. Sometimes it's nice to return these totems to the earth with gratitude for the help received. You must follow the wisdom of your heart on this.

I close this chapter with an image designed to help balance shamanic images elementally. The effect of the element a totem represents may not be the same on the abstract level as on the concrete level. However, all our images affect us with their energy, so it is wise to keep them balanced as well.

Medicine Circle • An Image of Shamanic Totems

Take a long, slow, deep breath.

Find that quiet place inside yourself.

Go into your place of inner vision.

Imagine yourself as an ancient shaman sitting on the top of a tall, sacred cliff at sunset.

You face the West and feel the last warm rays of the sun as it sinks below the horizon.

You honor the West as the place of sacred dreams and inner vision, balance and self-healing.

You have come to this sacred cliff to seek totems for your inner wisdom.

These totems may never have form on your Earth Walk planes.

These totems may come to you only in your place of inner vision.

They will be totems of great power.

And will bring you gifts of Self, gifts of Nature, and gifts of Spirit.

These totems may be your special secret medicine kept sacred in your heart.

These totems may reflect your higher Self in balance.

These totems may form your inner medicine circle, your circle of self-healing, your sanctuary of Source.

The evening sun sets behind the horizon, leaving a veil of twilight in its place.

In this quiet time between the world of day and the world of night, you call your sacred medicine circle together.

This circle represents your inner powers—known only to yourself, shared with no one.

You make your own medicine.

Still facing the West, you call forth your sacred inner totem from the West.

This is your Dreamspeaker totem. This totem calls forth images of wisdom from your inner vision.

Let this totem emerge in your inner vision.

This totem carries the Water of your Water, the depths of your inner-most emotions.

This is your Dreamspeaker self-connector.

Take all the time you need to communicate with your totem.

When you are ready, turn to face the North.

Facing the North, you call forth your sacred inner totem from the North.

This is your Elder totem. This totem calls forth your helping guides to sacred wisdom.

Let this totem emerge in your inner vision.

This totem carries the Earth of your Water, the wisdom of your intuition.

This is your Elder self-connector.

Take all the time you need to communicate with your totem.

When you are ready, turn to face the East.

Facing the East, you call forth your sacred inner totem from the East.

This is your Sacred Clown totem. This totem calls forth divine humor and inspiration.

Let this totem emerge in your inner vision.

This totem carries the Air of your Water, the creativity of your inner balance.

This is your Sacred Clown self-connector.

Take all the time you need to communicate with your totem.

When you are ready, turn to face the South.

Facing South, you call forth your sacred inner totem from the South.

This is your Guardian totem. This totem calls forth healing harmony in all aspects of your self.

Let this totem emerge in your inner vision.

This totem carries the Fire of your Water, the protection of your self-healing.

This is your Guardian self-connector.

Take all the time you need to communicate with your totem.

When you are ready, turn to face the West once more.

Stand facing the West.

Now slowly look upward and call forth your inner totem from Spirit.

This is your Creator totem. This totem calls forth the depths of your soul consciousness.

Let this totem emerge in your inner vision.

This totem carries the spirit of your Water, the gifts of your sacred dreams.

This is your Creator self-connector.

Take all the time you need to communicate with your totem.

When you are ready, lean down and touch the earth.

Touching the earth, call forth your sacred inner totem from the Earth.

This is your Sacred Mother totem. This totem calls forth nurturance from the inner mother.

Let this totem emerge in your inner vision.

This totem carries the heart of your Water, the compassion of your inner knowing.

This is your Sacred Mother self-connector.

Take all the time you need to communicate with your totem.

When you are ready, go deeper inside yourself to find your quiet place.

In your quiet place, call forth your sacred inner totem of self-image.

This is your Magic Lake totem. This totem calls forth self-recognition from within.

Let this totem emerge in your inner vision.

This totem carries the reflection of your Water, the strength of introspection.

This is your Magic Mirror self-connector.

Take all the time you need to communicate with your totem.

When you are ready, stand and face the West once more.

Give honor to the West, place of inner visions, healing balance, and sacred inner wisdoms.

Honor all of the totems in your medicine circle for the qualities they represent and for the elements they balance in your Self.

Allow yourself to return slowly from the quiet place of vision.

Know that you carry the energy of your sacred inner totems within your heart.

Know that your medicine circle is always there for your journey.

Return to the present time and place.

Go in balance.

There are seven directions, not four:
South, West, North, East,
Up (Spirit), Down (Earth), and Within (Self).
—*Grey Eagle*

Chapter 7

SHAMANIC HEALING

All healing is self-healing. No one heals another. No one. All we can hope for, in helping another person's healing process, is to be a catalyst and a channel for the healing energies. We can catalyst these energies with our training, our personal experiences, our heartfelt compassion, and our faith in the powers of self-healing. We can channel healing energies through ourselves and direct them to merge, awaken, and strengthen the healing energies of another. In order to be this catalyst and this channel for healing energies, we must be clear ourselves.

First and last on the shamanic path, we need to be self-healers. Until we have learned to tap into our own self-healing powers, we cannot catalyst the self-healing powers of another. Until we open ourselves and let healing energies flow through us, we cannot be channels of healing energies for anyone—including ourselves. We can use all of the methods, props, rituals, ceremonies, and totems imaginable. Still, we must ultimately learn to step aside and let the healing energies through. We must learn to get out of the way of our own self-healing.

The energies of shamanic healing are direct and powerful. If we are not clear, we cannot bring these through or focus them in the healing process. In order to direct pure energies, we need to keep our own energies and our own channels pure and direct. We learn to keep our flow of energies in balance. We find our own centers, through which we may direct these healing energies.

On the path of the shaman, we gain a new understanding of the value of self-work. We clear ourselves, we heal ourselves, and we share our experiences. When we do these things, we are setting the stage for another person's self-healing. We cannot hope for more, or take credit or accept responsibility for more. We are not healers. We are not martyrs. We are catalysts and channels for energy. We learn to work on ourselves.

We learn that even the work we do with others is still self-work. Energies come through our Self—and affect our Self—on the way to joining another person's energy. Any personal blocks we have can block the flow of healing energies for ourselves and for others. On the path of the shaman we accept the honor of being a catalyst and a channel for healing energies. We must also accept the responsibility for self-healing and self-clearing. This we must do with great tolerance, compassion, understanding, and love. If we can't bring these to self-healing, we can never really bring them into the healing process of another.

Shamanic healing is self-healing. It is often the hardest task on the path. In order to clear and heal ourselves, we must be objective, courageous, and strong. Self-healing is self-initiation. It is a rite of self-passage essential to the way of the shaman. When we choose to follow the path of the shaman, we open ourselves to energies and wisdoms from the highest levels of Self, Nature, and Spirit. These are our shamanic connections. As we involve ourselves in the work of self-healing and self-clearing, we may call on these connections to aid us in our journey.

We are not alone, nor are we being tested beyond our capacities. With faith in our highest self-healing abilities and openness to our clear intuition, we may make the journey of shamanic self-healing an experience of great personal growth and development.

Some traditions divide shamans (and witches) into two primary types: those involved with physical healing and those involved in the realms of the mind. This may be quite true in regard to the differences of vibrations used; yet there is a blended vibration of these two that is used in working with the body-mind connection. Simply put, the mind manifests itself in the body, and the body reflects the mind. These are inseparable.

Some shamanic practitioners approach disorders of the body-mind connection from the physical or body. Others approach these from the mental or mind aspects. Regardless of the approach, the process is holistic, particularly when we recognize the helping energies of spirit. As we move into the journeys of self-healing, it is good to honor the energies of mind, body, and spirit in our work. To this, we add the vibration of Nature, as we use our totems and balance the elements of our Self.

For the purposes of this chapter, I have divided the exercises in self-healing to correlate with the elements, or *tattwas,* reflecting in the chakra or energy point system. I did this to ensure that each self-element was tapped for its own energy and self-healing abilities. Also, by dividing these and examining them individually, their unique vibrations can be recognized for future use.

All of the exercises in this chapter can be used for holistic self-healing. They can also be distilled and concentrated for very specific areas of dis-ease or blocks. It is only through your own experimentation that you will learn which exercises work most effectively on which areas of your Self.

I have also included a chart on shamanic self-healing in the appendix, which you may use as an easy reference to get you started. As you experiment with various methods, I advise that you make your own charts. With all of the chaotic energies present on the path of the shaman, it is very easy to forget just what worked where, and how and why.

The journey of self-healing is an exciting one. Keep your protective South totems close by; call on the bear of the West for self-knowledge and healing. Invoke the coyote, too—you'll need your sense of humor!

All energies and elements flow through us. However, there are certain key points on our bodies where we can connect more specifically with each element. In this chapter we will connect with the seven primary energy points, or chakras, and with their corresponding elements. This is for the purpose of connecting and exercising these energy points and their related vibrations. We are not limited to this system; we are only using it as a foundation. As we all progress in our evolution, we are certain to find energy points and elements beyond our present knowledge. So, let's get in tune with the ones we know about now and get clear for the expanded energies of the future. Remember, the future is now.

The Chakra System

Energy Point	Area of Body	Element	Sensory Channel	Ray
Root Chakra	Pelvis	Earth	Smell	Red
Sacral Chakra	Below navel	Water	Taste	Orange
Solar Plexus Chakra	Center of abdomen	Fire	Sight	Yellow
Heart Chakra	Center of chest	Air	Touch	Green
Throat Chakra	Top of sternum	Ether	Sound	Blue
Brow Chakra	Center of forehead	Mind	Thought	Indigo
Crown Chakra	Top of head	Spirit	Experience	Violet

Before beginning work on specific energy points, it is advisable to do some general clearing of, and reconnecting with, your personal energies. Here are two exercises to help you do this. As always, you may do these as ceremonially as you choose.

The first is primarily a clearing exercise. I suggest that you do it with imagery alone the first few times. Later you may wish to use your totems as helpers for this. Because of the energies and emotions involved with this exercise, I do advise that you encircle yourself with white or golden light before you begin. You may also call up images of personal protection to support you. If you find that strong feelings are emerging, let them flow through you—don't hold them back! Let these strong emotions flow either upward to be released into Spirit or downward to be absorbed by Mother Earth. Don't worry, she can take it. She needs you to be strong and balanced.

Energy Clearing

Find a quiet time and place where you will not be disturbed. Make sure that you are comfortable, with your back well supported.

Take time to slow your pace.

Breathe slowly and gently.

Center your energies.

In your inner vision, see yourself surrounded by white and golden lights. Using your images, cast a circle of these lights around the area you are in. Feel yourself centered, strong and protected.

Next, imagine a beam of light flowing down on you from just above your head.

Let this light continue to flow down your back and into the earth.

This connects you to Mother Earth, to healing energies.

Now imagine another beam of light emerging from the earth and flowing upward.

Let this light continue to flow up your back and on into the sky.

This connects you to the Spiritual Plane of healing energies and consciousness.

You are the living tree, channel of the energies of Nature and Spirit.

Imagine yourself as this direct channel of energies.

Feel the strength of your shamanic connections and honor their support for you.

In your inner vision see yourself as you are now, encircled with healing, protecting lights.

You are connected to Earth and Sky, Nature and Spirit.

In your inner vision, call forth images of other connections you have in your present Earth Walk.

These may appear to you as beams of light, as silver chains, or as tubes or cables.

Let these emerge slowly.

Observe them with detachment and compassion.

Do not block them with judgment.

These connections may come from your chosen involvements with your family—your friends—your work.

Look at each of these carefully.

In your inner vision, call for images of energy moving through these connections.

Look at these closely.

Does energy move both from you and to you in these connections?

Can you send energy through the connections that seem to be only sending energy to you?

Can you receive energy from those connections that seem to be only pulling energy from you?

Consider very carefully the flow of each connection.

Without judgment, consider the choices you have made concerning each of these connections.

If a connection seems to be only pulling energies—consider that connection's relationship to your personal growth, progress, and self-development.

If a connection seems to be only receiving energies—consider your relationship to that connection's personal growth, progress, and self-development.

Take all the time you need to explore and examine these connections to your Self.

Ask your innermost teacher the wisdom of each connection—even those whose energies flow clearly to and from your own connections to Self, Nature, and Spirit.

Take time to rechoose those connections that you feel are a necessary part of your shamanic path.

Feel the strength of rechoosing for yourself.

Now take time to center yourself even more deeply than before.

Take time to stop the flow of energies to the connections you no longer choose to keep.

Disconnect these carefully.

As you do so, cast a healing beam of white and golden lights around the area where the connection was made.

Take all the time you need for this. If a connection is extremely difficult to break or release, do what you can for now.

Some connections take longer to release than others.

Know that awareness of your choice to disconnect with them has already altered the flow of energy.

Call for the healing energies of Mother Earth to absorb the connections you no longer wish to have.

Call for the healing energies of Spirit to help you release these connections and send them on to their highest good.

When you have finished with all of the connections that you can work with at present, breathe deeply and let your image of these connections fade.

Know that the work will continue within your deepest Self.

Take a moment to reaffirm your shamanic connections to Mother Earth and to Spirit. Feel the clarity increase in yourself.

Feel the healing flow of energies from your shamanic connections.

Honor the healing lights and let them fade.

Slowly allow yourself to return to the present time and place.

Take some extra time for yourself to adjust to the change of energy.

This clearing exercise has very real effects on those connections you have chosen to keep and on those you've chosen to release. In the event of a backlash, stay centered and strong. Continue to do this exercise for support. Focus on the release of the connections that you've chosen not to have in your life. If you feel a pull from a connection you no longer wish to have, center yourself, breathe deeply, and visualize the connection's releasing. Some take time. Be gentle with yourself and call on your deepest protective totems to help you stand fast. Also call on those connections you have chosen to keep. They can be a great channel for support and healing energies.

The next exercise is designed to stimulate your awareness of specific energy points and their elements. It can also be a great overall energizer when you need it. This exercise may also be done with imagery alone. However, I find it very helpful to use a small crystal or a piece of quartz for this. Rutilated quartz (with gold strands inside it) is excellent for this, as are the smooth, tumbled pieces of crystal available now. Another useful totem for this exercise is lodestone, which is very magnetic. Feathers may also be used. I suggest feathers of gentle-vibration birds, such as peacocks and ducks. Mandrake root and High John the Conqueror root may also be used effectively with this exercise.

If you do choose to use a totem, it is advisable to keep it only for this purpose and very closely related purposes, as it will hold your personal vibrations quite strongly after this.

I have a small double-terminated crystal that has become so charged, by continued use in this exercise, that I can just hold it for a few moments for a quick fix. After all, a quick fix is better than none at all, particularly if you have already opened the connections to deeper healing. I often carry it to keep my energies aligned. Once, when I was having particular difficulties with some 1st chakra energies of impatience, I taped this little double-terminated crystal to the base of my spine with a Band-Aid. I'm still hearing about that one from my husband—but it helped. Be creative with self-healing; we are modern, Aquarian shamans.

Elemental Energy Point Exercise

Take time to center yourself, as you did in the energy-clearing exercise.

Let energy flow down your spine into the earth.

Let energy flow up your spine into the sky.

Feel your shamanic connections.

Sit on the floor or the ground, with your back fully supported.

Beginning with your 1st energy point, feel the spark of energy within you just where your body touches the ground.

This is your root chakra. This grounds your energy and focuses the element of Earth.

If you are using a totem helper, touch the totem to your root chakra.

If you are using imagery only, you can imagine a Red Ray of light and energy encircling that area.

If you are using a totem helper, let this Red Ray encircle the totem as well.

Consider the element of Earth in yourself.

Honor the sense of smell—most primarily connecting you to the environment.

Honor the energy of that point and its connection to your personal growth and evolutionary development.

Continue this exercise until you have connected with each energy point or chakra. As you do so, recognize the evolution of yourself and of humankind through the developmental use of senses and self-healing abilities. Note your reaction to the energy of each point.

When you have connected with each energy point, take a few more moments to run the energies through yourself to clear and charge.

I have found it quite effective, for personal synthesis and center-ing, to finish this exercise by running the energies upward above the crown area into the White, Silver, and Gold Rays. Then I pull the energies back down through the crown Violet into the Indigo of the brow chakra area. This is the point of synthesis from which we tap into shamanic consciousness, inner work, images, and intuition. This is the magical third-eye area. Centering energy at this point can be very valuable for the perceptive abilities we need on the shamanic path.

Also, if you need grounding, run the energies back down into the earth *through* the root chakra. If you need uplifting, leave the energies at the crown level. If this makes you a bit too "blissy," you may have to slow the energy flow.

If you need to be more communicative, leave the energies at the throat level. If you need to be more compassionate, at the heart level. If you need to be more energized, at the solar plexus level. If you need to be more flexible, at the sacral level. If you need to be more secure, at the root level.

These energy points are a lot like valves. You will have to gauge your reaction to determine how open or closed to leave these points. When in doubt, close the chakra. It will not stop the proper balanced flow of inner energies. Experiment carefully and learn the balance of your energies.

You may find it helpful to imagine these energy points as blossoms of beautiful flowers in the colors of the vibrational Rays. When you become familiar with the energies of these points, you will deepen your perceptive abilities as well as your self-healing skills. Sometimes you will find that dis-ease will show up as a shift of energy at a certain energy point before it manifests in the body in other ways. Other times, you may focus on the stresses of everyday life and note the energy points affected by these stresses.

Chakras or energy points really can be a kind of shamanic keyboard whose notes and vibrations you can interpret in yourself as well as in others. There may be times, when you are working with another person's healing process, that you will actually manifest their symptoms in your own energy points. This is truly a shamanic attune-ment to the vibrations and a transpersonal connection to the self-healing energies.

The concept of the wounded healer has long been associated with the shaman. It reflected not only the intense journeys and trials of the shaman but also the experience of the shaman's self-healing. Today we do not need to seek endurance trials to find experiences— life provides enough for us all. However, the wounded healer is still quite valuable to us as a reminder of the strength of our own self-healing abilities and of the wisdom gained from our life experiences on the path of the shaman.

The remainder of this chapter is divided into seven sections. Each is based on an energy point and its element, sensory channels, and manifestations in our everyday symptoms of stress and dis-ease. Suggestions are given for self-healing activities and totem uses. Let these serve as a guideline and a catalyst for your own self-healing process. Each of the activities can be expanded and adapted for an overall self-healing exercise. They are divided only to give you a familiarity in working with specific elements and vibrations.

Several of these activities may be adapted for work with partners and with groups. So long as the energies are shared equitably, this can be very helpful for all involved. Ultimately, the work of self-healing is self-work. Working with others is not a substitute for self-work, but it can be a supplement and a support to it.

As you deepen your self-healing abilities, you may find blocks and obstacles that you feel need outside help. Do take the time to find someone whose energies you trust and whose light and love shine through clearly to you. Also, it is important to find someone who encourages you to participate in the healing process. A person who does this truly understands the power of self-healing. A self-healer is a shamanic healer and will be best able to deal with your energies as well. Begin self-healing with honor for the process, humor for the frailties, and openness to deep self-transformation.

Root Chakra • 1st Energy Point

Element: Earth

Sensory Channel: Smell

Ray Energies: Red, Scarlet, Rose

Dis-ease and Stress Manifestations: Anger, frustration, insecurity, depression, lack of grounding, blood and nerve disorders, lower backaches

Self-Healing Activities and Totems:

1. Participate in a sacred sweat lodge ceremony, if you can, for deep healing and Earth connection.

2. Adapt the sweat lodge earth womb for yourself by a personal camp-out. Touch the earth. Feel the heartbeat of the earth. Feel the healing vibrations.

3. Go outside, stretch out on the ground, face down or spine down, and let all your stresses flow out of your body into the earth. Cry, scream, rage—let it all out. Rest. Then feel the Earth energies flow into you, giving you strength, foundation, and deep healing.

4. Sit with your back against a large rock or a tree trunk and feel the energy of the Earth connection.

5. Imagine yourself following the roots of a tree deep into the earth. Smell the rich soil of Mother Earth.

6. Find a small cave or group of rocks. Construct your own sacred space to connect with the energies of Mother Earth and the element of Earth. Emerge renewed.

7. Work with clay—create figures of yourself and sacred totems.

8. Weed in the garden. Kneel on the ground. Smell the fragrances of Nature all around.

9. Collect perfumed oils or essential oils that have an earthy healing quality for you. Rub at the base of your spine and feel the energies realign. Patchouly is excellent for this area.

10. Call on the totem energies of burrowing animals who live very close to the earth. Imagine the experience of living in an earth burrow. Hibernate.

Sacral Chakra • 2nd Energy Point

Element: Water

Sensory Channel: Taste

Ray Energies: Orange and Peach

Dis-ease and Stress Manifestations: Repression, fear, inhibitions, lethargy, negativity, kidney and splenic disorders, indigestion

Self-Healing Activities and Totems:

1. Healing baths to soothe or energize: mix apple cider vinegar and epsom salts and add to your bathwater to balance energies, clear toxins, and cleanse repressions. Add crystals and stones (don't use pearls with vinegar).

2. Use Mineral World totems, such as carnelians, jaspers, and agates, to energize and give courage.

3. Place a crystal in a glass of orange-tinged water. Let it sit for a day. Drink and visualize tonic effects. Use crystals as a reminder. Rhodochrosite is excellent for disorders of the sacral chakra. Rhodochrosite gives a deep sense of self-confidence and self-peace.

4. Select a few healing teas, such as jasmine, hibiscus blossom, chamomile, and orange spice.

5. Take time each day to drink tea ceremonially. You may do this at sunset, like the Japanese. As you do, feel the soothing qualities of the tea and the gentle orange rays of the setting sun. Let these absorb the dis-ease associated with this area.

6. Drink water, water, water. Flush it all out.

7. Sit in a warm shower with a towel on your lower back; visualize tensions washing away.

8. Take a walk in the rain. This is good for the Earth and Water elements.

9. Fill a goblet, silver or glass, with pure water. Take it out in the morning sun. Allow it to absorb the energies of the Sun. This is an ancient Egyptian healing method. Add orange stones or crystals to the goblet if you choose. At nightfall, drink the water with ceremony and awareness.

10. Take time for a party for yourself. Be silly.

Solar Plexus Chakra • 3rd Energy Point

Element: Fire

Sensory Channel: Sight

Ray Energies: Yellow and Peach

Dis-ease and Stress Manifestations: Mental exhaustion, nervous dysfunctions, mania, agitated depression, intestinal disorders, poor circulation, liver dysfunctions

Self-Healing Activities and Totems:

1. Bead stringing—use lovely colored beads. String slowly; focus on each one at a time. If you're really manic, use only one color and forget about patterns. If not, create different patterns. String and restring.

2. Use art to create interesting designs, or scribble. Blend colors, try different textures, experiment visually. Display your work and enjoy it.

3. Go for a walk on a sunny, clear day. Stroll at a comfortable pace. Visually connect with your surroundings. See the subtle differences of Nature colors.

4. Read poetry that is inspirational and soothing.

5. Go to museums, zoos, places of pleasant, joyful visual stimulation with a variety of sights.

6. Go to a funny movie. Laugh. Let your abdominal muscles relax and laugh again. Loosen up. Breathe.

7. Make slips of papers with goals and achievements you wish to accomplish and qualities you wish strengthened so that you can do so. Use an iron pot, large ceramic bowl, or a fireplace. Burn to release the energy for your goals. Have another burning to release obstacles in the same way. Release—waning moon time. Attract—waxing moon time. Celebrate and heal—full moon.

8. Call for the energy of the hawk to give you vitality.

9. Take time to make Nature arrangements; carefully, ceremonially arrange stones, leaves, roots, flowers.

10. Meditate, meditate, meditate—and sleep more.

Heart Chakra • 4th Energy Point

Element: Air

Sensory Channel: Touch

Ray Energies: Green and Turquoise

Dis-ease and Stress Manifestations: Discontent, greed, envy, inconsiderateness, spitefulness, coldness, blood pressure disorders, heart palpitations, ulcers

Self-Healing Activities and Totems:

1. Take time to come into the present moment. Breathe deeply and feel the touch of your clothes on your body. Feel the weight of your hands, the position of your feet. Come into your body.

2. Feel a branch on a blooming tree. Feel the nurturing energies of growth and expansion, the wholeness of growth.

3. Light sage or thyme and carry it all around the house. Feel the vibrations change in yourself; feel the peace.

4. Use a feather to cleanse your aura of negative emotions. Sweep downward from your head, bringing the energy to the ground. Finish by brushing the feather across your chest and downward, as though you were drawing a large number seven on your chest.

5. Hug people you care about. Hug your pets, trees, rocks, teddy bears, pillows; hug yourself.

6. Use scented oils to anoint your heart area. Mint, lavender, and almond are good for this. Blend several and make your own heart strengthener.

7. Green moss agates are soothing for this area. Carnelians are stimulating. Malachite earths heart energies.

8. Take a walk on a windy day. Turn so that the wind sweeps you clean. Feel the wind on your chest and allow the wind energies to give you clarity and support.

9. Cook and prepare food that requires lots of tactile work. Knead bread; make Chinese food—chop, chop, chop. Make candies, whatever is most kinesthetic.

10. Experiment with new fabrics for yourself. Really feel the difference beteen textures, and note your reactions.

Throat Chakra • 5th Energy Point

Element: Ether

Sensory Channel: Sound

Ray Energies: Blue and Turquoise

Dis-ease and Stress Manifestations: Withdrawal, hyperventilation, selfishness, possessiveness, fevers, respiratory problems, throat infections, rheumatism

Self-Healing Activities and Totems:

1. Blend methods from the first four energy points for self-healing. Ether is a magnetic blending medium for all the others and reflects auric vibrations.

2. Chant *om* and lower vowel sounds to open expressive communicative energies.

3. Sing, hum, whistle, yell, scream, laugh. Express yourself vocally. No holds barred—in the shower or to the mirror.

4. Lie on your back on a blue-sky day. Breathe with your mouth open. Absorb the vast sky energy and fill yourself with the serenity of that blue color.

5. Write letters. Write in a journal. Write your feelings, your opinions, your advice—to send or not.

6. Harmonize to music. Practice your pitch.

7. Sip cool mint teas. Chew mint leaves, spearmint, orange mint, peppermint.

8. Make a collection of totems from various elements; place in a large bowl or cauldron. This is the energy of the 5th point or chakra. Arrange and rearrange. Express your reactions.

9. Wear amber beads for your throat area and clarity. Wear lapis for serenity; blue topaz for self-healing.

10. Design rituals and ceremonies to express your spirituality. Record these for yourself—and your book of shadows. Use candle burnings in your rituals. Observe the patterns of smoke as energies release into Ether.

Brow Chakra • 6th Energy Point

Element: Mind

Sensory Channel: Thought

Ray Energies: Indigo

Dis-ease and Stress Manifestations: Egotistical behavior, arrogance, totalitarianism, authoritativeness, obsessions, headaches, insomnia, disorders of the nose, eyes, ears, or sinuses

Self-Healing Activities and Totems:

1. Deep-level, Eastern void meditations. Focus on an indigo blue in your inner vision. Fall into the synthesis of the All-Mind.

2. Study symbols, such as ankhs, crosses, geometric shapes— focus on these and meditate. Observe your thoughts. Study the philosophies of your special symbols.

3. Candle-burning meditations. Focus on the deep blue at the center of the flame. Concentrate your attention fully. Feel your energies move together.

4. Create magical thought-forms and activate your imagery. See yourself as you wish to be; complete goals; stimulate self-healing; create and energize projects. Imagery plus thought plus control equals thought-forms.

5. Wear or carry azurite and silver for synthesis and receptivity. Rub smooth amethyst on your third-eye area to soothe. Use tourmalinated quartz for overall soothing.

6. Place small crystals on your face, sinuses, and your brow to help direct self-healing energies.

7. Light sandalwood, jasmine, frankincense, myrrh to deepen self-healing connections. Make sacred space.

8. Collect and wear symbolic jewelry. Sense changes in yourself.

9. Take up or increase your time with tarot cards.

10. Visit a variety of cultural centers and cultural museums. Note differences between the thoughts and philosophies reflected in cultural artifacts. Consider the universality and the uniqueness of symbols.

Crown Chakra • 7th Energy Point

Element: Spirit

Sensory Channel: Experience

Ray Energies: Violet

Dis-ease and Stress Manifestations: Hyperactivity, creative exhaustion, psychic debilitation, general lowered resistance, migraines, nervous tension

Self-Healing Activities and Totems:

1. Dance, move to music. Experience the energy, the flow, the spirit of music. Feel all your muscles moving in harmony with the music. Let Spirit move through you.

2. Light a gentle lavender or soft purple candle. Surround it with crystals. Turn off all other lights and absorb the soothing qualities of the color as it reflects in the crystal. When you are finished, take the crystals to your bath or to bed.

3. Take fluorite to bed—breathe a dream wish into it and place under your pillow. You may also place fluorite in a small pouch of mugwort to earth the dreams.

4. Do more rituals. Find old books of ritual and ceremony. Read long litanies. Do self-blessing rituals—feel spiritual.

5. Cast spells for the good of all—share Spirit.

6. Sugalite (royal azule) is ideal for the crown chakra. Use royal azule to tap akashic levels, read DNA codes, remember past lives—connect to your spiritual maps.

7. Cast a circle with crystals and amethysts. Use at least five: one for each of the cardinal directions, one in the center. Call on your spirit guides and helpers to communicate with you.

8. Write spiritual poetry or prose. Chant *om*'s.

9. Work with groups of people you know and trust. Share energy, do magick together, and be spiritual.

10. Go on a vision quest or sacred retreat in a Nature setting.

Chapter 8

SACRED DREAMS

I must shape my life out of myself—
out of what my own inner being tells me,
or what Nature brings to me.
—*Carl Jung*

Wind spirits danced a gleeful welcome as I walked through the deep waving grasses surrounding the ancient Mayan ruins. I had come to make an earth journey. I made my way around a tall crumbling tower to the medicine circle I had discovered there before. Ceremonially, I stepped into the circle and approached the center.

I placed a few small crystals on top of the flat column of stone in the center. Carefully I shifted the stone column from its position and uncovered a deep hole. I had emerged from this same hole on a previous earth journey, but it looked very different from above. The prospect of climbing down into that dark narrow hole held no charm for me. Still, I had learned through many journeys that this was the task.

I called for my wolves to join me. They were chasing one another through the tall grasses, sunlight sparkling in rich golden red lights on their coats. I was more than tempted to join their games, but I had already begun the journey; the wheels were spinning.

The wolves came bounding into the medicine circle, almost knocking me over with their exuberance. When they had settled down somewhat, I pointed to the hole I had uncovered beneath the center stone. They sniffed at it nonchalantly, then walked away to stretch out in the shaded area of the medicine circle and sleep. It was obvious they had no intention of climbing into the hole with me at all.

I wondered briefly about the benefits of having badger medicine at such a time. A badger would have been very useful about then. That hole was beginning to look smaller somehow. I called on the jaguar with whom I had connected on previous earth journeys in that area. I searched the jungle surrounding the ruins for shadowy glimpses of the great cat, but none appeared. It seemed I was to travel alone this time.

As I sat deepening myself for the journey, a butterfly flitted into the circle, danced around my head a few times, and then disappeared down the hole. There was nothing to do but follow. With a few unheeded words to my snoozing wolves, I began to climb down into the hole.

The ground was surprisingly warm as I slid down a steep angle deeper into the hole. Ahead I could see the butterfly dancing along the walls of the earth tunnel. I reached a narrower tunnel, barely lit from the entrance above. With some resignation, I entered this tunnel. It was only wide enough to allow me crawling space. I moved along quite slowly, feeling the earth very close around me. The butterfly flitted back often, as if to coax me along. The tunnel became darker and more narrow. This was by far and away not my favorite kind of place to be. Still, I was determined to see it through. Soon it was pitch black inside, and I shivered despite the relative warmth of the earth around me.

Although I had come to recognize the soft touch of the little butter-fly, I jumped each time she came back to check on me. Rocks tumbled from the sides of the tunnel, showering me with dirt and tiny stones. I gritted my teeth with irritation and kept going. The air in the tunnel seemed frightfully scarce. I struggled to keep my pace slow and to conserve the air.

After what seemed like hours, I caught the fragrance of smoke and burning herbs. Ahead of me in the tunnel I thought I could actually see the little butterfly. While I was wondering if mirages could occur inside an earth tunnel, I felt the tunnel bend sharply to the left. A welcome draft of air, fresh air, greeted me as I turned. A gentle light illuminated a short passage ahead of me. I could see my butterfly dance excitedly at an opening just a few yards away in the tunnel. She flitted back to touch me one more time, then disappeared through the opening.

By now I could hear a soft murmur of voices and the gentle sound of women's laughter. I struggled to reach the opening and poke my head through. After a few moments of breathing in the welcome rush of air, I cleared the dirt from my eyes and saw where I was.

I was peering into a large vaulted chamber in a great cave. The entrance to the cave was just above my head and cast enough light for me to examine the chamber. I was about a hundred feet or so above the floor of the chamber. Below me was a great kiva, a cere-monial room sunk deep within the earth. It was encircled with a series of steps leading down to a sacred fire burning in the center. To the far side were dark passageways. Just below me were several people I recognized from other journeys. Some I knew from my Earth Walk as well. They greeted me with some amusement and a great deal of teasing.

"Was that hard enough for you?" called one medicine woman I knew quite well. The twinkle in her eyes betrayed the irritation in her voice.

I was still breathing with some difficulty after my ordeal in the tunnel. I decided not to voice my thoughts.

"These young ones love to complicate things," said another

medicine woman I had seen before in my journeys. "All she had to do was decide to be here, and here she would have been. We had to wait while she gave herself the challenge she needed."

"Some people like to do things the hard way," said another woman; and they chuckled together.

I hate being discussed in the third person when I am present, but I felt like an idiot. I waited to get my emotions in check. At least I could breathe again.

The second medicine woman pointed out a vine reaching down into the cave from the entrance above. "You can climb down that, if it's not too easy for you," she said, teasing me.

"If all I have to do is decide to be there, then I decide that," I replied. The next thing I knew, I found myself at the center of the kiva, sprawled out most ungracefully beside the fire. Laughter greeted me from the group of women.

"Not bad," said my familiar medicine woman. "Try using your aim instead of your pride next time."

In the light at the base of the cave I could see more tolerance than teasing in the expressions on the women's faces. "Okay, Grandmother," I said, standing up and brushing off the dirt I had collected.

I recognized many of the women from journeys and Earth Walk work we had done together. Although I knew that some of these medicine women dwelled in spirit, and others on the concrete level, in this place there were no differences to be seen or felt.

I climbed the steps encircling the kiva and greeted the women warmly. One woman I had not seen before brushed my cheek with a gentle kiss. Her touch was strangely familiar, as soft as the wing of a butterfly.

"Thank you for your guidance in the tunnel," I said to her.

She laughed softly. "I thought you would never decide to get out of that tunnel. I was glad you finally had enough of it."

"Grandmother," I said to my old familiar medicine teacher, "I had not expected to see you all here."

I dug in my pockets and pulled out a tiny amethyst and a small fluffy owl feather. "Please accept these as gifts for all of your wisdoms." I handed her the tiny totems.

She smiled kindly. "It is not to me that you should give these gifts," she told me. "We are only here to prepare you for another wisdom, already deep in your heart and soul."

She put her fingers to her lips to signal for silence. In the quiet of the cave, I could hear the flames of the center fire crackle and hiss. I had learned to expect anything—and nothing—on an earth journey. All I could do was wait for the wheels to turn, to bring a new experience between the worlds.

The medicine woman with the butterfly-soft touch moved around me slowly. She chanted an ancient Native American rhythm, barely audible under her breath. Grandmother pulled a sacred crystal from deep inside her medicine pouch. She held it up so that the reflection of the center fire danced inside it. Then she placed it carefully on my heart and held it there until I felt its vibrations flow warmly through my body.

The medicine women who chuckled at my overcomplication of things came with herbs and a large striped feather. Humming to the rhythm of the butterfly woman's chant, she swept my energies clean and fanned sweet smoke around me. One by one, the other medicine women came to prepare me—brushing me with feathers, softly rattling beautifully painted gourds, blowing smoke from sacred pipes, and casting lights on me from crystals reflecting the flames.

"Now, my fierce little warrior," said Grandmother White Crystal Medicine Woman, "you are to meet the source of many wisdoms. You have pulled from the source many times, and you have served it well with what you have received. The path you have chosen has carried you far from your roots many times, only to return you there once again."

I felt wheels turning slowly deep inside my soul as she spoke. I watched the firelight cast shadows on the faces of these ancient sacred women. For the thousandth time I was struck by the earthy beauty of these Native American faces. I had seen the same beauty in the faces of my childhood—in the Pacific and in the Orient. Reflected in their deep brown eyes was the wisdom of ages past and ages to come. Only Grandmother's eyes sparkled blue in the firelight, like my own.

"You have learned the ways of the Earth Mother in many different lands," she said, reading my thoughts as always. "You have sought the wisdom of the people native to the land of your birth, and you have shared the wisdoms of the lands of your grandmothers' grandmothers down through time."

I thought of the many times I had stridently, proudly proclaimed the Nature wisdoms of my ancestors. I felt the frustration of trying to describe the horrors of our own persecution to these native people—

and to people whose ancestors had shared the land of my own ancestors.

"There is work to be done," I had finally stormed at one gathering. "Shall we continue this game of martyrs, or shall we move on together as Nature people? We have all been persecuted for our beliefs and for our allegiance to the ways of Mother Earth. Nine million, at least, of my people were tortured, maimed, and burned. Until we meet spirit to spirit as Nature people, the burnings will still continue—just in different ways. As long as we speak of our differences, we will not find our shared strength."

I had been furious. On and on I had raged, trying to make myself understood, until I realized that they simply could not see what I saw. I still felt the loneliness, the isolation of that realization.

It was then I had begun to work more frequently on the inner planes, sharing my thoughts with a few close friends, sharing my inner journey with no one. It was then I had begun the deep work of the shaman.

I had made the solitary quests and the earth journeys in search of direct, pure wisdom. It was then that new teachers of truth had come into my life—on the inner planes and on my Earth Walk as well.

One of these teachers stood before me in that fire-lit cave chamber, patiently waiting for me to return from my memories.

"I have not always shared my ancestors' wisdoms gently," I said flatly.

Grandmother laughed heartily. "No, little fierce one, you are Air, Fire, and Water. You will make things boil from time to time. That is the path you have chosen."

The acceptance and love in her eyes made me want to dissolve into tears.

"You seek the wisdom of the earth for your own balance," Grandmother continued. "And because it is the way of your deepest memories, you call for wisdom from a source thousands and thousands of years old. We are here to help you strengthen your ties with that same source."

I heard the whoosh of flames leaping higher from the center fire behind me. Shadows on the walls of the chamber lengthened and danced wildly about. The mists gathering in the cave were more than smoke from the fires. I felt the presence of people standing behind me, but I could not turn around.

A rustle of fabric and a fragrance long forgotten yet deeply remembered confirmed my feelings.

Grandmother looked behind me into the place of the center fire. She nodded her head in greeting, on her face an expression of deepest honor.

I wanted so badly to turn around and face what was behind me, but I couldn't move. I felt like a frozen flame. It was then I noticed that all the other medicine women had left the chamber. Only Grandmother remained—Grandmother and whoever stood behind me.

"You have journeyed hard, my little fierce one," Grandmother said, softly taking hold of my shoulders. "You have quested well for wisdom, and now you must return home."

"Home?" I wondered deep inside my mind. "Where shall I find that?"

"You must connect directly to the source of your deepest wisdom." Grandmother kissed me lightly in the middle of my forehead and turned me slowly around.

Before me stood the Lady, the goddess of my deepest memories. Her hair fell in golden red lights, the color of flames and embers. Her skin was the pale of moonlight. Her eyes reflected the cobalt blue of a deep mountain lake. Robes the many greens of a mystical forest, covered with fine embroidered patterns of silver, copper, and gold, swept the floor around her feet. In her arms she cradled a cauldron of silver with woven trimmings of gold, copper, and brass.

Beside her, watchfully quiet, were my wolves. Behind her were three women dressed in ancient Celtic robes. Their hair hung in long braids, brushing the floor.

I struggled to remember where I had seen them before, but my mind was transfixed on the Lady before me.

"Danu," I spoke without thought. "Danu."

I stood watching the fire cast lights on her face and considered what was before me. Danu, ancient goddess of the sacred flame of life, keeper of the fires of spring and rebirth, sacred muse of creativity and inspiration.

I had called on her energies many times, but I had never seen her—not even in my imagination. How was it, I wondered, that she would come to me now, on the journey levels of my inner vision?

"Daughter of Danu," she spoke, her voice crackling like wildfire in the cave. I jumped in spite of myself. Her face, once young, now seemed older, stronger and wiser; yet her eyes remained the same.

"It is I who named you Amber Wolfe. Do you not recall seeing me then?"

As she spoke, the red of her hair changed to a pale yellow-grey. The fine robes became the ragged collection of skins and furs I was used to seeing on Grandmother White Crystal Medicine Woman.

I looked to see Grandmother's reaction to this turn of events— but she was gone.

A familiar hearty laugh rang throughout the cave. Danu called to me across the center fire. "You have much to learn, little fierce one. It is good that we have time to kindle your fires."

At this point, I was completely confused. A soft chuckle from behind me made me leap out of my skin. I turned to face Grandmother White Crystal Medicine Woman once again.

Quickly, I turned back to the center fire and saw Danu, clothed in the fine green robes, golden red hair sparkling in the firelight. Both laughed with delight at my utter confusion.

I wanted to shout my frustration, but I cooled my energies and drew myself up with what I hoped was calm pride. "Explain, please," I said as evenly as I could manage.

Grandmother stepped into the kiva and stood beside Danu. She regarded me patiently with the cool blue eyes I had seen often in my inner vision, and spoke. "You came into this Earth Walk with ancient memories of your Sacred Lady, Danu. You were born into this land to be a bridge, as were many others born to wisdom. I, too, am a bridge. When I was in form, I carried the ancient memories of Native Americans and New Americans. Now I am in spirit and can be a helping bridge for you and many others."

"I suspected that," I said to Grandmother. "You came through both times I was named in the Native American traditions. The medicine helper who brought your message through told me you were in spirit."

"And you told her that made it easier to contact me." Grandmother looked at me with amusement. "We have made many journeys and vision quests together, but you are still the creator of your path."

Grandmother pointed to Danu. "And you created her as well; you know that."

"Well, I am certainly not the only one," I replied. I thought of the river Danube, named for Danu. I thought of the thousands of years she had been held sacred. I thought of the ancient race of Ireland,

Tuatha de Danaan—Children of Danu. I thought of the ancient Britains, who saw her as Cerridwen, and the Gaelic tribes of Ireland, who saw her as Bridget—all somewhat different aspects of the same goddess.

"She is far more than just a creation of my own mind."

I looked at Danu and felt a thousand memory wheels turning inside me.

Grandmother smiled. "Danu is energy, as are you, as am I. She exists in your mind because she has been held sacred for so long by Nature people. She is strong in your vision because you have reached the source of the energy from which she springs. She dwells within the heart and mind of all people whose ancestors held her sacred. Even if they don't feel or remember her, she is there."

"I have been with you always," Danu whispered softly.

I shivered, thinking of the litany of the Great Mother Goddess, sacred to the Craft of the Wise.

"I have many names," Danu spoke again. "You have called me thus."

She held the silver cauldron above the center flame. Beams of silver, gold, and copper lights shot across the chamber and bounced off the walls of the cave. The woven brass trim gleamed richly in the firelight.

"You and others like you have kindled the fires of the Nature ways during a long winter of fear and ignorance. Now the fires grow bright again as a new age dawns. You reached deep within your own soul and within the soul of Nature for this cauldron of wisdom."

Danu held the cauldron low, tilting it to reveal the contents. Inside were gemstones, cut roughly, as in ancient times.

"Choose," she said, offering the cauldron.

I spotted a piece of golden amber glowing with an inner fire of deep red. As soon as I had spotted it, Danu lifted the amber out of the cauldron and held it in the firelight.

"When you said you named me Amber Wolfe"—I spoke to Danu—"was it you, or was it Grandmother?"

"Why, you have named yourself," Danu replied. "You called yourself from the cauldron of life, just as you called for this fine amber."

She held the amber above the crown of my head. I felt a warm golden glow descend and fill me with a rush of power and energy. When she moved her hand down from my head, the amber was gone.

It was a sacred gift.

I remembered the tiny amethyst and the fluffy little owl feather in my pocket. I brought them out and offered them to Danu, to the cauldron.

"Keep the owl feather," Danu said. "There are many shadows cast by the kindling of sacred flames. You will need the wisdom of your owl to fly through the shadows."

She held the cauldron out to me, and I gingerly placed the tiny amethyst inside.

Danu spoke. "You may call on me as you need me. I am with you always. I have brought you other helping spirits who have guided your journey thus far."

I looked at the three Celtic women and remembered suddenly where I had seen them before. They had come to me once when I was quite ill. I had thought then that they must have come with the fever. Now I knew they had come to help.

I nodded to them in greeting and gratitude. They smiled and nodded back, long braids sweeping the floor. I felt I had found a wealth of help and protection I had not known existed. I knew then that there was much left to learn.

The flames were burning lower now, little flickers barely visible among the embers of the center fire. I knew that the time for the earth journey had come to an end.

I turned to bid farewell to Grandmother White Crystal Medicine Woman, but she had already begun to fade. The twinkle of her eyes hung briefly in my inner vision, like the smile of a Cheshire cat.

A rustle of robes on the cave floor told me that my Lady Danu and the Celtic women were also leaving. All that I saw when I turned around was a wisp of smoke from the center fire. All that was left of Danu was the fragrance of heather and the fresh grasses of spring.

I looked up at the tunnel I had come through and laughed at myself. I closed my eyes and decided to return home. When I opened them again, I was sitting quietly at my desk, just as I had been when I started. The clock beside me read twenty minutes later than it had when I began. Time, too, is a dimension to be traveled.

Shamanic Dreams

There is really no simple way to describe the processes of a shamanic journey. Perhaps the aboriginal shamans of the past (and those of the present) found the best approach. They didn't try to explain it. They accepted the validity of all their life experiences without concern for separating and designating the realms in which those experiences occurred. This is not to say that the shamans were unaware of what we would call different consciousness levels—only that they saw no difference in the value of the experience for their lives.

Much of the literature that we call visionary autobiography, or shamanic journey tradition, never attempts to designate the levels or realms of these experiences when describing them. While this is appropriate to the philosophy of the shamanic traditions, it is confusing to those beginning to walk in the way of a shaman. When these journey accounts are read, they are often regarded as fiction or fantasy by the reader. They are certainly not regarded as such by the shamanic author.

It may be futile to attempt to describe the processes involved in a shamanic journey. It must be experienced. Nevertheless, I hope to shed a little light on the subject and possibly some clarification.

When you have experienced a deep-level shamanic journey, you come to recognize the personal truths involved. Then you have undergone a self-initiation into realms of reality that you know are present for everyone, whether they are open to it or not. Shamanic journeys are not a part of what we call shared reality. They are the deepest exploration we can make into our personal reality. When we explore personal reality in this manner, we come full circle into the greater level of universal reality, which Jung called the collective unconscious. This is also called the soul consciousness. When we journey shamanically, it is as though we have dug a well so deep in our own consciousness that it reaches into the source of all consciousness.

The quality that sets shamanic journeys apart from other magical path journeys is the intensely personal, experiential nature of the event. Basically, we journey into the source level of, and through, our own images. Sometimes these images reflect more universal ones as well; but our approach remains strictly individual.

We also journey *into* our images. We do not see ourselves as we do in active imagery. We experience the journey firsthand. When clients have asked me whether an experience of theirs was a shamanic journey or imagery, I tell them two things:

> First, I tell them to remember that all inner-vision experiences have some validity.

> Second, I ask them to answer one question for themselves. That is: Did you watch yourself in the journey? Or were you there?

To understand our inner-vision experiences we must first understand what consciousness is. What is consciousness? This is a question asked by seekers of wisdom throughout the ages. Well, what indeed?! No one knows exactly what consciousness is, perhaps because it is so individual. Still, I'll attempt to give you a workable understanding to help you on your shamanic path.

Simply speaking, consciousness is awareness. It is awareness of our internal states—our inner images, emotions, and sensations. It is also awareness of our external states—our interaction with what is outside of our self, objects and activities in our environment. In general, our internal states are more abstract and undefined; our external are more concrete and focused.

If we arbitrarily place our familiar internal and external states on a continuum according to their levels of consciousness (or awareness), we may begin to see how they differ.

Table of Internal and External States of Being

Internal	Comatose	Total lack of perceivable awareness or consciousness (CS)
	Sleep (Dream State)	Deeply internalized awareness; CS absent; defocused external CS or awareness
	Hypnosis	Sharply focused internal CS and awareness; diminished external CS and awareness
	Meditation (Eastern Void)	Deep internal awareness and CS; mild external CS and awareness

Table of Internal and External States of Being (cont'd)

Active Imagery	Focused internal CS and awareness; slightly defocused external awareness and CS
Wakefulness	Focused external CS and awareness; mild internal CS and awareness
External Concentration	Sharply focused external CS and awareness; very mild or diminished internal CS and awareness

Basically, the sharper our external focus, the greater our sense of experiencing an event or state of being. At the same time, our focus on the internal states gives us access to states of being often masked by our interaction with our environment, or that which is external to us.

It seems as if we can't open the channels or mechanisms to allow ourselves access to both abstract and concrete levels at the same time. However, we are able to do this—sometimes with practice, sometimes by accident. We are able to do this effectively with active imagery. Active imagery allows us to receive information from the abstract internal levels, and to act on the information with concentration and focus on the concrete external levels.

However versatile and useful active imagery may be, it falls somewhat short of the deeply experiential nature of the shamanic journey. When we journey shamanically, we enter the internal states of being with the focused concentration of external states. When we journey we are more than just conscious or aware of our experience—we are there.

The Eastern mystics speak of being aware of the flow, aware of the states of being moving around and through us. In shamanic journey we are in that flow, fully aware and awake. We use all of the senses of our normal waking states to receive the experience of internal states. In this way we are able to receive the experience that we can only watch in other deeply internal states such as dreams, hypnosis, or meditation.

Sometimes dreams, hypnosis, or meditation can be gateways

to shamanic journey levels and can provide us with the sensory pathways to explore further. More often, though, the shamanic journey levels are reached by using the gestalt or integrated combination of all of our states of being. This allows us to tap a level beyond our understanding yet within our reach, and within our experience.

To journey shamanically, we must release our need to divide our states of being and open ourselves to the whole of our experiences. It is said that the shaman does not make arbitrary divisions and designations in states of being. Although this may make it difficult for us to live in a linear, concrete, outside world, we can adapt to meet the method of the shaman. We can learn to value the messages and experiences of our journey regardless of the level of consciousness we may assign to it. In this way we learn to become more open to deeper states, deeper journeys, and deeper experiences. We learn to be there.

I believe that the increased perceptive and experiential qualities of shamanic journeys (and some dreams) arise from our innate ability to shift our own vibrations in order to tap into a primal consciousness level. Consider that the tunnels so frequently encountered in shamanic journeys could be our own representation of the baser levels of the brain and spinal cord. These connect us primally to the earth—or the concrete level of form. The higher levels of the brain connect us to images, thoughts, and psychic energies.

Next, consider that the brain is a lot like the living tree of the shaman—rooted in the earth (concrete level), channeling the energies (physical senses) of Spirit (abstract level). It is just a thought, not a theory. Still, it encourages me to believe that we do indeed come to our Earth Walk awake, alert, and fully equipped for all of the journeys we make. All we need to do is learn to get out of our way.

The rest of this chapter gives some totems, activities, images, and suggestions for helping you make your own shamanic journeys. These are divided into various levels and grouped according to the worlds of Plant, Human, Animal, and Mineral. Blend and experiment with these to create your own formulas for shamanic journeys. They are "kitchen-tested" by me for effectiveness. Please let them help you create your own recipes.

Shamanic Journey Helpers • Human World

1. Spend a few minutes each day becoming aware of your "stream of consciousness" thoughts. Beneath this stream is a deeper level, often considered to be unconscious but accessible through journey work. Let thoughts and images flow freely, without structure. These may seem a bit swampy at first, but the stream and the channel will clear. Note patterns.

2. Make a drumming tape. The rhythm is the important factor here. Keep it steady as a heartbeat. Make the tape about twenty or thirty minutes long, depending on how long it takes you to reach deep levels of inner vision. At the end of the tape, make a loud noise or instruct yourself to return to the present time and place. After a minute, repeat the command or noise. Sometimes it's very pleasant to take long journeys, but it's psychically exhausting.

3. Select symbolic power objects that are sacred to you, such as grails, swords, shields, rattles, pipes, and deity figures. Ceremonially attune with the objects and request their energies on your journeys. Do accept that these objects will influence the journeys since they are links to specific energies. Start with short journeys and experiment with your symbolic or ritual objects as journey companions.

4. Form a small group of close friends and journey together. Either take turns and drum for each other, or go together, using a drumming tape or shamanic music. Share your experiences later.

NOTE: The shaman is constantly aware of the events of all levels of consciousness. The shamanic journey is but one—explore your images, dreams, inner visions.

Shamanic Journey Helpers • Animal World

1. Enter an earth tunnel or cave in your deepest level of imagination. Move through the cave slowly, calling for your special sacred power animal to come and aid you on your journey. Be certain that you feel comfortable with the power animal that emerges. If not, send the animal away. Then come out of the journey level and do some clearing with sage, vinegar baths, feather cleansings. Try again when you feel ready. Stay positive.

2. Call on the bear of the West for an all-purpose strong journey companion. Let the bear help you find a special cave. Go deeper and deeper with the bear as a guide. Let the journey flow. The bear is also very good for journeys of deep-level self-healing. If you have an area of dis-ease, visualize it as a cave to enter with the bear. When you are inside, do ceremony and let the healing energies of the bear and the flow of the West wash the area clean. Rest and hibernate afterwards. Bears love that.

3. Determine which positive mythical animals are sacred to you, such as unicorns, dragons, griffins, thunderbirds. Ceremonially request their presence on your journey. Like other symbolic totems, they will have a strong influence on the journey. The mythic animals have a special and distinct energy, as well as a connection to the energies of their origins in myth.

4. Journey with your pets. This is more in the Craft of the Wise tradition of familiars, but it opens wonderful connections for all levels. This is also possible with wildlife in your close environment. Be ready for surprises.

Shamanic Journey Helpers • Plant World

1. Make a special journey incense. Blend sage, mugwort, dragon's blood resin, frankincense, cedar, juniper, and thyme (whichever ones you can obtain). Add herbs special just to you. Burn only when you wish to journey. Soon the scent alone will get you started.

2. Select and blend oils such as rose, sandalwood, lavender, and mint. Add an oil distinctly yours. Sprinkle in nutmeg, mugwort, myrrh, rubbed sage, or cinnamon (any combination—make your own). Anoint your chakra points sparingly. For earth journeys, start at the crown chakra and work down. For sky-spirit visions, start at root chakra and work up.

   This oil should be saved only for journey purposes. It is extremely effective when placed on the spinal energy points or on the heart, back-of-the-neck, and third-eye areas. Anoint the third eye before sleeping, for dream-state journeys.

3. Buy a plant that thrives on low light, such as amarantha, spathifillum, Chinese evergreen. Keep beside your bed (gifts of crystals and feathers are nice for such a plant). Take time to attune to the plant. Share your visions, images, dreams. Imagine that plant growing just inside the entrance of a sacred cave. Let it help you enter.

4. Gather flowers that bloom between darkness and dawn. Dry the blossoms and place them in a pouch. Use for journeys between the worlds.

NOTE: Whether you use mind-altering substances to journey or not is your business. Just remember that shortcuts can turn out to be dead ends.

Shamanic Journey Helpers • Mineral World

1. Make a circle of crystals, however many you have, all sizes. Place them point down into the ground if you can. If not, in cups of salt or soil. Ceremonially enter the circle and request a crystal pathway into the earth journey levels. Points straight up can be used for a sky-spirit vision; points toward you, for healing journeys and energy rebalancing. Points outward can be used for protection or for sharing energies. You are the programmer.

2. For various levels of inner vision and journey, I suggest the following stones. Work with them interchangeably to determine what works best for you. When you have chosen, ceremonially adopt the totem for that purpose. Save in a special place.

   A. Dream stimulators—Herkimer diamonds, quartz crystals, blue topaz, fluorite.

   B. Deep-level void journeys—Dark amethysts, azurite, apache tears (obsidian), black coral.

   C. Earth journeys—Smoky quartz, tourmalinated quartz, citrine, topaz, dioptase, emeralds, turquoise, malachite, amber, amber calcite.

   D. Sky-Spirit journeys—Rhodochrosite, rose quartz, fluorite, rutilated quartz, celestite, amazonite, all crystals.

   E. Healing journeys—Double-terminated quartz, crystals specifically programmed by you.

3. Choose two stones or crystals to be Dreamspeakers for you. Sleep with these on your pillow or under your pillow, in your hands or on your heart.

Part III

NORTH

SACRED WISDOM

SHAMANIC CEREMONIES

EARTH

ATTRIBUTES OF THE NORTH

The **Element** of the North is Earth.

The **Wheel of the North** is the wheel of
    Wisdom
    Practicality
    Symbols
    Ritual
    Ceremony
    Materialism and Prosperity
    Sacred Knowledge
    Teaching and Learning
    Patience

The **Energy** or pace of the North is steady, rhythmic. The heartbeat of Mother Earth.

The **Journey of the North** is the journey of wisdom.

The **Traditional Colors** of the North are
    Green
    Violet
    Brown
    Black
    White
    and the Deep Blue of the earth seen from space

Some **Sacred Spirits** of the North are
    Gaia—Earth Mother goddess
    Demeter—goddess of grain and abundance
    Rhea—mother of all deities
    Herne—horned god of the Green Wood
    Pan—god of joy on earth

Auriel (Uriel)—archangel of the North, keeper of sacred wisdom

Ghob—servant of Auriel, earth gnome, guide of the earth journeys

Gnomes—elemental spirits of Earth, ruled by Ghob

Agla—elemental king of Earth

Some **Animals** of the North are

Buffalo—for wisdom and practicality

Wolf—for teaching earth wisdom

Owl—for sacred knowledge

Dragon—for symbols

Stag Deer—for ritual and ceremony

Heron—for organized wisdom from intuition

Mythical Beasts—of all types, for learning the symbols of wisdom

Some **Minerals** of the North are

Crystal formations or clusters—for gathering wisdom and energy

Dark Crystals—for sacred knowledge and ceremony

Onyx—for practicality

Jasper—for earth wisdom

Aventurine—for prosperity

Green Jade—for growth and prosperity

Black Jade—for patience

Deep Violet Fluorite—for ritual and symbols

Royal Azule—for symbols and DNA codes

Marble—for steadfast practicality

Amethyst—for ritual, wisdom, and ceremony

Some **Plant World Helpers** of the North are

Oak Trees—for all magick, ritual, ceremony

Redwood Trees—for sacred wisdom

Myrrh, Sagebrush, Patchouly, Magnolia—for ceremonial incenses

Some **Human World Helping Activities** of the North are

Nature Ceremonies

Pagan Festivals

Shamanic Philosophies
Nature Retreats
Woodland Walks
Mountain Journeys
Cave Explorations

Helping Thoughts for the North:
With Patience do I seek
sacred knowledge and wisdom.
With Practicality do I prosper.
With Ceremony do I learn earth wisdom.
With Ritual do I support my soul's growth.
With Symbols of Earth do I teach.

Riding the Wheel of the North

It seems that I have been teaching and working forever. I am in desperate need of ceremony and Earth connection. Fortunately, it is time for a sacred sweat lodge day at the Seneca Wolf Clan South Lodge. As I make preparations to leave, I continue to psychically "bump" into my ritual staff. Each time I enter my room, it seems to jump at me. Finally, I stop to gaze at it reflectively. It is sitting in the corner, as it has been for far too long. Academic demands, motherhood, and the intensive study of Native American wisdom have left little time for the ritual staff of my Craft. It seems lonely, and I'm horrified to see dust on the crystal set at the top.

I take it from its place in the corner and carefully examine it. It is cut from a branch to be just my height. The branch came from an old ash tree. It was cut by a small tornado spawned by a major hurricane. The tornado had damaged the tree heavily. But when the storm had passed, the tree stood fast. Wrapped around the top of the staff is blue-green sash, trailed by a violet ribbon. Within the loops of ribbon and fringe I see stones, crystals, and bits of shell.

Secured in special places on the staff are symbols of my Craft and sacred symbols of the spiritual warrior. An enameled Celtic cross, a gift from a dear Craft brother, gleams up at me forlornly. The crystal at the top seems cloudy, even after I wipe it clean. I have the very real sense that I must be as cloudy as that crystal.

I muse on the protocol of bringing a Wiccan Craft ritual item to a Native American sweat lodge ceremony. No doubt some there will see it as more of my rebellious "witch business." I think it is indeed witch business—and witch business is Nature business. I decide to take my staff—or rather, my staff decides to go—it's difficult to say.

After I have arrived, I feel the energy in the staff stir. Not wishing to be too pushy with my "medicine things," I decide to place the staff against one of the sacred elder trees at the lodge. On the way, I find Grey Eagle, Seneca elder of the lodge, discussing crystals with a good friend of mine.

I listen for a while; then decide there must be a reason for all this synchronicity. I ask Grey Eagle to tell me about the energies he feels in the crystals set on my staff.

He spends a long time with my staff. Finally, with those gently piercing eagle eyes, he looks at me and says, "Well, it used to be a

Grandfather Crystal."

I feel a miserable mix of emotions. Part of me rages—part of me feels guilty—part of me knows why the staff had to come. A Grandfather Crystal is a sacred spirit crystal in Native American wisdoms. Tradition holds that the energies of shamans in spirit may return in crystal form. What Grey Eagle is saying is that my shaman spirit left the crystal, or can no longer be felt.

But this is a ritual tool of the Craft of the Wise, I think to myself, quiet for once, it has been charged in highest ritual and used ceremonially for many years. If I put what Grey Eagle is saying more in my own terms—the energies of the crystal are no longer charged. The crystal is not channeling the energies shamanically, so to speak. This is no time for a semantic discussion, I think, practical for once.

I think of the Native American ceremonial objects that people bring for Grey Eagle to awaken their energies. Can a Wiccan staff be recharged by someone else? That is not in my philosophy, I think. Still, the staff seemed determined to come to the lodge. I hold the staff and consider the situation carefully.

I have spent quite a while on the Rainbow Path. The whole point of my work has been about blending traditions, like colors in a rainbow; but I've kept my staff at home. Maybe it needs blending too.

"Can it be reawakened?" I ask Grey Eagle, wondering if I can bear to let anyone, even someone as special as he is, do ritual ceremony with my personal staff—my Craft symbol.

He looks at me very quietly for a time. I try to maintain a composed attitude and not clutch my staff and run.

"Take it over to the medicine wheel at the center of the land there," he finally says. "See what happens."

So that's it—I do it myself after all. Part of me is glad. Part of me wishes fleetingly that I were the type who could say "You do it." I'm not—and especially not with something as personal as this.

I make my way slowly through the great trees surrounding the medicine wheels and the sweat lodge. As I approach the great medicine wheel, I try to think of the many shared wisdoms of Nature represented by traditions all over the earth. I try not to think about the difference between high magick and ritual. That is not the issue today. Then the significance strikes me full force. The staff is symbolic of my philosophy, my air, my creative force. I have been experiencing Native American wisdom in many ways, but I had not run the energies through my own philosophical symbols. I had done no real ritual or ceremonial blending.

Well, time to practice what I preach, I think, as I walk around the circle, waiting for a sense of which direction to enter.

As I make my way around the circle for the third time, I feel the strength and wisdom of the North pull me. Part of me hesitates. Entering from the North can be tricky. I still remember the incredible rotten odor I unearthed once, entering unprepared from the North. I feel that the energies of the North are deeply at work this day, but I must approach them rightfully—ritually.

I circle to the South and enter ceremonially. I move to the center of the wheel and lay my staff crystal point toward the North. I stretch out beside it, with my head in the North, and feel the energy of the sacred medicine wheel.

There in the warm sun, with blue sky overhead and great old trees encircling me, all the arbitrary symbols seem to fade. I feel my energies realign gently. I let the strength of Mother Earth support me. All my plans for ceremony and ritual pale in comparison to the natural sacredness of this Earth connection.

After an hour or so I feel complete. I have journeyed into Nature wisdom, using my philosophy—my staff—to guide me. It is a private experience. I take my staff and place it in the car. The energies seem very strong in it now; yet still renewed and delicate. I do not discuss my experiences.

A few days later, I decide to recharge my staff in my own tradition as well. I cast a circle in my den and lay the staff crystal point in the North. I sit beside it in the South, facing North. It's approaching full moon time, and I feel the energies building. I have a shield in my hands with bells on it, which I shake gently, and I chant to summon helpful energies. I have just begun to chant when a piercing howl from the back yard sends rushes up my spine that give me colors.

The next thing I know, I am in another room with the door closed. I always knew I could fly, given the right formula—I don't even remember opening the doors. Every hair on my body is standing on end. That was the howl of a wolf. There are no dogs that sound like that south of Alaska. Besides, I know that is a wolf. I can feel it. I know what it is—I don't know why it is.

I manage to get myself back out into the den. Slowly. I know I have to deal with the circle I cast, I tell myself repeatedly. Everything is still and calm. I'm still trying to figure it out in my head. The experience is quite real. Maybe that would account for the goosebumps I have. Wolfbumps, I think—ha, ha, ha. Why do I still have them? And why is it so quiet now? I begin to think I've imagined it. But it was so close. But why only once? What is it that feels so different about this experience? I have certainly encountered a great deal of phenomena in my life.

The wise-woman shaman in me is delighted. The psychologist in me skeptically mentions the possibility of auditory hallucination. I've heard of auditory hallucination, after all. I've even known a few people who were pretty well acquainted with them when I was working at the state hospital. Great. That's it. Other people get angels speaking to them—I get a wolf howling in my back yard.

I'm not telling anybody, well, not many. The next morning I call a special, close friend, who lives nearby.

"Cindy, do we have wolves?" I ask her, trying to sound casual. We often talk about our wildlife adventures.

"Oh yes," she says. "I see them sometimes, way across the fields in back of the house. My husband thinks they're coyotes, but I know they're wolves. I can tell by the way they walk. They walk connected to the ground."

I tell her about my experiences of the night before. We laugh about the scary aspects. It's so good to have someone to laugh with about these things. I'm glad she's seen wolves. "I'm relieved," I tell her. We both laugh and hang up the phone.

Relieved! Oh my God! There are wolves in my back yard! I watch the moon from inside the house for a few nights.

A few days later, on a cold, full moon night, we're doing a Native American pipe ceremony in my back yard. We've all worked hard and we're feeling cohesive. We're one under the night sky. As we begin to pass the pipe around, a wolf howls, not too far away on the bayou.

Immediately, every dog for miles begins to bark hysterically. This is something I hadn't heard when the wolf had howled in my back yard a few days earlier. Hmmmm. Of course, I could have missed it. I was too busy jumping out of my skin at the time. This time the wolf doesn't scare me, but I do check to see if anyone else heard it.

The dogs finally stop, and the night is quiet again. We finish our pipe ceremony and begin to hug our way out of the circle. It's a nice custom.

"I told you I heard a wolf," I say to my close friends as I hug them. Validation may not be necessary, but it's nice from time to time.

After everyone has left for the evening, a wolf begins to howl, followed by the dogs' barking. Then more wolves howl, and still more, until the dogs have to shut up.

Only the wolves can be heard.

The wolves howl for three nights. The dogs don't even try to interrupt anymore.

I call Grey Eagle and Gentle Earth Woman to tell them about the wolves. He tells me that the full moon of February is called the Wolf Moon in some traditions. It is February.

Still later, I have the opportunity to see Lynn Andrews give a talk in Austin, Texas. During the break, I tell her about the wolves. "What do they want?" I ask her, laughing, but serious.

"Maybe they like you," she says, smiling.

Still later, I learn that the wolf is the teacher of earth wisdom.

Still later, I find a wolf claw pendant in the out-of-ordinary way I'm becoming accustomed to. I hang it on my ritual staff in honor of the connection it has helped me make. I do ritual to welcome the wolf.

Even now, my dance with the wolf has only just begun. I am honored to share my Earth Walk with such a special spirit.

I find my place in the North.

From there I can be the wolf in all the directions I may journey.

The Wheel of the North is the wheel of wisdom. In the North we find our place and define our Earth Walk journey. The North gives us the strength, the practicality, and the patience to teach—and learn— earth wisdom. The North is the place of precision, measurement, and self-architecture. In the North we learn the recipes and formulas for ritual and the keys to wisdom through symbols. In the North we find our sacred center through ceremony. We accept the sacred gift of power—and we walk in balance.

Here is a brief ceremony to use when you're beginning the work of the North. Approach the North with the energies of ritual and deep ceremonial reverence. The North is the place of spiritual connection through symbol and sacred wisdom to strengthen your path.

North Ceremony

Stand in the West, facing East.

Feel the energies of the West and inner vision flow through you. Let them return to the waters of consciousness and sacred dreams.

Now turn to face the North.

You are standing in the South, place of Fire and protection. You have journeyed through the West, place of Water and inner vision. You have ridden the wheels of higher Self and emotional self.

Now you are clear to seek the sacred wisdoms of the North journey.

The North is the place of the element of Earth. It is here that you receive the sacred symbols and wisdoms through the shamanic channels you have opened and cleared in yourself.

As you stand facing North, feel the deep, steady vibration of the North pull you. Take all the time you need to connect with that vibration. Match your energies to the steady heartbeat of the North—the heartbeat of all Nature wisdoms held sacred throughout time. This is the heartbeat felt beneath all sacred symbols, even when their origins have been forgotten—or misplaced. This is the heartbeat of Mother Earth.

Take a few moments to center your energy. When you have done so, walk from South to West, to North, to East, and return to the South. You have walked a symbolic, magical circle.

Now you may approach the North from within this sacred circle. As you approach the North from the South, remember that sacred wisdom comes to us clearly when we receive it from a place of sacred trust and faith.

Face the North just a step away from the inside edge of your circle. Take time to honor the wisdom and energies of the North. Take time to pledge yourself to sacred wisdom—as student—as teacher—as Earth Walker.

When you feel ready, turn and stand in the North, facing South.

Feel the sacred Pentagram Shield of the North declare your sacred journey and fill you with the strengths it represents.

Honor all the lessons you received in the South and the West. Honor the help you have had on your journey. Honor the lessons of the East still to come and the energies still awaiting your progress on the path of the shaman.

When you are complete, absorb the energies of your sacred circle into your heart. (You may make an image of this in your mind.) Then feel the energy drop down, deep into the heart of your wisdom. Begin the journey of the North with patience and self-honor. Honor self-wisdom.

Chapter 9

SHAMANIC CIRCLES

The circle represents the wheel of the universe. Within the circle, as within the universe, there are many other wheels. These wheels are represented in ceremony and ritual by the elements, the deities, and the spirit keepers, or gates to the inner planes. There are many other symbols, totems, and tools used in different traditions. A set of books could possibly list all of these—one book of shadows cannot.

In this book, I have endeavored to present the commonalities present in Nature traditions. This is because the shamanic path deals so directly with the elemental energies of Self, Nature, and Spirit. The path we undertake now, in an age of blended wisdom, allows us to experience the energies of symbols and wisdoms from many different traditions.

Some occultists feel that we must exercise caution in using symbols and wisdom outside our own inner codes. Others feel that it is important to study different traditions to deepen our connection to the universal source of energy that flows through all wisdom, in many different ways.

It has long been a tradition in the ancient Craft of the Wise to explore the wisdoms of other Nature-based systems. Because of this tradition, my natural curiosity, and my land of birth, I have been privileged to study Native American wisdom. In doing so, I have felt my Earth connection strengthened and my dedication to the ways of Nature become more determined. I have also felt my appreciation for my own Craft expand and develop new dimensions.

The path of exploring other traditions can be filled with tremendous growth. It can also be a struggle as you sort for what has deepest meaning to you. Sorting wisdom to find your own connection to wisdom is a dance of deep self-power. Approach with the same blend of humor and honor that has carried you through other journeys, and you will fare well. Look for the underlying heart of Nature wisdom in all of the symbols and traditions you encounter. That is the way of the shaman.

Follow your own path to wisdom, regardless of who seems to be heading in another direction. We do walk side by side from time to time on the path of the shaman, as on any magical path. We do not share the same path. The journey of the North gives you the experiences to walk steadfast, connected to the earth on your path.

The shadows I share here are most basic to Nature traditions. My own Western occult work and traditions in the ancient Celtic ways color these, as does my work with Native American wisdom. If an aspect of some of these shadows intrigues you, I urge you to study the origin of its wisdom for yourself. Only you can define your own wisdom and symbols—however, you may choose to experience many others while you do so.

In the North, we learn a great deal about living ceremonially and creating ritual space. The very words *ceremony* and *ritual* have so many different interpretations that we may become confused and frustrated. To simplify the matter, here are three basic approaches to the concepts of ceremony and ritual. (These are generalized.)

Native American. Ritual has to do with acts of Nature energies, primarily shamanic. Ceremonies have to do with set forms of spiritual connections.

Western Occult. Ritual has to do with the energies of soul or spiritual levels, set form. Ceremonies have to do with Nature or elemental energies, some set form.

Aquarian Format. Ritual is set form; specific words are used, although you may construct these beforehand from your own blend of traditions. Once ritual is begun, it follows a set format, regardless. This can be most important for acts of active magick when the energies become intensely focused and specific. Ceremony is free-flowing. Emerging energies are incorporated in the basic format. Some traditional ritual formats are used in ceremony to begin and to end the events, but new energies are welcomed and even solicited in ceremony.

I believe there are times to do set ritual. I believe there are other times for free-flowing ceremonies. More than any choice of format, I believe in living ceremonially—every day. That is the heart of Nature wisdom and the way of the shaman.

When you live ceremonially, you are centered in personal power, in balance with yourself, in harmony with all of the energies of Nature, in direct connection to Spirit. You walk within your own circle of power. Within that circle, your path becomes a kind of moving altar of spirituality.

Every time you stop to touch a tree or share energy with a friend, you do so with the sacredness of set ritual in the circle you carry with you. You do so with the creative energies of ceremony in the ongoing free-flow of shamanic living. Living ceremonially deepens your shamanic connections and your self-power.

When you live ceremonially, you do still take time for set rituals and ceremonial events. When you live ceremonially, you come to these with a stronger connection to all the energies and wisdoms. The symbol of the shaman is the living tree—living in ceremonial connection to Self, Nature, and Spirit. You need not wait for times of ritual and ceremony. Walk in power—now, and always.

Here are some methods to help you develop your skills and learn to live ceremonially, shamanically, magically. I am primarily a ceremonialist. The methods I present may be developed as ritual if you so choose. To do this, you may have to delve deeper into the various traditions and find their formulas. Mine are derived from doing just that many, many times. I still do it, and I still learn something new each time.

Casting a Circle for Ritual or Ceremony

NOTE: I have included a chart called Sacred Wheels in the appendix. It gives a variety of types and variations of the basic Nature circles, or wheels. These may be adapted to suit your personal path.

The following is a basic Nature circle consisting of the four cardinal directions and their elements. Within each direction I have included another circle to represent the wheels-within-wheels aspects of energies.

This may be adapted for group or individual use. I have found that shared group rituals fare best when the most basic sorts of circles are used. Each person is a wheel of energies all by himself. When too many symbols are used with too many people, the energies can become chaotic and essentially useless for working.

However, there are times when a group of people honestly share enough symbols and connections to the same origins of wisdom to make for very powerful work. These things take time, so I suggest you begin group work with a basic approach and add more symbolic totems as you become cohesive.

For individual circles, you may experiment a bit more freely. Just remember that you are the channel of the energies of whatever you choose to use in your circle.

This is a circle I use for healing, magick, journeys, adopting totems, and dedicating or charging ritual items. It is designed to be a foundation for all purposes.

Any of the ceremonies, exercises, and images I have given you may be amplified in this circle. Blend and create your own rituals or ceremonies with an openness and honorable attitude to sacred wisdom.

This takes some time to assemble at first. If you make fair-size batches of the ingredients, you can store them, add to them, and use them repeatedly. You can even take the ingredients of only one wheel and use as a complete circle. Experiment.

Nature Circle • Shamanic Wheel

For this circle you will use

>   incenses for Fire in the South (some traditions use candles here)

>   mineral totems for Water in the West

>   mineral totems for Earth in the North (ritual is a North journey and shamanism is an Earth Walk; this circle emphasizes the journey and elements of the North)

>   candles for Air in the East (some traditions use oils here; I oil my candles) and one for your Self

Begin with a point in the South. It is useful to use a stone or a special mat to mark the point. I use large round trays to symbolize the wheels—and to put my totems on.

South

In the South you will have four different incenses. Small bowls or saucers from clay flower pots are excellent for this.

In the South of your South, have incenses such as cinnamon, dragon's blood resin, cedar, sweetgrass, frankincense, or nutmeg. (Choose or blend.)

These are the Fire of your Fire.

In the West of your South, have incenses such as sandalwood, thyme, hyacinth, lotus, or vanilla.

These are the Water of your Fire.

In the North of your South, use incenses such as myrrh, patchouly, sagebrush, honeysuckle, or magnolia. (In a pinch, use dried grasses or broom straw.)

These are the Earth of your Fire.

In the East of your South, use incenses such as lavender, mint, clover, or lemon grass.

These are the Air of your Fire.

For the center, select one personally meaningful incense to represent you. Place just South of the center of your circle.

West

In the West you will have four Mineral World totems associated with Water. To signify this, you may also put your totems, such as stones or crystals, in a bowl or tray of water.

In the West of your West, have mineral totems from rivers or creeks, from moving, flowing bodies of water. River stones are ideal.

This is the Water of your Water.

In the North of your West, have mineral totems from dry creek beds or paths of ancient rivers. Cave stones are often just right, or canyon or arroyo stones.

This is the Earth of your Water.

In the East of your West, have mineral totems from lakes, ponds, or still pools of water. Stones from a lakeside are fine.

This is the Air of your Water.

In the South of your West, have mineral totems from hot deserts or sunny beaches. Shells are fine if they have been in the sun awhile.

This is the Fire of your Water.

In the center, select a Water/Earth totem that represents you. Stones with holes are magick here. Run water through the hole to represent flowing energies and place just West of the center.

North

In the North you will have four Mineral World totems associated with Earth.

In the North of your North, have mineral totems such as ores, metals, steel, clay, or peat. A pot of rich soil can be used here and later sprinkled on your plants for added growth energy.

This is the Earth of your Earth.

In the East of your North, have mineral totems such as crystals or gemstones. Meteorites have an added energy that is very powerful here. High-mountain stones are also good.

This is the Air of your Earth.

In the South of your North, have mineral totems such as lava, stones from around old volcanic craters, or obsidian. Apache tears are excellent here, and tumbled obsidian.

This is the Fire of your Earth.

In the West of your North, have mineral totems such as river stones, shells, coral, or clay from creek beds—as long as the connections to Water and Earth are clearly combined.

This is the Water of your Earth.

In the center, place a mineral totem that represents you. Crystals are good here, especially if you have not used one elsewhere. Place just North of the center of your circle.

East

In the East you will use candles anointed with oils, if you have them. If you don't have oils, extracts for cooking or flavorings are fine. Just blend with pure vegetable oils. Almond oil is superb, as is olive.

Anoint a candle from the center upward to the point of the wick, then from the center downward to the base. This signifies the connection of Earth and Spirit for this circle.

In the East of your East, use a yellow, orange, or white candle. Anoint with oils such as lavender or mint. Mint extract works well here. In a pinch, use mace or marjoram sprinkled in oil.

This is the Air of your Air.

In the South of your East, use a red, orange, or white candle. Anoint with oils such as frankincense or cedar. Lemon or orange extracts work well here. In a pinch, sprinkle cinnamon or cloves in oil.

This is the Fire of your Air.

In the West of your East, use a blue, violet, or white candle. Anoint with oils such as sandalwood or violet. Cherry or raspberry extracts work well here, and especially vanilla.

This is the Water of your Air.

In the North of your East, use a green, violet, or white candle. Anoint with oils such as patchouly or honeysuckle. Extracts of maple and almond work well here. In a pinch, sprinkle ground grains such as cornmeal or oatmeal in vegetable oil. (Messy, but effective.)

This is the Earth of your Air.

In the center use a candle in a color specifically chosen to represent you or use white. You may anoint this candle with personal oils meaningful to you. You may blend these oils, in a pinch, by mixing a favorite perfume or cologne and oil together. You may also carve your name or special symbols in this candle. Place just East of the center.

A circle is activated or opened on the outside points first. Beginning in the South is always fine. Honor each direction as you move around the circle and attune to its element. Whichever direction you decide to begin with, attune with the element of its element first. For example, in the South, light the South incense and move around the circle.

For any circles or wheels, I advise clockwise direction to start. Some traditions hold that counterclockwise is a spiritual path and clockwise is an earth path. My own Craft traditions are quite specific on this point, so I use clockwise to cast all circles. Within that circle I may move in any direction to do the work I need. Basically, clockwise (Deosil) attracts, and counterclockwise (Widdershins) banishes.

My Seneca Wolf Clan mother stresses the importance of always moving in a circle, whichever direction you go. I completely agree with this when it applies to an outer circle that you are casting. To move crisscross could block the energies you are working with. Inside the circle, the way you move depends more on the "mood" of the work and the energies you're working with.

In the Nature circle or shamanic wheel I have just given you, I move about freely. In a more symbolic or ritualistic circle using deities, sacred symbols of wisdom, or power objects for specific directions, I move in a circle always. You will have to work with these yourself to find the right measure and pace, as well as direction. We're here to learn—we're not expected to come in knowledgeable. Just use the equipment you were given: your brain, your physical senses, your intuition and, most of all, your sacred common sense.

After you have activated the energies around the circle, move inside to the center. Basically, this is an altar of your Self, representing your personal connection to the energies of Nature. Moving to the center also represents your path as a shaman, centered in the energies, balanced in power. Doing this literally centers the energies.

The center elements can be activated from the South as always. This is good, because you begin in faith, move through inner vision, through wisdom, and illumination. Beginning in the East is a bit chaotic in energy at times, but it is excellent for divination and journeys. It illuminates you—coming and going.

If there is a specific element or attribute or journey direction that you are working on, or with, activate your center altar with this energy. If you need to earth or attract energies, move clockwise. If you wish to banish energies or to attract a more spiritual connection, move counterclockwise—within the circle. Just state your intentions clearly; and be specific!

As you work with circles, you may want to attune with the various symbols and deities or sacred spirit keepers of the directions and the elements. At the beginning of each section, I have listed a few of these. The ones I listed are ones I am familiar with. As you explore other wisdoms, you will find others to use. Please do it honorably.

The best advice I can give you is to approach all deities, symbols, elemental spirit keepers, and unfamiliar power objects as a student. Too many people want to command these very powerful vibrations or tap their energies far too soon. Remember two things:

> Your attitude determines the energies you connect with, *absolutely.*

> Whatever you do with energies must flow through you first and last.

State your intention to learn for the highest good the wisdoms represented by the deity or symbol or spirit keeper.

Invite the new vibrations by name. Spell them if you are worried about pronunciation. Use titles, attributes, and whatever other associations you know. Invite these to stand on your circle and share their wisdom or receive your tribute. This may seem a bit flowery, but it's very good practice when you're tapping into energy vibrations, which have been around an extremely long time in deity or symbolic form. It is just a more ritual approach to natural energies, and it pays off to do it right.

Each of these deities or energies must be honored in the same formal manner—individually. This can take some time, believe me. Having done this with a full regalia of deities and symbols many times, I now know why sorcerers truly had apprentices. I advise that you stick with no more than four at a time (one from each direction), and never call an elemental spirit without its ruler. The energies are far too direct, chaotic and seductive.

It's best to keep a hierarchical sort of approach here. This is ritual, and it's a North journey of measuring patiently and learning. Guess who is the apprentice in the North? We are—even, and especially, when we're teaching.

Perhaps you are not interested in ritually calling the various deities and rulers, but you wish to attune to the symbolic energies at a higher vibrational level. For this, I call the archangels of the directions, also called angels of the winds by some traditions. The beauty of doing this is that their vibrations have such strong positive energies, you can connect to them quite confidently.

I once called the archangels at a Native American naming ceremony, because the energies were extremely chaotic and because there were people present who I knew were actively siphoning energies—some from me, and some from others. Although I did it quietly and I thought unheard, the medicine teacher present was fascinated to learn what I was doing. To her, it was a new concept to call the deity. The deity usually called her. I explained that it can happen both ways: the energies are there to use when the need arises.

Usually I call the archangels before doing serious ceremony (some emerging energies get included as they arise) and set ritual. I also call them on occasions when I really need to feel that their power and protection are there. This is effective for me, since it springs from my own occult and Craft traditions. If you call them in circle for the first time, do it as with elemental rulers and other deity energies. Be the student. You are anyway, no matter how long you have been doing shamanic or magical path work. I keep finding this to be true.

Some people find the archangels far too patriarchal or over-Christianized. At one gathering I was amazed to find that a nun and a former priest had never heard of Auriel (or Uriel), archangel of the North. When I mentioned this to my husband, he said, "Maybe that's the one they made into God." Hmmmm. It is true that Auriel has a very all-father quality. I'm still thinking about that one.

As far as the patriarchal aspects are concerned, I feel this is a personal choice. I try not to confuse sexuality and spirituality—or sexuality and energies—too much. It's true that the archangels have very active energies. When I call for them, that is what I want.

However, I have also considered the real need for a more "feminine" counterpart—or aspect—of the spiritual vibration energies of the archangels. When I journeyed and called these to come with the traditional archangels, I found that what emerged gave a nice balance to the energies.

Here are the traditional archangels and the feminine goddess aspects that emerged and, for me, vibrated harmoniously. Together they can form sacred energy pairs for your highest ritual work and needs. Experiment for the ones that are meaningful to you.

North

Auriel (Uriel)—high lord of all that is attributed to the North.

Traditionally, Auriel appears as a serious-faced man of mature years, with flowing silver hair and violet eyes. He wears a cloak of rainbow colors that flashes and glows in his aura.

Athena (Minerva)—Greco/Roman, high lady goddess of wisdom. She traditionally appears as a strong woman in full armour: her breastplate symbolizes earned wisdom, and her helmet, the protection of knowledge. Athena was goddess of war before she was goddess of wisdom. Her energies are strong and direct.

East

Raphael—high lord of all that is attributed to the East. Traditionally appears wearing the garments of a traveler—a kind of astral bard. Wears winged sandals, broad-brimmed hat, and yellow cloak, and carries a staff with serpents.

Kwan Yin—Oriental high lady goddess of serenity, good fortune, and peaceful enlightenment. Traditionally appears as a beautiful Oriental woman, often seated or standing on a lotus blossom, sometimes holding a small vial or vase, representing good fortune and abundant growth.

South

Michael—high lord of all that is attributed to the South. Traditionally appears as a golden-haired warrior clad in golden armour, plated kilt, and curved breastplate. Right hand holds an engraved runic sword. Left hand is behind a battle shield. Some recent traditions hold that Michael became St. Michael who slew the Dragons (i.e., destroyed the powers of the Druids). Don't you believe it. It's probably a rumor started by the bishop Pattricus (St. Patrick), who is credited with driving the Snakes (i.e., the Druids) out of Ireland. Don't you believe that either. Just look at what those ancient followers of Druidic ways have done with St. Patrick's Day! All those people wearing the sacred green of Nature—consider that festive energy!

Danu (Bridget of the Gaelic Celts, Cerridwen of the ancient Britons)— high lady goddess of the inner flame of Nature and creation, keeper of the cauldron or womb of all life and sacred wisdom. Traditionally appears holding a cauldron, chalice, or bowl. Appears young (Maiden), middle-aged (Mother), or old (Crone), to represent all of the cycles of life continuing. Represents spiraling wheels of Nature, life and renewal.

West

Gabriel—high lord of all that is attributed to the West. Traditionally appears as a young man, strong and wise, with an inner glow. He wears a luminous cloak, and on his forehead, the curved crescent horns of the waxing Moon—which he does not blow, contrary to popular modern myth.

Selene (Selena)—European, high lady goddess of the Full Moon. Traditionally appears as a mature maternal woman, quite gentle in her power. She wears robes made of silvery fabric reflecting moon-beam lights, and also wears a silver crescent, points upturned, on her forehead.

All deities, symbols, rulers, archangels, lords, ladies, devas—whatever—are energy forms. We are energy forms. There may not even be matter, just denser vibrational patterns of energy. (We all know a few of those, admit it.)

We create our images of these powerful spiritual vibrations to help ourselves make connections to these energies.

All of the traditions of wisdoms, from the most aboriginal shaman-ism to the most esoteric metaphysics, are concerned with tapping into these energies in different ways using different images and forms. Some of these have been used for magical and spiritual channels for an extremely long time and subsequently have a very significant vibration of their own.

You study the attributes of deities and symbols not to be limited by their traditional meanings but to know what sort of vibration you're tapping into. It's a good idea to study these before working with them, but it can happen the other way.

Notes on the Journey

Once when I had been working academically very, very hard for a long time, I journeyed using active imagery. The image had to do with seeking a source of inner strength. When I entered the chamber containing this source, I found Athena. Not only did I see her in imagery, I tapped into that very distinct Athena vibration. There is no mistaking some deity energies.

I had spent many years working with moon goddesses and woodland goddesses and probably needed Athena energy to get my academic projects completed. After Athena emerged so strongly in my journey, I actively used that energy channel for my work. I found some wonderful molded-plaster faces of Athena and Mars, and I brought them both home because the symbolic deity energy of my house is Mars. Then I hung them on a wall in my bedroom, just above the headboard of the bed. Athena on one side and Mars on the other. My intention was for both my husband and me to pull on their strength for the active work we both had at the time.

As long as I was pouring lots of energy into my projects, everything was fine. When I finished my projects, all hell broke loose. It seemed that Athena forgot she was goddess of wisdom but remembered how to be goddess of war. Shamanically speaking, I had left that channel unused, open wide, and the aspects clashed.

Every discussion in our house became a fiery debate over nothing. At first I attributed it to just being tired and cranky. Then I caught sight of my two plaster plates of Athena and Mars one day. I wondered what I could have been thinking to have put those two energies together, especially side by side in our bedroom. Venus or Aphrodite would have been fine. Venus tamed Mars, so to speak, and they created, among other things, Harmony; but Athena and Mars—never.

I considered calling the store where I had found the plates and asking for an Aphrodite face, but I knew it had gone beyond the point of substituting the energies. I had to break the energy pattern that was developing from the interaction of those two fiery symbolic energies. I had to stop the energy being manifested all over the house.

I took the plates dramatically off the wall, to match the dramatic energies of course. I strode outside with all the fire and warrior spirit I had, which was plenty after having those two around, and smashed the plates on the patio. I swept the pieces together and placed them in the ground under my garden faucet, which I let drip for a while. Let them cool off and work it out somewhere else.

The difference was immediate. If nothing else, it signaled to our deepest levels to slow the flow of fire and find better balance of energies within ourselves and together. Sometime later I did a little ceremony to honor Athena for her helping energy, and at a different time, a ceremony to honor Mars. I was taking no chances.

Almost five years after that, I found a tiny cameo of a warrior on black onyx. Upon closer inspection, I recognized Mars (or Ares, as he is also called). I brought it home to my husband for a Yule present. I may need it myself, though, with all my Ares family here to dance with.

I close this chapter with a few suggestions for making altars. A personal shamanic altar can be made for one specific direction for journeys associated with that direction. As a follower of the shamanic path, you carry your sacred circle inside you.

For group altars you may need to use a little adaptation. And when you are working with a group, always be sure to encircle the altar. To do this, honor all of the directions, their energies, and their elements. Then encircle the group and the altar with these balanced energies. This harmonizes the energies of the group.

When you do anything in reverence, honor, or celebration, you have created an altar of sorts. Just placing an offering at the base of a beautiful rock or tree makes that a sacred altar space. Altars are the focus points for energies. If you walk in balance at the center of sacred energies, you are indeed an altar yourself.

Altars and altar instructions are the subjects of many books. Study traditional altars to help create your own. The chart on sacred wheels has several forms of circles that may be adapted as altars on a smaller scale. The charts of totem properties of the worlds of Nature may also provide some helping catalysts.

I have found it to be an added depth of connection to make direction altars to represent journeys or wheels I am working with. When I do these, I try to emphasize the element of the direction. With some I use only the element of the direction, but this can be limiting and out of balance. It's good to include a tiny representative, in some form, of each direction or world in Nature. For example, a tiny feather, a dried flower, and a small charm or colored ribbon on an altar made of stones can be enough to give the balance. I also try to let the style or the movement of the altar match the energy of the direction.

> North altars are quite set and orderly, with lots of symbolic items.
> East altars are a creative, expressive, and seemingly chaotic jumble.
> South altars are exuberant and vivid—never quiet.
> West altars are mystical and use soothing lines and colors.

Some traditions hold that an altar must be constructed to stay in one space only. As long as the altar itself doesn't become a sacred monument, this can be good for ritual. It's the energies and the shamanic connections of Self, Nature, and Spirit that we hold sacred.

Be able to set an altar anywhere, anytime.

Bring the circle from within you.

Still, you may have certain sacred spaces in your environment for work just on your own.

Change symbolic items. An active altar changes and energy flows.

Make a good basic altar from the center items of the Nature circle I gave you, or from those of any wheel.

A dark candle and a light one set side by side make a fine altar.

I use a vanilla- or mint-scented candle for the Lady/Goddess. You may use this for receptive energies, the Moon, or your inner emotions and visions.

I use a cinnamon or musk (watch out) candle for the Lord/Consort God. You may use this for active energies, the Sun, your outer character and relationships.

Four crystals representing the directions make a harmonious altar. Other totem objects, such as jewelry totems and symbols from the worlds of Nature, can be recharged on or inside the crystal circles.

Chapter 10

SACRED SPELLS

The energy of the North is steady and grounded. When we ride the Wheel of the North, we learn to weigh and measure our growth and progress on the path of the shaman. It is in the North that we apply our knowledge as well as receive deeper wisdoms. We combine sacred wisdom with practical wisdom to enhance our journey.

This chapter is designed to present workable formulas, rituals, and spells useful for all of the wheels. Each wheel or direction has specific energies that lend themselves to our work on the path of the shaman. When we learn to flow with these energies, we find our work strengthened and our growth enhanced.

The following spells, formulas, and rituals can be adapted to work in all of the directions. I have divided them to give you a foundation to work from, and a variety to become familiar with.

In the North we work with

>sacred keys—activating symbols and spirituality
>patience—grounding and personal pacing
>prosperity—using energies for material growth
>practical wisdom—using magick for daily application

In the East we work with

>creativity—tapping the energies of expansion
>divination—learning to read the energies
>mental powers—sharpening our awareness and per-

ception
peace—finding and sharing the flow of harmony

In the South we work with

protection—establishing personal security
love—balancing the energies of our relationships
self-power—developing our gifts of strength
purification—cleansing our Self and clearing our path

In the West we work with

journeys—mapping our inner quests
inner vision—finding formulas for consciousness
self-healing—maintaining personal wellness
balancing—harmonizing aspects of Self

Totem helpers from each of the four worlds—Animal, Plant, Mineral, and Human—are available to help us focus energies directly and manifest our intentions specifically. As always, please use these only as samples to add to your own medicine bag.

North Ritual • Sacred Circle

You will need

> a round light-colored or white tablecloth (these are available very inexpensively or can be made from double-bed sheets)
>
> permanent marking pens in colors: red, blue, green, yellow, or just black
>
> one light candle and one dark candle (these will need to burn completely for this spell, so I suggest votives or dinner tapers)
>
> plain white or manila drawing paper and a pencil or crayons in red, blue, yellow, green, and black
>
> drawings of sacred symbols (you may have these in your personal library, or you may use the symbols in the appendix; you may also do this with no "notes" and let symbols emerge; it's okay to do both)

Set aside a few hours when you will not be disturbed. Spread the cloth out on the floor. Place the candles side by side in the center. Place all of your notes and drawing materials on the tablecloth as well. (I use a tray to hold these.) You may use incenses, other candles, and music if you need to outside of the circle to set the mood. However, silence and as few other types of sensory stimuli as possible are preferable at this time.

When you are ready, sit in the center of the cloth, facing North. Take a few moments to center your energies and pace your breathing. Close your eyes and call on the keepers of each direction to be present and bring you sacred wisdom. Cast a circle of white or golden light around the perimeter of your cloth. This is now a sacred circle. With your eyes still closed, state your intention to be a channel for sacred wisdom and a student of spiritual knowledge. In your heart, feel your willingness to learn. Open your heart and mind to sacred wisdom. Feel the energies flow through you.

Now open your eyes and light the darker candle, which symbolizes your receptivity to sacred wisdom. Light the lighter candle next, to symbolize your willingness to activate the wisdom you find on your path. These candles have many symbolic meanings in different traditions. For this ritual, I find it useful to think of them as the sacred pillars forming a gateway between the worlds to let wisdom channel through.

Some other symbolic meanings for these candles are:

Dark Candle	*Light Candle*
Yin	Yang
Female	Male
Night	Day
Form (Matter)	Force (Energy)

When the candles are lit, face North and ask for a sacred symbol to come into your inner vision to represent the Ray to the wisdom of that direction or wheel. If one doesn't come into your inner vision, take time to look through your notes. Sometimes a symbol will seem to jump from the page as you connect with its energy. You may also find it useful to sketch or doodle on your drawing paper until a symbol emerges for you. If you design your own, this is perfectly fine. Keys to sacred wisdom can be traditional or personal. This is shamanic magick.

When you have the symbol for the North, take time to sketch it carefully on paper. Place the paper in the North, just at the edge of the circle. This symbolizes wisdom coming from inner and outer energies. Later, you will draw the symbol on the cloth. For now, honor the energies of the North and turn to face the East.

Repeat the process in the East—then South—then West—and return to face the North.

Facing North, look up to honor Spirit; then down to honor Earth. Close your eyes and go inside your heart for a symbol that connects you to the core of all the energies. This will be your most personal symbol and the key to your special energies. Your monogram or your sacred name may be used here quite effectively. Sketch it on paper and place in the center of the circle.

Take a look at all of the symbols. Connect with the energies that each one represents for you. As you do so, you may find that you want to make additions or even changes. The energies are very chaotic at the center of the shamanic journey. Sometimes a symbol that came from one direction may actually work better for you in another direction. Move the sketches around if you need to. Energies in the North are steady but not static, and all symbols are wheels, so moving these can be necessary at times.

When you are comfortable with the placement of your sacred symbols, you may draw them on the cloth in the directions you have chosen. Traditional colors for the directions vary, but these are in keeping with the energies:

North—Green	South—Red
East—Yellow	West—Blue

You can use your markers to draw these symbols and mark the directions in traditional colors. You can also use only black. If you use black, you may decide to omit marking the directions. That way, you can spin the symbols in different directions when you work with this circle. Of course, you can make more than one of these ritual circles; so do what feels right for the time being.

When you have finished drawing the symbols, honor all of the keepers of wisdom for their help in creating this ritual circle. Gather your sketches together and place them in a notebook. These may be used as meditative keys and symbols for other rituals.

With this cloth circle, you have created a very sacred ritual object for yourself. You may use it in a variety of ways to signal your deepest spiritual and magical work times. One woman I know made hers into a kind of poncho to use as a magical robe as well. You can also use it as a magical coverlet when ill, stressed, or in need of protection; as a cover for a large dream pillow; as an altar cloth on a table; as a decoration hung on the ceiling or on the North wall of a room; or as a large medicine bundle for sacred objects.

Rituals, formulas, and spells can be created from the most basic or the most elaborate items. How you put these together depends entirely on you. It has always been a part of high magick and ritual to have lots of regalia. However, I am always humbled by the endurance of the simple ways of magick.

In the days of the witch craze and the time of burnings and persecution, magical regalia was a deadly bit of paraphernalia to own. Many in the Craft of the Wise adopted the simple methods of the pagan, or country folk. A grail could be made quite well from an earthen cup. A staff could be a broomstick without its straw. A simple twig could be a wand, and a bit of wool or hide could be a shield.

Metaphysically speaking, all energies are present in all things. We can be very creative with what we use. It's the spirit that counts in all ritual and magical work—not the finery. Certainly, the shamans of old had to fashion their ritual items from simple things in Nature. If we do choose to have elaborate regalia, it's wise to balance it with simple items as well. This way we connect with a variety of energies that we need at different times. In this time of blending, we can use modern technology as well as ageless methods and create our special Aquarian combinations.

The rest of this chapter lists spells, rituals, and formulas to use for magical, shamanic living. These were designed to be as simple or as elaborate as you choose to make them.

North Wheels

I. Sacred Keys

1. Draw symbols, runes, or talismans on slips of plain paper. Write your intentions specifically on the back until you have worked with these for a time. Burn in a silver or blue candle flame to receive the energies. Burn in a gold or red candle flame to activate or release.

2. Draw symbols on flat smooth stones and place on your altar to connect with those energies. Four or five stones can be used as a circle of symbols.

3. Burn symbols in a mixture of frankincense and myrrh to awaken their deepest spiritual energies.

4. Burn symbols in a mixture of sage, thyme, and cinnamon to activate their energies in your life.

5. Burn symbols with bay leaves to honor the energies. Call on symbolic mythic animals to unlock doors to wisdom.

II. Patience

1. Have a quiet cup of jasmine tea. Breathe and meditate.

2. Carry dolomite, chalcedony, rose quartz, moonstone or blue lace agate to channel soothing energies of patience.

3. Make a list of all the things that make you impatient (ALL of them—you're not being petty). Without anger, burn your list in a mixture of sage and sweetgrass or rosemary to soothe your energies. You may also write these on bathroom tissue and flush them. It's difficult to do this without laughing—and laughter is a powerful tool in and of itself.

4. Weed your garden. Visualize each weed as a source of your impatience being removed.

5. Call on the spirit of the buffalo to slow the pace of impatience. Feel your energies become strong and steady.

6. Call on the spirit of the blue heron to organize your energies and make priorities clear to you.

III. Prosperity

1. Just as the moon turns from dark to new, place a black stone, such as onyx or obsidian, and a green stone, such as aventurine or malachite, on your altar or ritual circle. Visualize all obstacles to prosperity flowing into the black stone. Visualize all supporting energies for prosperity flowing into the green stone. Carry or display the green stone to keep the energies for prosperity flowing. Place the black stone in the earth or in a pot of salt or soil. At the time of full moon, charge the green stone in the moonlight and celebrate increased prosperity. After the full moon time, take the black stone out of the earth. Display in a prominent place and visualize obstacles continuing to flow into the stone.

    Continue this process until the energies of prosperity are balanced in your life. I find aventurine to be excellent for cash; malachite, for business growth; and emerald, for overall wealth. Some people use pyrite to attract prosperity, but this can be tricky. After all, it is "fool's gold."

2. Burn saffron and bay leaves to attract the energies of prosperity. Cedar, juniper, and live oak are also good for this. Visualize and manifest your intentions clearly.

3. Use a piece of rich green ribbon or fabric and attune with the expansive Green Ray energies. Money and prosperity are a form of green energy.

4. Place five silver coins under five green candles. You can arrange these as the points of a star, or in the four directions and a center. As you burn the candles down, visualize the prosperity increasing. When the candles are burned, take the coins to a young, growing tree or a very old strong tree. Leave these as a gift.

5. Take a dollar bill and write your prosperity needs on the money. Use symbols or talismans if you choose. Burn at the new moon or full moon for extra power. Sprinkle the ashes around where you live or combine with salt to make energies earth quickly. Use additional dollars for deeper spells. Consider it a gift to the gods. Place in Nature.

6. Make a contribution to a cause or charity you really support with your heart. It can be a small donation if need be, but do it wholeheartedly. This can rebalance the flow of giving and receiving in your life. If you have more time than money, give of yourself. Giving energy begets giving energy and flows through you. Give willingly.

7. Use a peacock feather as a wand to cast a prosperity spell. Focus on the opulence and splendor of the colors in a peacock feather.

8. Do a vision quest or inner journey to tap into past lives of great wealth. (You certainly had a few. Where else do you suppose you got that taste for luxury?) Examine patterns in your past lives which you may use to increase prosperity now. Examine your karma—karma is choice.

IV. Practical Wisdom

1. Cast a ritual circle (use your cloth here) and call for specific guides to help you ground the energies of wisdom for everyday use. When you put out a call like this, be prepared for a new spirit energy to start sharing your home. This has resulted in everything from a British nanny and a medieval friar to an old Irish wise woman and an Oriental Zen master showing up. Take time to establish a working relationship with this helping guide. But remember, you are the person in charge of your life. Be as practical about the advice and wisdom that you choose to receive as you are about that which you choose to share.

2. Use a wooden spoon and sprinkle salt or cornmeal around where you live. If you have an apartment, just put a little in the corners. If you have a house, put it outside. Don't worry about the neighbors; they will have a lot stranger things to adjust to as you follow the shamanic path. You can always tell them it's an old Indian trick to nourish the earth.

3. Visualize a warm golden brown or copper screen surrounding you. This screen filters out extraneous static and only allows useful, practical wisdom to enter. Carry copper coins as a filter.

East Wheels

I.   Creativity

1. Buy inexpensive paints, such as tempera, finger paints or watercolors that primary schoolchildren use. Take freezer paper and roll out long lengths on the kitchen floor or in the garage. Immerse yourself in the flow of colors. Paint as though you were a small child, free of creative inhibitions.

    You may also do this with pastels or colored chalk and with colorful play dough. These may seem a bit like simple, childish activities, but creativity is inborn and may need to be re-awakened in just this way. Express yourself freely, without judgments or expectations about the product you are creating. Creativity is a process. The product is a side result.

2. Burn lavender buds or make a little sachet of lavender buds to summon light creative spirits. You may also do this as an honor to the sacred muses of creativity.

3. Call on the spirit of the eagle to bring high ideals to your creative forces. Find an inexpensive figure of an eagle to use as a fetish or totem symbol. Paint it silver for poetic, musing creativity. Paint it gold for overt, active creativity.

4. Carry a white, yellow, lavender, or gold fluorite when you need clear, concise creative energies. Carry citrine clusters for expansive creative energy.

5. Tie white feathers or hawk feathers to a yellow ribbon. Wear or use as a meditative touch totem for creative energies.

II.   Divination

1. Carry a dark bowl or iron cauldron filled with water outside on a clear moonlight night. Let the moon reflect in the water and wait until the water is completely still. Ask a question and dip your fingers in the water. As the reflection of the moon dances on the dark water, watch for patterns and listen to your inner wisdom.

2. Call on the spirit of the dark timber wolf to scout answers for

you and divine the direction of your shamanic path. Ask this wolf to relay messages to your own special totem animals. These wolves are very illusive.

3. Buy a mirror from a dime store. Using your permanent markers, decorate it with symbols sacred to you. Light a votive candle and place it in front of the mirror. Gaze at the reflection of the flame in the mirror and watch for patterns to emerge behind the reflection.

4. Call on the spirit of the great horned owl to help you fly through shadowy times of the unknown. Watch for owls to show up in your environment.

5. To divine answers with a fire, ask your questions, then throw tobacco, sage, or even broom straw on the fire. Watch how it is consumed. Fast usually means yes, or favorable. Slow means no, or unfavorable. Watch for patterns in the flames.

III. Mental Powers

1. Drink spearmint tea. It will soothe your body, as well as clear your mind.

2. Burn sandalwood incense. Take a small bell and ring it once (wind chimes may also be used so long as they are delicate in tone). Listen very carefully until the last tiny fragment of the bell tone has gone. Breathe in the scent of sandalwood and repeat the process. Concentrate and focus until you are in the absolute moment and nothing exists but the bell tone, the sandalwood, and you. Use jasmine and lower-tone bells for a more meditative effect. Learn to "be here now."

3. Call on the spirit of the hawk to sharpen your perception and your awareness. Be a hawk, and make your aim true.

4. Take a piece of mandrake root or a lodestone and charge it in your sacred circle as a little wizard or wise woman. Carry, to help you have clear wisdom.

5. Call on the jaguar for deep shamanic awareness. Be the jaguar—attune to the energies, even in the chaotic jungle of everyday life.

6. Burn an incense of cinnamon and rosemary to energize

mental awareness.

7. Blend oil of lavender and oil of carnation. Anoint your third-eye area and pull energies through your brain. Lily of the valley is also good for this.

8. Image your brain as a great tree with strong branches and deep roots. Honor the strength of your mental capabilities.

IV.   Peace

1. Light white- or peach-colored candles in a dark room. As you focus on the glow of the candles, visualize warm, peaceful energy spreading and creating a flow of harmony world-wide.

2. Take light-colored blossoms of flowers and breathe a prayer of intent on each one. If you are near water, let these blossoms float away, carrying energies for peace. If water is not nearby, take the petals of the blossom and sprinkle on the ground to earth peaceful energies.

3. Plant a magnolia tree with blessings for harmony and peace. Its dark, evergreen leaves and white blossoms symbolize the peaceful balance of heart and mind together.

4. Mix oils of lavender, violet, gardenia, magnolia, or lotus. Anoint yourself for personal peace. Pass at gatherings for harmony in the group. Sprinkle or dab on doorways at businesses or schools for a balanced atmosphere.

5. Call on the spirits of white water birds, such as herons, egrets, and cranes, to help you connect with peaceful energy flow.

6. Buy spools of peach, white, and blue ribbons. Braid these together in seven-inch lengths. Knot at each end and give to friends as a talisman for peace.

South Wheels

I. Protection

1. Call on the spirit of the badger or porcupine to give you lessons on staying undisturbed.

2. Mix rubbed sage, basil, dry mustard, cinnamon, and dragon's blood resin (if you have it). Sprinkle on tobacco, rolled oats, or rice. Burn this mixture for protection or carry it in a small medicine pouch. This mixture can also be burned in the four directions to give you added protection when you need it.

3. Stones in the shape of crosses, star sapphires, amber, amber calcite, stones with natural holes, and stones in the shape of an animal or person can be very protective to wear or carry.

4. Mandrake root, St. John's wort, and buckeyes are protectors from the Plant World.

5. Cactus plants on the windowsill of a South or North window are great protectors.

6. Plant junipers and wisteria in your garden for protection and beauty.

7. For instant protection from Spirit, make the sign of the Cabalistic cross. Touch the third-eye area and say "Ateh" (Thou/Spirit); then touch the heart chakra and say "Malkuth" (True Self); right shoulder, "Ve Geburah" (Power); then left shoulder, "Ve Gedulah" (Glory). Bring both hands together, clasp at the heart chakra, and say "Leolahm" (Universe), "Amen" (Eternal). Separate your hands slowly, bringing them around to meet at the back of your neck. This is powerful and is effective for several hours.

II. Love

1. Place two small candles at opposite sides in a plate of salt. Each night for seven days, bring the candles closer together. Light and concentrate on strengthening a relationship in

your life. It is helpful to carve names in the candles and to mark seven sections, one for each night of the spell. You may also add rose petals or rose oil to the salt to symbolize your heartfelt emotions. Remember that it is not advisable to force any relationship or to try to bind another person's spirit or affection. This spell is excellent for relationships that need renewing and for giving that "one more chance" to work things out.

2. Call on your most sacred power animal or helping spirit guide. Ask it to communicate your affections for another through your beloved's spirit guides or power animals.

3. Mix rose oil and clove or cinnamon oils for a powerful love potion. For a more romantic relationship, use more rose. For a more passionate relationship, use more clove or cinnamon. This can be dabbed on a crystal or on a candle to share with your beloved. A few drops can be mixed with almond oil or baby oil for a wonderful massage oil. Test on wrists first, as this can be very strong on the skin.

III. Self-Power

1. Go to a rock shop or store where stone beads are sold. Select beads that make you feel strong and that reflect aspects of power for you. If you find enough for a necklace, fine. If not, string with quartz crystal beads to amplify the beads you have selected. You may also make a shorter string to carry as a Mineral World power totem. Pattern is not important here. Let it emerge for you.

2. Buy ribbons or fabric in gold, royal blue, and deep rich violet. Wear, carry, or wrap a small crystal in them to use as a power totem.

3. Call forth power animals that reflect your deepest strengths. Dragons are excellent here, as are lions, wolves, and eagles. When you feel your energies ebbing, call on these animals to restore your sacred gifts of power.

4. Mix ginger and rubbed sage. Sprinkle on rosemary and burn for a power incense.

5. Buy carnations to wear or display in your home. Red carnations are excellent for vitality; white for serenity; pink for relationships. All of these balance self-power harmoniously.

6. In your inner vision, use active imagery to design images of great power. Let these come forth as dramatically as you can. Tap into the vibrations of these images' energies.

7. Use your ritual cloth or a smaller piece of fabric with sacred symbols. Wear or display on your altar to connect with power energies daily.

IV. Purification

1. During the time of the waning moon, select one day to cleanse your body, mind, and spirit. Drink teas such as clover or raspberry. Burn sage or thyme to smudge your home. Bathe with salt and a few cups of vinegar added to your bath. Place crystals and special stone totems in the water with you. When you are finished bathing, let the water drain. Visualize any negative energies flowing out and leaving you clear and purified.

   Eat light, simple foods, such as rice and good breads. Avoid salty, spicy and rich foods for at least that day. Fill a pitcher with pure mineral water. Place a crystal in the water and drink throughout the day. When the water is gone, carry the crystal for a few days to absorb any residue. Later you may place the crystal in full-moon or noonday-sun energies to recharge.

2. Use your ritual circle to call forth your highest spirit guides or the archangels. Ask for help in keeping yourself clear and purified.

3. Burn a brown candle in your home. Visualize any negativities being consumed and released from you. Let these vanish into the ethers, where they may be transmuted to their highest good. Stay positive.

West Wheels

I.   Journeys

1.   Mix nutmeg, mace, bay leaves, and thyme to burn as a journey incense. Add sage for an earthy journey, sandalwood for a meditative journey, and frankincense or myrrh for a deeper spiritual journey.

2.   Sit in the middle of your ritual cloth, or a circle you have cast. Chant the vowel sounds repeatedly: a-e-i-o-u (say oo). It often helps to rock or sway and find a personal rhythm. Continue this until the chanting becomes automatic. For sky-spirit journeys, visualize your etheric self lifting out through your crown chakra. For earth journeys, stretch out with your head in the North or sit and visualize your etheric body being absorbed into the earth. You are protected within this circle. Still, if you are new to this, I advise that you set a timer or arrange for someone to signal you when ten or twenty minutes have passed. It is also valuable to do this strictly with imagery a few times.

3.   Buy five small crystals. Fluorites are excellent, as are amethysts or double-terminated crystals. Clarity is not important for these crystals. Place in the four directions of your circle and hold the fifth crystal. Chant vowels or om's.

4.   Call on the bear to be your journey guide.

II.   Inner Vision

1.   Spread out your ritual cloth, or cast a circle. Walk clockwise around the circle nine times, spiralling inward. State your intention to be receptive to wisdom from inner vision. Sit quietly in circle and allow images to emerge. When you are complete, spiral out counterclockwise nine times. The spirals symbolize your earth journey inward to inner vision and your spiritual journey outward with new wisdom gained.

2.   Make a tea of mugwort or thyme. Bathe your crystals, amethysts, rose quartz, or moonstone in the tea. These may then be taken to bed with you for dream visions, placed on

your altar, taken into your ritual circle, or worn during psychic work.

3. At the time of the dark moon, take a black stone into a darkened room. Light one small candle and let the flame reflect in the black stone. Let this symbolize the quest for inner wisdom in the midst of shadows. Carry the black stone to increase your inner awareness.

4. Call on the spirits of the dolphins and porpoises to guide you through the oceans of consciousness and to develop your psychic gifts.

5. At full moon time, draw the moonbeams down through your crown chakra for vision and enlightenment.

III. Self-Healing

1. Sit with your back against a North wall, or lie flat with your head in the North. Begin with your feet and focus your awareness there. Breathe deeply and release with a strong, sharp breath (groan if you want to—be dramatic; it helps). Visualize any kinds of dis-ease being released with your breath. Continue slowly up your body, down your arms and out through the crown chakra. Take your time and pay special attention to areas that need extra work.

    When you have finished releasing dis-ease from your body, take a few moments to steady your energies. Next, connect with the magnetic energies of the North. If you are sitting, feel these move into your spine. If you are lying down, feel these energies move into your crown chakra. Breathe deeply and pull these magnetic energies throughout your body to heal and realign you completely.

2. Whenever possible, sleep, journey, or meditate with your head in the North. Place a crystal at the top of your head and a piece of mandrake root at your feet for added healing. Burn sage or thyme.

3. Every day, take a few moments to run the energies and vibrations of the chakra or Ray energies up and down your spine. Use Red—Orange—Yellow—Green—Blue—Indigo—

Violet up the spine. Use Violet—Indigo—Blue—Green—
Yellow—Orange—Red down the spine. Finish by surrounding
yourself with white, gold, or healing green light.

IV. Self-Balancing

1. Place two mirrors so that you can see your left or female/
    receptive side in one and your right or male/active side in
    the other. You can do this just with your face, if need be.
    Examine each reflection without judgment. Look for signs
    of strength or weakness. For example, if the active side
    seems agitated or stressed, let energy flow from your recep-
    tive side to soothe and nurture. If your receptive side seems
    tired, let the active side energize it. Watch for signs such as
    small injuries, rashes, et cetera, on either side; they may
    indicate an energy deficit.

2. Take time to gaze at your face in one mirror. Focus on the
    area between your eyes and breathe balanced energy into
    that place. Doing this regularly can keep your energies in a
    state of increased harmony.

3. Select a dark stone or crystal (I use a smoky quartz or
    amethyst) and a light stone or crystal (I use citrine or clear
    quartz). Hold one in each hand and swap sides every few
    minutes to balance your energies.

4. Choose a soothing, receptive oil, such as vanilla, and an
    energizing active oil, such as clove. Dab sparingly on your
    wrists to balance the needed energies. Blend and dab on
    your third-eye area for personal harmony.

Chapter 11

SHAMANIC CYCLES

The greater cycle of Nature is made up of many smaller cycles or wheels. These we may connect with to enhance our shamanic journey in the work of our chosen path. We attune to the cycles of Nature and balance our lives to the rhythm of the seasons. When we do, we deepen our connections to the energies of the world around us.

This chapter gives some of the traditional activities, meanings, and energies of Nature cycles. Mother Nature has provided us with a complete system to balance our life journey. This chapter will show us how to choose and connect with our totems appropriately and in tune with the cycles of Nature. We will explore methods for balancing the energies of our totems, regardless of the time or season.

Although totems and their energies may be used at any time, some are very helpful at specific times to connect with the cycles and the vibrations shamanically. These are totems that best reflect the energies of those times. This is also a very useful way to develop relationships with new totems, and to build a foundation of shamanic connections.

Attuning to the elements of Self, Nature, and Spirit is the core of shamanic journeying. Even in modern times, our ancient souls and spirits call us to act in different ways, according to the cycles of Nature. Many of our shared holidays are based on very ancient Nature cycles and festivals. Some of these festivals were based on the vibrations of the sun's energy. These are solar cycles and festivals. Other festivals were based on the vibrations of the moon energies. These are the lunar cycles. Because the lunar cycles are more frequent and more closely related to our daily lives, we begin with these.

Lunar Cycles and Totems

New Moon
The new moon is a time of beginning projects. It is also a time to renew relationships and projects already in your life. The new moon is a good time for personal initiations and self-affirmations. The energy of the new moon is very light and gentle. I advise that you begin your lunar cycles in this way.

Plant
Plants for the new moon include any newly budding plant or new growth from a plant. This is a symbolic representation of beginnings and can be placed on your altar, or carried or worn to remind you of new growth and energy. If you have a new project beginning, I suggest that you get a new plant and let that remind you. You can take it to work, or you can keep it in your home.

Incense totems for the new moon are vanilla, because of its gentle healing and goddess energy; cinnamon, because of its spicy, active god energy; mugwort, for opening your psychic centers; jasmine, for a delicate way to begin attuning to spirituality; myrrh, for an earthy yet spiritual incense that helps you open those channels; and rosemary, which is an overall good inspirational sort of herb.

Animal
Some animal totems for the new moon include the heron and the hawk. This is particularly true of the great blue heron. The blue heron is good for organizing spiritual energy. Hawks are good for the new moon because they have focus and great perception. They take aim at a project or a result, and they achieve it.

Other animal totems for the new moon are cats and bears. Since cats are very inquisitive and, of course, curious, they represent that fresh new energy of the new moon—inquisitive, anxious, childlike energy. Bears are good for the new moon because they're gentle companions for the journeys that we make shamanically. Foxes are notable for their cleverness and elusiveness; energy is very quick and new with the fox. Butterflies are excellent because, of course, they represent the renewal of metamorphosis. Doves, because of their gentle, loving spirit. Cardinals, because of their quick flash of energy and color. Wrens, because they're very industrious.

Human

Human World totems for the new moon include Zen meditation because it helps develop a very one-pointed awareness, and gives a "be-in-the-moment" meditation.

Another good activity for the new moon is burnings. Burn slips of paper with your desires written on them, or your goals and your projects, and release them into the ethers, into Spirit.

Art is another good activity. At new moon, you want to design new a project. Instead of just doing it in a linear, written way, you can draw and sketch it. This helps develop it. You can save that art to concentrate on, or you can release it by burning it in a fire at new moon.

Exercising is excellent for new moon, dancing out what you want by movement. It's a good way to initiate your energies within yourself.

Mineral

Crystals are good at all times, because they can be programmed. Specifically for the new moon, though, lodestones are quite good because they hold a magnetic charge for such a long time. You can program them for an entire cycle of the moon to help you achieve your goals.

Rose quartz is another excellent Mineral World totem for the new moon because of its gentle, loving energy. It is a very soothing and yet a very inspiring Mineral World totem.

Carnelian is quite good for the new moon because it has a gentle fire. I advise that for the new moon you use the lighter peach-colored carnelian. Later, you can use the darker ones.

Amber is quite good for the new moon because it represents that golden energy of growth.

Of course sand and soil, or a combination, are good for the new moon because they represent what we plant our goals into.

Another good Mineral World totem is peridot. It has a yellow-green energy that makes it very much like the new budding plant Ray energies.

Waxing Moon

The waxing moon is a time of energizing the projects that you already have and the new ones that you have begun. It is a time for adjusting and adapting your projects. As time goes on, you may see that you want things changed. This is the time to begin doing that.

The waxing moon is a good time for healing and self-healing. It's a time for doing the kinds of activities that build your strength.

The waxing moon is also a good time for protecting yourself and your environment. It's excellent for sharing that loving protection with the world.

Plant

A very good plant for the waxing moon is the pine. It's traditionally a tree that has to do with emotions, growth, and support. Its varied forms make it easily accessible to all.

Honeysuckle is excellent for the waxing moon because of its prosperous energies. And sandalwood is good for its meditative and deepening energies.

Holly is good for its evergreen qualities. It's strong, it lasts, and it has red berries. It's a balance of newness and renewal. It symbolizes constant growth and growth within growth.

Any blooming flowers are good during the waxing moon time. Buds are better at the new moon, and blooming flowers are better at the waxing moon.

Blooming plants and plants whose leaves are obviously growing are quite good to use. You can put these on your altar or on your desk at work, if you want to.

Animal

For the waxing moon time, the deer is especially good for pacing. The deer holds the energies. This is a good totem to call on to keep you on track with your projects.

Working dogs, like border collies and Saint Bernards, make good totems because they represent industriousness and the joy of achieving something in life. This is what you're doing as you build energies in the waxing moon.

Bobcats are quite fierce, and yet they are very small. They have a kittenish quality, and they also have a big-cat quality. Bobcats are excellent because they represent the balance of energy that you need at the waxing moon.

Some of the bigger cranes and egrets are quite good, as are the snow geese. Because of their cycles and the way they change and adapt to the seasons, these are very good for waxing moon times.

Squirrels and chipmunks, who live in a very interesting relationship with the earth and the trees, are very shamanic in their own way. They're very industrious. Chipmunks, of course, live very close to the ground and are good connectors.

Human

The waxing moon is a time for more structured spiritual rituals. Be a little more formal during the waxing moon time and really pull that building energy in. It's a time for set rituals. It's a good time to pull out books of rituals, or to write rituals and follow them.

This is also a good time for business updates. That is like your own strategy session with yourself. I call up sort of a "Board of Directors" in my mind, and this is a good way for you to do that.

Mineral

Carnelian is also good during the waxing moon. At this time you move into the somewhat darker, richer shades, where the vibration moves from being kind of peach and yellow into orange and red.

Jasper and agates are quite good because they help you pull that building moon energy down into the earth, in other words, into your daily, practical life.

Malachite is good, because it is a very prosperous, expansive energy stone. Chrysocolla and turquoise are also good because they have the green of growth and the blue of spirituality.

Citrine is good for its golden growing energy. And dioptase and tourmalines are good for their deep green growing energy. If you get a watermelon tourmaline, this can be very useful for the balance of active and receptive (red and green) energies.

Rutilated and tourmalinated quartz are also quite good at the waxing moon time. Rutilated quartz has gold-colored inclusions, which are very active and stimulate growth. Tourmalinated quartz has darker inclusions, which have to do with being focused and attuned to energy.

Full Moon

The full moon is a time of celebration. You celebrate energies that you want in your life. You celebrate energies that are already present in your life, and you celebrate growth achieved. It's also a time of honoring energies. It's a time of being in a place of gratitude and thanks. The full moon is a time when you celebrate completions in your life—even if they aren't quite there yet.

Plant

Traditionally, one of the greatest plants for full moon time is the oak, which is a great tree of strength and wisdom. Other trees that make good totems are ash trees, for life/source energies; and evergreens of all sorts, for eternal strengths. Palms are quite good for their flexibility. There's a sense of celebration in palms.

All full white blossoms are good for the full moon time. Flowers such as gardenias and lotuses are very feminine, seductive, and luxurious. Magnolias are excellent.

An incense you can use would be allspice, good for burning at full moon time. Bayberry is good for celebrating fullness and growth. And almond is quite good. You can blend bayberry, allspice, and almond together and sprinkle on sage or thyme. Burn to celebrate at full moon.

Animal

This is the time to celebrate your relationship with personal animal totems and to empower your shared connection to the realm of spirit.

Full moon time is especially good for attuning with mythic and symbolic animals such as dragons, gryphons, and unicorns.

The white owl (or gwenfar) is very powerful at full moon as a symbolic representation of the goddess energies.

The great stag of the forest represents the god and the sacred white doe symbolizes the goddess. Together, they represent the reflective relationship of full sun (active/male) and full moon (receptive/female) in a mutually empowering balance.

Human

Full moon is the time for expressive, joyous celebrations, ceremonies, and rituals. These may be either solitary or shared.

Celebrate the successful completion of projects even if they are not quite fully manifested in your life—yet.

Full moon is a time for expressing gratitude to self, to nature, and to spirit. It is a time to accept, graciously, where you are on your path to power.

Full moon ceremonies and rituals are times to connect with your personal vision of deity and your own source of spiritual nurturance. This is the time to pull yourself together and celebrate your power. Make a concerted effort to blend elements of your persona into a more harmonious creation of self.

Key words—and concepts—for this time period are Expansion—Enjoyment and Enlightenment.

Full moon is the time to use lots of candlelight and beautiful music to celebrate and dance to honor the Light and the Beauty in your life—in all Life.

Mineral

Clear crystals of all kinds may be used effectively at full moon time to amplify and empower rituals, ceremonies, and magical projects.

Milky white quartz provides a gentle source of amplified power and also represents the healing white light as well as deeply maternal energies. Selenite provides a slightly more structured version of this white light, maternal power.

Silver correlates most directly with the lunar energies. At full moon, use silver to increase personal gifts of psychic power and inner receptivity.

Moonstone in all shades symbolizes inner vision, psychism and spiritual receptivity. Since moonstone is, by nature, a most absorbent stone, it may be charged at full moon to bring gentle empowerment throughout the entire lunar cycle.

Pearls and mother-of-pearl are quite good during full moon

time to connect with the deep, inner flow of "oceanic" consciousness.

Platinum is also excellent at Full Moon. Platinum is particularly good for high magick ritual at this time since it reflects the powerful balance of lunar (silver/receptivity) and solar (gold/activation) in its natural energies. Platinum is a multidimensional mineral.

Waning Moon

The waning moon time, as the moon gets smaller, is a time of releasing, banishing, and purging things in your life that are obstacles for you. You want to be careful not to banish everything. We all need some of what we think of as obstacles to give us balance. When you do banishings, be very careful that you are specific when you banish obstacles.

The waning moon time is also a time for purifying yourself, your environment, and your activities. It's a good time to clean house—the house being your environment or your Self.

Plant

For the waning moon, a good herb to use is mandrake, because it is a root herb. It's a very dark-force herb in the sense that it connects with deep magnetic energies, and you can put a lot into it. You can take a mandrake and put what you need to banish into it and return it to the earth.

Garlic is also quite good. It's good to have garlic in your house because it absorbs negative energies quite well, as do onions. Rue is good in the garden with other herbs because it keeps negative influences out.

Frankincense is quite powerful burned in the waning moon for purifications. It keeps a spiritual tone. Juniper is good for releasing and for protecting you during purification.

Willow, with its flexibility and its movement, is a very helpful plant. Sage and sweetgrass in combination are good for releasing because the sweetgrass helps you maintain a positive balance while the sage dispels negative energies.

Cedar is good for purification. Also any sort of night flowers are good at waning moon time. Night flowers symbolize the ability to blossom even in times of darkness. They're very powerful flowers. You can put them on your altar. It's best if you can go outside and be with them before you pick them. This is because they close as soon as you pick them.

Animal

Animal totems for the waning moon time include the raven, which is quite good for these dark times. Ravens have had a very bad reputation in some traditions, but they are great messengers of spirit and of psychic knowledge. Sometimes very powerful psychic images come during the waning moon times, because the energy is softening and you can be more open to listen and hear. Ravens are helpful for this.

The wolf, of course, is good for many other occasions, as are many of these totems. The wolf is especially good for waning time, because it's a very good protector and a teacher of wisdom while you're doing these purifications.

The bear is helpful for self-healing and banishing dis-ease.

Jaguars and panthers or jungle cats are quite good for being aware when the energies are darker and slower. The owl is symbolic of being able to fly through shadows. Night hawks are also quite good since they keep that focus, even in darkness. At waning moon time, we find that shadows have a lot to do with all reflections of our Self on our shamanic journey.

Mythic animals, such as dragons, griffins, unicorns (whatever calls you), are quite good for the waning moon time. You can tune in to the symbolic energies when the moon is waning and quieter.

Human

Shamanic journeys are often made during the waning moon time because the energy deepens. Earth journeys are best at this time, as you feel your connection to the earth deepen when the moon lessens in its intensity.

Eastern void meditations are healing at this time. Allow yourself to go into the nothingness and the quiet. Listen for what your needs are in your life, and for what you need to banish or change.

This is also a good time for deeply personal rituals that are not shared and that come from you alone. It's very deeply personal. You can move and dance and sing. You can do burnings. You can take things and put them in the earth. You can cast things out. Also, the ashes from your burnings are wonderful for sprinkling onto the earth and casting into the winds.

Mineral

Obsidian or Apache tears are good for carrying during the waning moon time. They help absorb the negative energies that you are banishing, and allow you to focus. You can clean them later by running them under cool water. Other minerals that absorb energies well are jet, onyx, black jade, and hematite. Hematite also helps in purification.

Smoky quartz is good because it has that crystalline structure. It's very powerful and amplifies the waning moon energies. It's a very good journey companion.

Darker amethysts (some of them are quite dark violet) are quite good for waning moon times to give spiritual-level help.

Lava is good because it represents the upheaval that sometimes comes with renewal.

Soil, peat, moss, and marble are all quite earthy symbols that pull on energies of the earth, and this is more pronounced at the waning moon time.

Dark of the Moon

Dark of the moon is when the moon has no energies in relation to the earth. It's just before it turns to a new moon. The way you determine this is to find calendars that tell you what time the new moon will be and figure a few hours before then.

Traditionally, dark of the moon is a very tricky time. Energies are literally void, and you can't be sure what your energies will do. This is a very good time to surround yourself with your personal protective totems. When you decide you're going to do work at this time period, deep-level release work is quite good. What you may have begun in the waning moon you can complete at the dark of the moon, but do use familiar totems.

Dark of the moon is not a good time to begin a new relationship with a totem or to try a new kind of project in any way. It is a good time to go into that deep spiritual place within. Ask for the deepest kind of shamanic connections and renewal that you can achieve on the path.

Solar Cycles and Totems

Winter Solstice

Winter solstice is a time to celebrate the birth of the sun. This is the crest of winter, when the days are the shortest and the nights are the longest.

Primitive man would celebrate the return of light to the earth at this time. This is a time for celebrations of joy and abundance to coax the return of light and energy from the sun.

Plant

All evergreens are good during winter solstice, especially pine, juniper, cedar, and holly. Mistletoe and oak are quite sacred for winter solstice because of their relationship to eternal growth and the strength of cycles.

Excellent herbs for incenses include frankincense, for its deep spirituality; myrrh, for its earthier spirituality; and bayberry, for its abundance and prosperous energies.

Animal

Horned goats symbolize the male sun energies.

Reindeer, of course.

Owls are quite good because of the darkness into the light.

Stag deers with horns. This celebrates the time of the hunter protecting while Mother Earth rested.

Mythic animals are quite good to celebrate with at this time for their symbolic connection to Spirit.

Eagles are good because winter solstice is a time of very high spiritual ideals. The eagle flies highest, closest to the sun.

Human

This is a time of many celebrations and holidays. It's also a time for healings. The energies are very warm and giving throughout the world at this time period. It's a good time for having sharing circles and healings.

It's also a good time to do journeys. Shamanic journeys with groups are good at this time.

Vision quests are quite good at the time of winter solstice because the idealism and the spirit of oneness is quite clearly in the air. Vision quests can be very spiritual at this time.

Mineral

Gold is an excellent Mineral World totem for this time, because it represents the sun energies and the energies of renewed growth.

Topaz is also good for this, and it has the increased crystalline structure that leads it to Spirit. Citrine can be used, as well as topaz, for sun energy.

Malachite is very good, its green color representing continued abundance.

Garnets and rubies are good for the blood of life.

Candlemas (also called the Feast of Waxing Light)

It's a time of celebrating the light and the energy in your life growing stronger, and to celebrate the return of the growing season in Nature. This is the time when the first plants stir below the ground. It's a time to celebrate the fires of spring and growth being kindled in the earth and in the light. It's also the festival of Bridget, the white goddess of creativity.

Plant

A good plant for Candlemas is the crocus, which makes its appearance in the midst of very cold weather.

Camellias, which are winter flowers, represent growing strength and abundant energy, even in the midst of winter. This is particularly true of the crimson and red camellias.

Shamrocks and clovers are quite good for Candlemas, to celebrate the ancient Irish connection with Bridget.

Animal

Rabbits are quite good for this time of year because they are sacred. In winter they provide food for predators, and they survive by burrowing in the earth. They are prolific and signal us to remember that life goes on and multiplies.

Owls are also good here because of their wisdom. The darkness of winter and the darkness of night are very similar in energy. Owls are creatures of this energy.

All hibernating animals are good to use at Candlemas, especially bears. We ought to remember that hibernation is an important part of life. Just as sleep is a part of daily life, having a time period to rest and hibernate in during the year is a good thing. In the days when there were not climate-controlled homes, people had to hibernate. Now we have to choose to do it about the time of Candlemas, which is around February, the 1st of February. It's a good time to hibernate like the bear. Take some time for yourself.

Human

Music is quite good at this time period. Write it, dance to it, move to it, draw to it, or just listen to it. Music is called the gift of the gods—or the Goddess, the Muse.

It's a time for writing and art. Again, let it emerge from you.

This is a time to tap into the deep sources of creative energy and do creative work.

It's also a time for inner journeys. Go inward. Renew yourself deeply and find those first fires of creativity kindling within you.

Mineral

Marble is quite good at this time of year because it's cold and yet has veins of activity and growth in it. It's a very good symbol for Candlemas.

Copper represents earthy, warm, fiery aspects.

River stones are good for the flow of creativity they represent.

Lava is good because it represents the inner fires of the earth.

Jasper, especially the red jaspers, represents the red energies of growth and warmth in a cold dark time.

Smoky quartz is used for its clarity, even in darkness, and for the light that is within it. It's a very good stone or crystal to put on your altar to celebrate Candlemas.

Spring Equinox (also called Festival of the Trees)

This is a time of solar balance. The sun and the earth are in perfect alignment. Days and nights are the same length. This represents our receptive and our active aspects being in balance, male and female. Mother Earth energies in us are awakened by the Father Sun energies being in balance. This is a time of renewing and rebirth. We have resurrection of our own spirit and our growth, which has come through the winter. It's a time when the trees begin to bud out and show the growth and the promise for the new year.

Plant

Any spring flowers or new flowers of delicate colors and any new green leaves, which also represent the energy of the new moon, can be used for the energy of the new sun.

Animal

Use newborn, gentle animals. This is not the time for predators. This is the time for the gentle-spirited animals, like the lambs and little chickens we are familiar with at Easter. These are truly totem animals for this particular time period, to remind us of the gentler side of our lives.

Any new birds, baby birds or spring birds, are quite good at this time as are doves.

Human

This is a time for ceremonies rather than set rituals. It's a time for being fanciful, and having ceremonies that are light and gentle. Have festivities of gratitude. In a way, it's another kind of thanksgiving time. Give thanks for the newness and celebrate. This coaxes the growth to continue.

Mineral

Rose quartz is excellent for spring equinox because it has the gentleness of energy that's needed.

Lavender-colored amethysts, the lighter ones, have just the right vibration for spring equinox. It's a gentle yet very spiritual energy, and a very healing energy.

Blue lace agate has a very similar vibration to the lavender amethyst, but it's a little earthier and can be used for a more physical healing.

Carnelians are also good, especially the lighter ones, for spring equinox because of their gentleness and the way they help you connect in relationships.

Beltane (also called May Day)

Beltane is a time for celebrating the growth and balance in your life and for celebrating the fertility of your life. Celebrate the fertility of your spiritual growth and the fertility of your material growth as well. This is the time when Mother Earth and Father Sun were considered to be in union. This is when we have May Day picnics and celebrations. Go a-maying.

Plant

Wildflowers are excellent for Beltane as they represent the beauty of natural energies blooming and energy from Mother Earth.

Tuberoses and lilies are quite good, too, being deep spring flowers. We also use oak, because of its sacred wisdom; ash, because of its representation of life; and willow, because of its flexible and friendly nature.

Animal

As the sun grows stronger, the hawk is a fiery representative of this energy.

Use the stag deer to represent the male energy, the active energy of Nature.

Use the white doe to represent the receptive female energies of Nature.

Rabbits represent proliferation and fertility. Rams and ewes (for the male and female energies) celebrate the balanced, productive side of life.

Human

This is a time for weddings. This can be a wedding of mind and spirit. This can be a wedding of a relationship in your life. This is a time for celebrations of joy and fertility: dances, picnics, and ceremonies of Nature.

Mineral

Malachite is excellent for Beltane because its deep green represents prosperity and fertility at its fullest on the earth.

Agates bring the energy of the season and inspire you with their vibrations.

Darker carnelians are also good because they warm your relationships and the fires of love within you.

Rubies, again, represent life's blood.

Silver represents the growing fertility of life and receptivity of the female principal.

Summer Solstice (also called Festival of Midsummer)

This is a time of celebrating nurturance and growth and prosperity in your life. It's a time to relax and enjoy the work that you have put in. Bask in the balanced energy of the sun and moon and the sky and earth. It's a very high growth time. It is not a time for starting new projects as much as it is for energizing ones that you have begun. It's a time for healing yourself and sharing that energy with the planet.

Plant

Roses symbolize the full-blooming energies of summer.

Jasmine is good for the luxury and the opulence of summer.

Hibiscus, especially red and yellow hibiscus, is good for its rich tropical energies.

All blooming plants and summer plants are good for summer solstice time.

Animal

Peacock and peahen are excellent. If you can get a peahen feather, that's quite good. Peacock feathers are easily available; peahen feathers are a little harder to get. They are used to symbolize the sacred marriage of Jupiter and Juno, of sky and earth, and the time of great balance that is solstice.

The white doe is good for deep female energies.

The jaguar is good for the deep earth energies. It's a very good time for shamanically calling the jaguar.

Doves are good for summer solstice time because they represent that expansion of peace and the message of harmony.

Human

This is a time for healing circles of all types. It's a time for self-healing. This is a time for Nature ceremonies outside. Dance under the moon, dance under the sun, and *be* outside.

This is also a time of shamanic journeys of all sorts. It's especially good for sky journeys, because the high energy of the sun is uplifting.

Mineral

Malachites are good for summer solstice (as well as Beltane) because the green of malachite is a very prosperous, nurturing energy.

Emeralds have an additional benefit in their crystalline, gemstone quality. They have a higher vibration to use in celebrating prosperity and growth in your life.

Sapphires are good for personal synthesis. Their dark blue symbolizes the deep spiritual connections we make when we keep ourselves healthy and growing.

Lapis is also good for spiritual connections at this time and has a little earthier energy with practical applications.

Turquoise and amazonite are symbolic of the marriage of earth and sky and are very sacred at this time.

Silver is good for being receptive to growth and to celebrate the nurturing receptivity of female growth.

Moonstone is also useful at this time. It's very gently healing and soothes us and nurtures us during this time period.

Lammas (also called August Eve)

This is the time of the first harvest festival. The summer growth has begun to be harvested and preparations are being made for the fall and winter to come. This is a time when we begin to move those lazy sun-nurtured muscles and begin work for the winter. This is a time to remember to celebrate what we have harvested, but not to forget to save some projects for the next planting in our life.

Plant

Corn symbolizes the harvest. We use corn and we also save some for seed to plant later.

Wheat and barley are also good as they are products of the earth, born of the sun's energies and the earth's nurturance.

The first leaves of fall are good on a Lammas altar to symbolize the change in the cycle, and in the seasons.

Sunflowers are also quite good to celebrate the energies of sun, which have grown crops and grown your energies all summer.

Animal

Stag deer celebrate the active male energies of sun, which have energized the crops and the products of our lives.

Buffalo are celebrated for their strength and patience.

Bears remind us to make preparations for winter. Even in this high-energy time, they remind us that we will need to rest and hibernate.

Wolves help us connect and learn from the wisdom that we have gained through our time of nurturance in the summer.

Hawks give us focus again. We sometimes lose our focus a little in the summer, when we are healing and relaxing. Hawks help us sharpen our focus.

Eagles give us the ideals with which to begin preparations for new plantings, and keep us from resting on the laurels of our first harvest.

Human

This is a time for spiritual housecleaning. It's a time to make preparations for balancing your mind, body, and spirit. Organize programs of self-healing and meditative times and times for spiritual journeys, rituals, and ceremonies. It's a time to organize and make sure you have time to do these things. The harvest time is a busy time, and we forget to take time for ourselves. This is the time to remember that.

Mineral

Carnelians capture the last rays of sun's energies and warmth.

Amber is good for clarity at this time of harvesting and preparation for winter.

Tourmaline, particularly dark green tourmaline, is quite good because of the full last green energies of summer.

Malachite is also good here because it reminds us that even in harvest and in the fall to come, there are still plants that continue to grow, projects to nurture, and prosperity to create in our lives.

Soil reminds us to be grateful to the earth of our own being, and to the earth that brings us products and crops.

Ores of any sort are also good to connect us to the earth.

Marbles are good to connect us with the steady, deep foundation energies of earth.

Shells remind us to be receptive to growth, even in a time of harvest, and to be aware of the tides of our life.

Copper celebrates the warmth of earth fires to come in midwinter.

Fall Equinox (also called Alban Efel by the Druids)

This is the original time of thanksgiving. It's the second of the harvest festivals, and a time when we really have to work hard getting things organized.We feel the seasonal energy begin to change and realign, and this tells us it's a time of recycling and of celebrating the changes in our lives. Any equinox is a time of alignment. The sun and the earth are in alignment again. In the spring they're aligned and they are awakening. In the autumn, they are in alignment but they are beginning to rest. Days and nights are closely balanced. This is the time to balance the aspects of ourselves in preparation for rest and inner work.

Plant

Maple with its bright vibrant color reminds us of that last blaze of glory which promises that there will be new growth later.

Hickory and nut-bearing trees are symbolic of the harvests of our life.

Sandalwood is a good incense to use at this time. It has a very woodsy, earthy and spiritual, meditative vibration.

Sage and sweetgrass are used for purification as well as for their renewing and recycling energies.

Animal

Bighorn sheep symbolize the ability to survive in a very sparse climate and a sparse environment, as do mountain goats. Both represent male/sun energies.

Squirrels are very good for this time period. They remind us about preparing for winter. They teach us to have an active, frivolous nature even as we do this. Have a celebration of harvest while making preparations for winter.

Human

This is a good time for group and circle work. Share the tasks of preparation, organization. Some things are accomplished very well in the winter, such as very mental activities; and this is a good time to have groups get together and plan for these.

It's also a good time to work for balancing healing energies throughout the world. Equinox is a time of balance. You can send restful, peaceful energies at this time.

Mineral

Gold is quite good for this time. It represents the sun's gift of activation energies.

Emeralds, again, because of the prosperity.

Jasper, agates, and citrine all have a golden and earthy quality. Citrine is a bit more spiritual. Stones that are grey or brown, or earthy, ore-colored stones, and red stones are quite good at this time to remind us to have gratitude to the earth for the harvests of our own life.

Samhain (also called Halloween)

Traditionally, this is the time when the veils between the worlds of Spirit and form were considered to be the thinnest. These veils lifted, so that there was better opportunity to communicate. This is the time to communicate with spirit guides, with friends or family members who have passed on. It's also a time to release people who have passed on.

This is a time to celebrate the final harvest of the season and begin winter in earnest.

Plant

Lavender is excellent for summoning spirits.

Ivy symbolizes friendships of friends past and present.

Harvest vegetables are good for Samhain altars, as are fall leaves and roots, which remind us to reconnect to the earth. Of course, the pumpkin is a harvest vegetable, and we carve it to scare off negative spirits. This can be a celebration of harvest and abundance.

If you have a pumpkin to spare and carve, you certainly have had an abundant crop.

Animal

Black cats, because of their shadowy, wisdom aspects. This is a good time to call on the black-cat aspect. Panthers are black jungle cats, and they can be used effectively.

Ravens are quite good for Samhain. They carry messages into the darkness and to what we consider to be the shadow worlds.

Owls are also good for Samhain for the same reason. They are messengers. Some traditions have superstitions about owls being negative, but owls have the ability to find clarity in darkness. This is a good totem animal for Samhain, when spirit energies are very, very close.

Any shadowy animals, or night animals (such as night hawks), are good at this time period. This is the period of transformation within the time of darkness.

Human

This is a good time for very deep shamanic journeys. Be sure that you circle yourself protectively, because there are a lot of frisky energies out there. When you are journeying, you are open. At this time, do it in a circle or use your crystals and protective totems.

This is also a good time for seances and communicating with spirit guides. It's a time to begin to communicate with ones you didn't know were around. I advise that you do this with groups of friends— at least to begin with—and try to keep the spirit light yet still reverent. This is a very welcoming time, not a scary time. Stay positive.

This is also a good time to release any energies which seem to be holding on. These can be personal energies or energies that have to do with the world. If something seems to be hanging around, this is the time to do releasing. Group work is best for releasing negativities to the world.

This is a time for great Nature rituals. This is the beginning of the wheel of the year in many of the Wiccan traditions. The wheel of the year changes at this time when the veil between the worlds is the thinnest.

This is a very good time to have a gentle, loving communication between yourself and your totem animal, and to reaffirm your abilities to journey between the worlds.

This is a time for deep, personal vision quests. Take time by yourself in your own shadow aspects. Chase away and release what needs to be released in your life.

Mineral

Copper is very good for this time. That warm, orange glow reminds us of the kindled fires of the earth even when we cannot see their energies.

Gold is also good to remind us of the sun, even at this time when the sun's energy is waning.

Silver reminds us to be receptive to the energies of wisdom coming in through the winter.

Amethyst helps us attune to the greater spiritual energies that the darkness of winter brings.

Obsidian gives us protection in the dark times of winter and the dark times of our lives.

Granite symbolizes the solid foundation of the earth.

Soil or peat reminds us of the richness of earth even when it is resting.

Nature provides us with a system of balanced energies. It is for us, in our using Nature connections, to provide our own balance. I have designed a chart to give you some ideas on how to balance the energies of totems from the various worlds. These are just samples, and you can use these to give you ideas about how to work with your own.

Sacred Totem Objects Balance Charts

In general:

Balance predatory animals with prey.
Balance prey animals with Plant World.
Balance Plant World with Mineral World.
Balance Mineral World with Human World.
Balance Human World with all others + Spirit + Love + Light.

Animal World Totems

In general: Remember that Animal World totems reflect personal aspects of our selves as well as having elemental associations. If a traditional association does not agree with your interpretation, use your own.

Balance earthy, fixed animal totems with
   water animals for flexibility
   fiery predators for motivation
   wingeds for perspective

Balance fluid, water animal totems with
   earth-connected herd animals
   fiery predators for courage, protection
   wingeds for inspiration, creativity, focus

Balance airy, philosophical animal totems with
   earth herd animals for sociability
   fiery predators for sure focus, goals
   water animals for sensuality, compassion

Balance fiery predatory or defensive animal totems with
   airy, intellectual teacher animals for perspective
   water animals for insight, consideration
   earth practical animals for planning, organization

Human World Totems

In general: Harmonize spirit helpers by calling for your helping guides from the four directions to work together with their special gifts. Then try to stay centered, out of the way; and keep a sense of humor.

Utilize the human vibrations in several kinds of philosophies to keep harmony in Self. Balance overdoses of specific philosophies.

Balance work-oriented tasks, career, overachieving with
   Oriental, Zen mindfulness for perspective, self-healing detachment
   Eastern intuitive meditation philosophies for resting in the void, the all
   Nature philosophies for strength from all Nature totems and for recycling of pace
   physical body-mind philosophies to relieve stress, strengthen body and mind

Balance overemotional, spiritual "blissiness" with
   task-oriented philosophies specifically for reconnecting

with patterns and cycles
Nature philosophies for grounding spirituality
Oriental mindfulness for perspective and detachment (this is tricky; try earthy tasks and Nature connectors first)

Balance detached Oriental mindfulness with
Nature philosophies to connect with Earth energies
Western physical tasks for applying insight to Earth Walk, daily life path
Eastern intuitive meditation philosophies to deepen spiritual connections (this is tricky because it can cause delusional separations; use task-oriented, physical, Nature cycles first)

Balance out-of-proportion, chaotic Nature animism with
task-oriented, physical philosophies for practical reality applications
Oriental mindfulness for perspective
Eastern intuitive meditation philosophies for deep-level rest, renewal, and connection to inner healer

Plant World Totems

In general: Plant World totems, not ingested, are practically self-balancing. However, here are a few pointers.

Balance evergreens with deciduous plants to keep cycles of Self in awareness and understanding.

Balance luxurious, blooming plants—such as gardenia, magnolia, jasmine, etc.—with good, hardworking plants like cedar, holly, juniper, "common" flowers like daisies, and clover, grasses, and grains for the "common touch" in healing.

Balance highly sacred trees and plants—oaks, redwoods, ash, mandrake, myrrh, frankincense—with
grains, grasses to earth wisdom
wildflowers and steady bloomers—mums, zinnias, etc.—to personalize wisdom for humor

Balance grasses, grains, weeds, clover with
sacred trees and plants to deepen spiritual connection and empower magick and healing
blooming flowers to lift spirit and increase ceremonial awareness and celebration of earth wisdom

Mineral World Totems

In general: The Mineral World, like the Animal and Plant worlds, is
   naturally self-balancing. For example, since crystals grow on
   rocks, this is self-balancing. It's when we isolate members of any
   world that the imbalances take place. This we can deal with by
   using our good, shamanic earth sense.

Balance shells, corals, and river stones with crystals, gemstones and
   translucent stones for increased flow of spiritual energy and
   dream work.

Balance crystal's high-energy vibrations with
      salt, soil, sand to slow your pace and ground energy
      gemstones and translucent stones for magick, self-healing, ritual
      plain old rocks to rest crystal energy (also to rest gemstones)
      gold to direct intense energy and wisdom
      silver to receive and absorb energy and vision
      copper to mellow energy, earth healing
      iron and other ores to hold energy

Balance earthy stones—agates, jaspers— with
      translucent stones for gentle lift of spirit
      semiprecious stones and gemstones to move energy upward
         and aim self-healing vibrations
      sand, soil, salt to rest energy
      crystals to open psyche and spiritual psyche
      metals and ores for practical, self-disciplined work

Chapter 12

SHAMANIC SHIELDS

Sacred power objects represent the shaman's connection to Self, Nature, and Spirit. It is the depth of these connections that causes the objects to hold such strength and fascination for us on our shamanic path. I have said before that power does not dwell in objects. It is our shamanic interaction with any object that activates it and gives it the vibrations we feel.

When we create sacred power objects, we are giving form and focus to the energies we work with. We are expressing power tangibly so that we may connect with the energy more easily. We are also expressing power to honor its gifts and contributions to our lives.

Like the shaman, power objects are channels for energy. Neither shamans nor power objects hold energy. The flow of energy comes when we learn to honor power as a gift of Spirit. As we learn to express and honor this gift by creating sacred power objects, we deepen our shamanic connections and open ourselves to greater wisdom.

All sacred power objects that we create express our personal relationships to shamanic energies. Even when we create objects that have strong traditional meanings and symbolic connections, it is our personal connection that activates and energizes our creations. Objects created to represent traditional symbolic energies strengthen our personal channels for that energy.

The path of the shaman is the path of the Self. Our sacred power objects reflect our soul's journey. Sacred power objects declare our intentions and our affirmations of faith, wisdom, and strength. These objects declare who we are, how we make our journey, and where our supporting energies come from. Sacred power objects are manifestations of personal totem energies. Our interaction with these centers our energies and attunes us to the special vibrations of Self, Nature, and Spirit.

I have called this chapter Shamanic Shields to clarify the concept of a shield. The most commonly held concept of a shield is an object we use for defense in battle. Shamanically, though, a shield is an object that declares our Self in connection to power. In that respect, all sacred power objects can be considered shields.

A shield represents the wheel of energies we work with personally. To awaken the energies of our special sacred power objects, we have only to spin the wheels and release our Self to the flow of Spirit. This is the way of the shaman as a warrior of Spirit. When we learn to ride the wheels of Self, Nature, and Spirit, we are learning to balance the shields of connection to power. As we do this, we create objects that celebrate and declare the sacred connection.

In this chapter, we will learn some methods for creating sacred power objects for ourselves. We will learn to let our sense of Self, our inner vision, and our practical skills help us create these very personal totems of power. As wheels, all power objects can be used to tap into the energies from all of the directions. I have chosen twelve useful totem objects and categorized them according to the energies and directions they are most easily attuned to. As always, this is an arbitrary decision. Choose your own categories as you become familiar with these. Make your own medicine. Here are the categories I have chosen.

North • Earth
Shield or Pentacle
Fetish Pots and Smudge Pots
Sacred Salt Mixture

East • Air
Talking Stick and Staff
Feather Fans
Herbal Blends

South • Fire
Shamanic Mask
Totem Necklaces
Talismanic Jewelry

West • Water
  Shamanic Drum
  Spirit Rattles
  Sacred Baskets

The methods presented are designed to make use of ingredients and supplies that are easily obtainable. As you travel on the path of the shaman, you may choose to create power objects from special and rare objects more difficult to obtain. This is certainly fine and understandable. It is still good to remember that no one thing is to be valued above another, regardless of the energies that travel through it. All things are sacred to the shaman. All worlds are holy. Here's a story to illustrate that point.

One of my Wolf Clan brothers told me that the Dalai Lama had come to the Wolf Clan lodge along with some of his lamas, or monks. (You can just imagine these Tibetan masters of wisdom connecting with the beautiful Native American energies and lessons.) These lamas shared in the comfortable atmosphere of the lodge and enjoyed a wonderful home-cooked meal.

After supper, the Wolf Clan mother announced it was time for ceremony or circle. The Dalai Lama and his lamas looked around at the Wolf Clan members assembled in the kitchen, like the family that they are.

"But where are your holy people?" asked one of the lamas.

"Well, here," replied the Wolf Clan mother. "All people are holy people." (And all objects are sacred to Spirit.)

North • Earth

Shield (or Pentacle of Self)

A shield declares your sacred intentions and your connection to shamanic energies. A shield represents the wheels within wheels. Shields can be made as generally or as specifically as you choose, to reflect your personal journey. The pentacle with its five-point star is also a wheel and declares a Wiccan connection to power.

You will need

> a hoop (embroidery hoops made from wood are excellent, or wire hoops, which you may wrap with yarn and ribbon)

> a piece of fabric or hide large enough to overlap the hoop by several inches (natural-fiber fabrics that you can fray and unravel are good choices, as is fabric you can draw on)

> glue or sewing equipment (I don't sew, but some prefer this as being more traditional)

> paint or markers, stones, feathers, dried flowers, herbs, scraps of ribbon, fur, yarn, jewelry (one earring or a cuff link that has lost its mate is very good to use here to represent your Self), buttons, shells, nuts, seeds, assorted beads, and objects of Nature (check the Appendix for totem meanings if need be)

Take time to smudge all the objects you've collected. Sit in circle as you do them and call for the energies of the objects to flow through you. Connect the fabric to the hoop and hum or chant to it. Smudge the blank shield and offer it to the directions. Spend time gazing at the blank shield. (Some choose to leave it just so.) Connect individually with each object you have collected.

When you have done this, arrange the objects on the shield. Sometimes these form a pattern very rapidly. Other times, many different arrangements need to be tried. Take all the time you need to let these emerge for you. For your first shield, it is good to concentrate on your special connection to the shamanic energies. Create a shield that declares your Self and your personal gifts of power.

Fetish Pots and Smudge Pots

Many of us use large shells, such as abalone, for smudge pots. You may prefer to make or decorate a clay pot or bowl. The clay saucers used under plant pots make fine smudge pots. You can paint them to express your individuality. You may glue stones to the bottom of the saucer, pot, or shell. This lets air underneath and prevents heat damage. It's good to burn sage or thyme in a smudge pot first to clear the energies. Follow with sweetgrass or rosemary to seal positive energies.

A fetish pot is used by some to house the tiny totem figures of animals and birds. I use mine for this, as well as to charge or rest jewelry and small talismans. You can make a wonderful little fetish pot from self-hardening clay (available at craft stores). Roll the clay into long "snakes," as you did as a child. Coil these from the inside spiraling outward. This represents wisdom spirals and the greater wheels of life.

After you have coiled these, begin to pull them upward gently to form a bowl. As you do this, smooth the coils and press them together. Clay sticks well if it is moistened with just a little water and scratched with a twig or fork before you join pieces together.

While the pot is still wet, you can roll it gently in sand, tiny beads, or chips of stone (available at rock shops; ask for the residue of tumbled rocks).

While the clay is still soft, you can press shells or stones gently into its walls, or stick feathers, ribbons, or rawhide strips through it. Be creative—not judgmental. As with all objects you make, take time to smudge and connect with each item you use.

Let the pot air-dry for several days on a high shelf. Then you can place it outside on a warm sunny day or in an oven at very low heat for about four hours. After it has cooled, you may paint or mark the pot with symbols sacred to yourself. Charge in circle.

Sacred Salt Mixture

This is an excellent medium to charge totems in and to "simmer energies." After it has been blended for a few moon cycles, a pinch can be added to spells, bathwater, or as a gift to Nature. I often make a starter salt for special friends. It's a lot like sourdough and can be shared, if desired, to start some for others. Blend rock salt or table salt with chopped or ground herbs, crystals, small stones, nuts, seeds, jewelry, locks of hair, ground incense, and a few drops of your special oils. Store in a covered earthen jar. Feel free to continue adding to this mixture. It "grows on you."

East • Air

Talking Stick and Staff
The talking stick has to do with communication. You can pass it at a gathering with the understanding that only the person holding the stick (and the elder or group leader, if desired) can speak. This works somewhat better in theory than in practice, but it does hold the energies down well.

You can also take it into your personal ritual circle to communicate with totems and spirit guides; it serves as a focus for the energies. Sacred talking sticks usually show up in Nature. One medicine woman I know found hers "swimming" toward her in a river, looking far too much like a snake for her taste. She felt strongly that it was a communicator of wisdom, so she adopted it as a talking stick. I found mine on the beach, sticking straight up in the sand with what looks like one eye wide open.

Another stick I have is a branch shaped like a y, which was carved with symbols for me by my husband. (I do well to slice bread.) I wrapped this with a rainbow-colored ribbon to use at workshops and gatherings. I find it best to keep talking sticks fairly simple. Ribbons or strips of fabric in your sacred colors are often enough. It's also nice to tie a few bells to the ribbons to help summon spirit guides and to shake if there are too many interruptions.

A staff or rod is used to receive, direct, and channel higher spiritual energies. Traditionally, a staff connects you to the strongest, most pure energies of your philosophy and spiritual ideals. A staff is declarative of your deep shamanic and magical gifts. Staffs are often made from strong branches of oak or ash trees. However, one of the most wonderful staffs I have seen was made from a long copper pipe wrapped with rawhide laces. The important thing is that the staff be created from natural elements that you connect with.

One staff of mine, which I described earlier, is quite formal and declares my work as a priestess of Spirit. All of the symbols, crystals, and sashes on it are fixed. Being predominantly Aquarius, my element is fixed Air. This staff reflects that for me. Another staff I have is constantly in the process of receiving new carvings and changes of ribbon colors. This is my journey staff and supports my work as I progress on my path. I use my formal staff to cast the circle for high-magick ritual and my journey staff for more free-flowing ceremonies.

Staffs are very much shamanic shields. Because of this, they often take some time to emerge. One of mine sat for a year on my front porch before being decorated and adopted, another for three years. If you find a branch that has appeal for you and potential as a staff, be ready to follow its timetable. In the meantime, feel free to take it out in the moon or just use it as a walking stick. A little smoothing and sanding are also nice in preparation. I also rub mine with oils that are special to me. When you think of the staffs carried by wizards, wise women, and medicine teachers, remember how smooth and worn they often are. A staff is a lifetime totem. Develop the relationship carefully.

Feather Fans

Feathers are traditionally messengers and communicators of energy. When feather fans are used to smudge, they are directing energies to communicate with our self-healing and self-strengthening abilities. One single feather, or an entire wing of feathers, can be a fan.

As with all totem objects, it is good to "feed" or balance the energies of the feathers when you can. One hawk fan I have is made from a short branch of oak. The feathers are stuck in small holes drilled into both ends of the branch. At the top are several varieties of hawk feathers. At the bottom are duck feathers, since ducks are prey for hawks.

Another fan I have is made from owl feathers with strips of rabbit fur wrapped around them to hold it together. A heron fan I have has a tiny dragonfly wing and an iridescent fish scale attached. If you cannot find the actual item that will balance a totem, you can do it symbolically with drawings or carvings. The effect is the same.

An excellent way to make a feather holder is to cut the top off of a disposable razor and stick feathers into the handle. If this doesn't seem very shamanic, you may be glad to know the idea came from a special Seneca elder and medicine teacher. You can wrap the handle with ribbon, fabric, or strings of beads.

Some traditions hold that the quill of a feather must be uncut or undamaged in order for it to be used shamanically. Cut feathers are only used for decoration, according to this tradition. I have not found this to be true for me. However, if you are concerned about it, simply stick cedar, juniper, or pine needles in the open quill. It's how you feel that most influences your shamanic connection with power objects.

Feather fans can be used for personal or group smudging quite effectively. They are also useful energizers just by themselves. I use fans to sweep my aura or to awaken the energies of the totem feathers for my own work. Feather fans can be very sacred energy connections when placed in the East or South of a ritual circle.

I often place small feathers in my letters to people. I also give feathers to special friends, with tiny stone beads, shells, or bells tied on with natural-fiber yarn. Large feather fans can be very deep journey aids. Hold the fan, or fans, and dance the energy of the winged ones. You may take flight!

The feathers you use are not as important as the intent you have, or the meaning you give to them. One of my most special feathers is a white turkey feather colored black to look like an eagle feather. (There is a lesson in that somewhere.). This feather was given to me with great ceremony by a dear friend. As she presented it to me, my puppy grabbed it and ran across the yard, followed closely by my son. In the tug-of-war that ensued, the feather came out with a huge bite in it. I saw it as a wonderful symbol of the kind of chaos we sometimes have to be spiritual and shamanic in the midst of. When the confusion of everyday life threatens to close in on me, I take out that feather (bite and all) and remember the strength that humor has on the path of the shaman.

Herbal Blends

Although I burn a lot of herbs in ceremony and ritual, I also keep large bowls and jars of herbal blends for their beauty and their energies. In these blends, I place crystals, stones, shells, and other Nature objects I use to connect with. I also use these to house, charge, and rest some of my power totems, such as talons or symbolic jewelry. One jar is so beautiful that I often journey into it. I imagine myself as a tiny wood spirit and jump right in. It is very meditative and energizing just to stop and smell the fragrance or touch the earth energies of these blends.

It is fine to use a premade potpourri to start your own herbal blend. You can add oils, herbs, and other Nature objects to make these especially yours. One blend I have began as gardenias and irises that had been dried and sprinkled with orris root powder (available at craft shops). I was fortunate to have a friend with an incredible knack for starting these blends, one who was magical enough to understand my need to add to her mixture. If you do add your own herbs and flowers, be sure and give them plenty of time to dry beforehand. Patience really pays off with this.

South • Fire

Shamanic Mask

A mask can be made to represent any aspect of the shaman's medicine or totemic connections. Masks can also be made to represent the shadows or darker sides of ourselves that we need to dance through on our journey as shamans. If you do make a shadow mask to help work through an aspect of yourself, it is good to honor the lessons it has brought you. When you have reached a point where you can do this, you have taken power over aspects that were once obstacles or shadows for you. It is not advisable to keep such a mask when you have achieved this. Return it to Nature as a gift for the growth that the lesson has brought to you. Release it with gratitude.

Whenever you connect deeply or "take on" the aspects of a totem helper, such as a power animal, you are symbolically wearing a shamanic mask. These masks can be made as simply or as elaborately as you choose. You can make or buy masks meant for wearing or for displaying like a shield of self-power. If you do buy a mask that has already been created in a totemic form, be sure to smudge it carefully. Wait for at least one moon cycle to cleanse. Then energize it with the vibrations you intend for its use. Even then, work with it carefully. Test the waters of totemic energies before you dive in.

Masks are most often made to celebrate our shamanic connections to Self, Nature, and Spirit. These are displayed or worn in journeys, ceremonies, and rituals. I advise you to begin by making a mask of the shamanic strengths and gifts of power in your life.

You can make a simple mask by painting your own face. This is an ancient method to signal your readiness to journey between the worlds, and your powers as a spiritual warrior. This is also an excellent way to begin detaching from your judgmental self so that you can observe your own sacred gifts.

A more permanent mask can be made from cardboard, art tissue paper (available in wonderful colors), sequins, ribbons, beads, feathers, crystals, and scraps of fabric. Be creative. When you have made such a mask, "dance it" and act out the energies it represents, to awaken it.

Another good way to make a mask that earths your shamanic energies is to use clay or even Play Dough. Roll newspaper in the shape of a large face-size egg and secure with masking tape. Take a flat circle of clay large enough to cover the newspaper form. Drape the clay circle (a lot like pizza dough) over the form and begin to mold a face shape. Use additional clay to give your mask features and decorate with personal objects and objects from Nature. Use the same processes as with your fetish pot to shape the clay features and later to dry the mask. Let this mask emerge and take its own form. To make it truly yours, add a bit of your hair and adopt it formally in circle. Let it reflect your strengths.

Totem Necklaces

A necklace is used for much more than decoration. Like the shield, it can reflect your power gifts and connect you to the totem energies. The circle of the necklace can represent a circle of self-power or specific self-healing energies. Most necklaces should be made long enough to touch your heart area or your solar plexus for maximum effect. Some totems, such as amber, peridot, and blue topaz, are best left at the throat area to facilitate their natural abilities as communicators and soothing clarifiers. Keep the properties of the items you use in mind when you make any necklaces.

I am a great one for stringing together beads to create a specific effect. One necklace I made, though, was of leftover lapis lazuli, turquoise, malachite, and bone. It has become one of my most powerful totem helpers for shamanic energies. Whatever you put together, be sure to save one or two beads. Place these in your sacred salt or your herbal blends to charge. Sometimes the most dynamic combinations come from leftover beads you had not originally intended to put together.

When you buy beads that are expensive, remember that you can amplify them with crystal, clay, bone, or less-expensive stones of similar Ray energy. (Check the Appendix for ideas.)

A friend of mine has a very wonderful necklace that she calls her "gris-gris" (Louisiana magic!) necklace. It is primarily made of fiber, to which she has added beads, charms, shells, and stones for several years. The effect is uniquely hers and quite powerful. Let some necklaces develop slowly.

Talismanic Jewelry

In the Craft of the Wise we often make magical jewelry that is engraved or painted with symbols or talismans for specific purposes. Check the Appendix for a good basic selection of common symbols and talismanic squares. Instead of drawing these on paper for use in burnings to awaken the energy, you can wear these for continuing effect. Talismanic or symbolic jewelry will need to be cleansed and re-energized to maintain its properties.

You can make talismanic jewelry with specific stones, often called fascination gems, which have traditional attributes. Symbols can also be drawn on simple clay or wooden disks with specific colors to activate the energies. One of the most interesting pieces of talismanic jewelry I have seen was made from a wooden bracelet (available at the dime store) that had been decorated with symbols marked in permanent ink.

It's really very magical to make do with what you have. The energy you put into these more than balances the energy of an expensive stone or charm that you buy. You are the magick in your life; you are the center of the energies.

Traditionally, talismanic jewelry in the Craft of the Wise has been made according to astrological systems that are quite ancient. Here is a brief chart to get you started. Remember that your astrological sun sign is only one aspect of your Self. The main three to consider are your sun, moon, and rising signs. If you don't know these already, check your bookstore for astrological guides or have a chart cast. You may be surprised to find that you are already connecting with stones and colors that are attributed to your astrological signs.

Use these as a guide only—there are many variations to explore.

Talismanic Jewelry

Sign	Mineral World Totems	Color
Aries	Carnelian, jasper, garnet, iron, steel	Red
Taurus	Peridot, emerald, turquoise, copper	Light Green
Gemini	Amber, topaz, amazonite, aluminum	Light Blue
Cancer	Emerald, pearl, moonstone, silver	Rose Pink
Leo	Ruby, diamond, gold, copper	Orange
Virgo	Jade, sodalite, rhodochrosite, tin	Grey-Blue
Libra	Opal, lapis lazuli, quartz, copper	Peach
Scorpio	Bloodstone, onyx, garnet, silver	Crimson
Sagittarius	Coral, topaz, turquoise, tin	Violet
Capricorn	Malachite, agates, citrine, lead	Brown
Aquarius	Aquamarine, zircon, sapphire, aluminum	Electric Blue
Pisces	Amethyst, bloodstone, alexandrite, silver	Lavender

When you are making talismanic jewelry with fascination gems, feel free to substitute stones and Mineral World totems that have similar Ray energies. As always, use what you feel strongly connected to, regardless of what any traditional system calls for. You may find later that there are quite specific reasons for your sense of connection to a stone or color.

West • Water

Shamanic Drum

In many shamanic traditions, the drum is considered the steed or the vehicle that the shaman rides to the journey worlds. The rhythm of the shaman's drum is a powerful tool to use for earth journeys and vision quests. The beat and the vibration of a drum can be effectively used to channel energies for self-healing and magical work as well.

If you make any significant purchase to add to your shamanic tools, a drum is a good investment. Many varieties of drums are available at various prices. I advise that you put a little time into your search for a drum and try to resist the first expensive ones that invariably show up.

Some traditions hold that the drum makers call for spirits to enter the drums they create. I don't know about that, since I can't imagine any of my spirit helpers agreeing to this. I do know that each drum has a rhythm that is uniquely its own. Each drum has a vibration or resonance that you can find by experimenting with it. When you tap that resonance you have effectively connected with the energies, or what some call the spirit, of that drum.

Drums can be found in wonderful places like secondhand shops and charity sales. Of course, my first drum came from just such a place. I took a lot of ribbing about buying an old set of beach bongos for shamanic work, but they had an immediate appeal for me. I've spent most of my life on or close to beaches, and bongos have great associations built into me. When I adopted my beach bongo drums, I placed two symbols on them to declare my shamanic intentions. On the larger drum I drew my pentagram, complete with flying Aquarian astrological symbol. On the smaller drum, I placed a simple arrow, the rune of the spiritual warrior.

Some time later, as my connection to drumming work deepened, I received an unexpected gift. My in-laws, somewhat amused by what they call my "interest in Indians," said they would send me an old drum they had stored somewhere. After all, no one was using it since the children were grown—right?—hmmm.

Imagine my surprise when a package came bearing an antique Cree drum, which had been brought down years before from Canada. Along the outer edges of the drum some child (no one could remember who) had painted large green arrows. After I had spent some time connecting with the drum, I outlined the arrows with copper paint to honor the Earth connection that had brought that drum into my life. I've collected several drums since then, each for special purposes; but when I journey deeply, I always use my old bongos or that wonderful Cree drum I was gifted to receive.

When you first start drumming to journey, it's best to learn to match the rhythm of your heartbeat. Doing this can create a deep meditative effect and start you on your inner quest. At a shamanic intensive I attended, a woman came with five large drums. Her ability to match several heartbeats at once was astounding. When I asked her how she'd learned to do that, she said, "Listen and go one beat at a time."

Grey Eagle advises us to keep a steady rhythm so that spirits can "climb" down it, like a ladder. I also advise you to experiment until you find the beat that resonates the connection between you and your drum. This is the shamanic connection.

For hide drums that get loose in damp climates, one shamanic teacher I know uses a hair dryer to tighten it up.

For drums that become too tight and have more resonance than you want, an Irish folk musician showed me a great trick: Rub the surface of the drum with ice until you can get a true beat without too much ring.

Spirit Rattles

Rattles are used shamanically to signal beginnings and endings of spiritual journeys, to break up blocks, to attract and direct energies, to call totem helpers, and to maintain dance rhythms.

A very effective, if not aesthetic, rattle can be made from taping two cups together with dried beans inside. Before you purchase a rattle, you might try the cup rattle to see if you are attuned to rattling. Some people I have worked with much prefer a drum or bells to the sharper-edged vibration of most rattles.

A large gourd rattle (available at most esoteric supply stores) can serve a double purpose. Tapping the rattle with the palm of your hand can give a deeper rhythm, similar in vibration to a drumbeat. Of course, it can also be shaken for a true rattle vibration.

For me, the sound of a rattle is very important, regardless of the type. I have used my children's rattles at times when I wanted a soft effect on my journey. I created a sacred rattle from a very commercial "tourist trap" rattle, complete with dyed chicken feathers and stenciled symbols. I covered the rattle with indigo paint to symbolize synthesis. I glued tiny soft feathers to the top and to the handle. It may have been just my imagination, but the tone of that rattle seemed to change after I had transformed it.

I took a similar rattle apart and placed dozens of crystal beads inside. The energy of that rattle is most spiritual and I use it for vision quests or high-magick work. If you construct a rattle with crystals from an old rattle, or from a dried gourd and a stick, be sure to energize and adopt it formally.

Sacred Baskets

In most traditions, baskets are considered to symbolize the female receptive aspects. As such, they make excellent houses for more active totems, such as feathers, which can be quite direct in their energies. Most of us are not skilled in basket weaving. If you are, know that it is an ancient sacred craft, and be honored by the gift of that ability.

If you buy a basket to make into a sacred power object, take time to choose one that invokes primitive energies for you. Some baskets obviously are machine-made and do not carry that personal vibration of caring. Other baskets look as though they could have been made in just the same way thousands of years ago. These are the best baskets for shamanic work.

When you use a basket to house sacred objects, be sure to balance their energies. The basket I have to keep my hawk and owl feathers in has a fine rabbit skin stuck at the bottom. To this I add dried wildflowers for the rabbit. A covered basket filled with moss and sage can be an excellent place to keep crystals and other stones. A basket of shells and driftwood can become an altar for crystals and feathers on a moonlight night. A tiny basket can be used to dry a single rose and a few ferns. This can be placed fresh on an altar and later used as a house for other totems. Many of us in the shamanic tradition keep a basket near the front door, to which we add feathers of all types that we find along the way. This helps keep the energies focused and pro-vides a pleasant vibration to the house as well.

Journey inward whenever you feel the need to create a sacred power object but are at a loss as to how it should come together. Imagine your creative energies flowing in a great black cauldron deep inside the earth. Sometimes this cauldron is being stirred by a wizard or a wise woman who looks surprisingly like you. Ask that person for help in constructing your sacred power objects.

Part IV

EAST

SACRED KEYS

SHAMANIC SOURCING

AIR

ATTRIBUTES OF THE EAST

The **Element** of the East is Air.

The **Wheel of the East** is the wheel of
> Free Mind
> Creativity
> Illumination
> Divination
> Brain Stimulation
> Philosophy
> Mindfulness
> Awareness
> Perception

The **Energy** of the East is swift, mercurial, changeable.

The **Journey of the East** is the journey of perception in chaos.

The **Traditional Colors** of the East are
> White
> Yellow
> Scarlet
> Peach
> Turquoise Blue
> Gold
> and the Rainbow Colors of illumination

Some **Sacred Spirits** of the East are
> Danu—goddess of creativity
> Mercury—god of communication
> Athena—goddess of wisdom
> Kwan Yin—goddess of mindfulness
> Buddha—teacher of illumination
> Nuit—goddess of the skies

233

Raphael—archangel of the East, mystic illuminator, star traveler

Paralda—servant of Raphael, shape changer in the mists of mind

Sylphs—elemental spirits of Air, ruled by Paralda

Yod He Vawhe—elemental king of Air

Some **Animals** of the East are

Doves—for messages of peace and illumination

Hawk—for focus and perception

Eagle—for philosophy and ideals

Wolf—for communication and perception

Deer—for perception, awareness

Raccoon—for thinking

Cardinals—for creativity

Some **Minerals** of the East are

White or Clear Fluorite—for illumination and creativity

Moonstone—for receptivity to illumination

Turquoise—for focus and awareness

Single-Point Crystals—for perception

Amethyst—for meditation and illumination

Rhodochrosite—for brain stimulation

Royal Azule—for brain codes

Some **Plant World Helpers** of the East are

Wildflowers—for creativity

Spearmint, Lavender, Clover, Sage—for meditation incenses

Some **Human World Helping Activities** of the East are

Divination	Martial Arts
Fortunetelling	Brainstorming
Sourcing	Philosophical Debates
Vision Quests	Expressive Arts
Zen Meditation	Flower Arranging
Tai Chi Chuan	

Helping Thoughts for the East:

Illumination through Creative Communication.

The Mind is Awareness.

Perception in all Philosophy.

Focus for Peace in Chaos.

Riding the Wheel of the East

Vision Quest

to Grandmother White Crystal
Medicine Woman

I am climbing a rugged mountain path.
The wind dances through my hair and whispers in my ears.
I listen for the messages, but the wind spirals upward,
Leading me higher.

I am wearing a woolen cloak with many pockets.
My shoes are of the softest leather. I feel every stone.
I breathe deeply and balance my step.
I place the soles of my feet onto the well-trod ground.
The path smooths out before me.

The mists of evening sweep away my footprints.
The night clouds come to blanket the peak of my mountain.
The last ray of the sun silhouettes a soaring broad-winged bird.
Twilight stars beckon through the branches of a golden tree.
I light my lantern.

Darkness drapes me. It stills my sight and clears my vision.
I hold the lantern high above my head.
I walk on in a circle of light. All heights and depths are one.
The fragrance of herbs brewing drifts past me.
I can hear the gentle crackle of a campfire.

The path narrows as I make my way around a great boulder.
I press my back into the rock as I pass. I breathe in its power.
The path opens to a clearing, and fire lights a shallow cave.
By the fire sits an old woman wearing a cloak with no pockets.
Her smile warms the night air.

We sit on woven mats. She gives me tea in an earthen cup.
She has the clear eyes of a mystic, and the lined face of wisdom.
Her hair falls around her shoulders in gold and silver lights.
Beads of every color sparkle against the whiteness of her robes.
In her lap, a basket holds crystals of all shapes and colors.

She bids me to choose four crystals: red, yellow, blue, and green.
With a twig, she slowly draws a circle in the earth.
One at a time, she places the crystals on the circle.
Yellow to the East. Red to the South.
Blue to the West. Green to the North.

She waves her hands over the yellow crystal, and hums deeply.
Color lifts out of the crystal, into her hands. She touches me.
Images explode inside my head.
Smiling Buddhas. Kwan Yin on a lotus blossom. Mandarin splendor.
Fujiama, sacred mountain floating on the sea. Painted silks.
I see the Great Wall of China from far above the indigo earth.
In mindfulness, I am all things. I am Air, the Tao, the Aum.

She waves her hands over the red crystal, and touches me again.
Pagodas fade, and pyramids rise in the desert. Isis and Osiris.
Acropolis stands in linear perfection. The golden mean.
Zeus throws a thunderbolt. Jesus of Nazareth dies on a cross.
The Senate of Rome becomes the Capitol building in Washington.
I am a rocket launching into space.
I am Thrust. I am Active Energy. I am Fire.

She touches me with the light of the blue crystal.
Temple bells caress the peaks of the Himalayas. Tigers roar.
Siva dances in a brass ring of fire. Paisley mandalas drift by.
Marble palaces in reflecting pools. Carved stone jungle ruins.
I am a jeweled Lakshmi, goddess of fortunes. I am Jasmine.
I am the Ganges spilling out to sea.
I am Water. I am Flow. I receive. I return.

She touches me once more, and green crystal light pierces me.
A shaman, in hides and antlers, dances to empower the hunt.
Medicine men pray to the Great Spirit. An eagle flies free.
A wise woman gathers herbs by the light of the moon.
A clan feasts to celebrate the harvest, gifts of the Mother.
I am Grain and the Grower. I am Seed and Sower. I am roots.
I am Demeter. Corn-Mother. I am Gaia. I am Earth.

Visions fade. Sensations slip away into the night sky.
I am aware of the sounds in the darkness. An owl calls to me.

The old woman stirs the crystal colors into circles of light.
Higher and higher, they swirl and blend. A rainbow spiral.
The colors crystalize into pure white light. Radiant Energy.
I breathe in to receive.

The Light is absorbed into all that it touches.
The old woman and I sit by the fire, sharing one heartbeat.
She takes the crystals and places them in my pockets.
They glow through the fabric of my cloak, then softly fade.
I feel them inside my mind.

She looks into my eyes and I know my Self.
She smiles a farewell, and is gone.
I hear her gentle laughter on the wind as I turn for home.
Dawn rays glisten on the morning mists in rainbow hues.
As I walk on the path, I face the rising sun. It warms my being.

The Wheel of the East is the wheel of divination and illumination. The image you have just read came from a vision quest I made to divine the future of my path. I had explored many types of wisdom and found great value in them all. Still, I was not certain that I could continue with so many different philosophies and ways of illumination in my life. I felt I must put them together somehow or select just one to follow. I had reached a place of crisis on my path, and I went to Spirit, "crying for a vision" to guide my journey.

It was in this vision quest that I first truly understood the meaning of following the Rainbow Path. From it I gained the strength and spiritual support I needed to make my own blend of wisdom, magick, and shamanic medicine.

In the East we learn to seek answers from the energies of Self, Nature, and Spirit. There are countless guides to help us when we learn to recognize, use, and accept this help. We do this through ancient systems of divination and fortunetelling; we do this by psychically attuning to our inner wisdom.

In the East we learn to center our energies in the midst of chaos. Illumination, creativity, and inspiration rarely come to us in a measured, ordered fashion. Because of this, we learn to sharpen our focus, our perceptive awareness, and our mental capacities. We learn to divine patterns in the midst of confusing energies and stimuli.

Traditionally, the Wheel of the East is shown as an unfinished or open circle. This symbolizes the need to stay open to illumination. The structures we impose on ourselves in the North break down a bit when we make our East journeys.

In the East, the shaman learns to be centered in receptivity with clarity of mind and sharpness of sensory channels. In this way, the shaman can stay balanced while activating the energies received from Source. The East is the wheel we ride to understand our function as mirrors for ourselves, as well as for others. We learn to reflect energies, whether ours or others we work with. In order to do this, we must learn to read the energies clearly. When we do so, we are better able to follow our own shamanic path.

When we have divined the flow of energies, we are less influenced by those not meant for us to dance with. We learn that our lives are not framed by others' expectations. Ultimately, we learn that our lives are not even framed by what we call our own expectations. The illumination of the East teaches us who we are—clear of any goals, patterns, and expectations we have arbitrarily imposed on ourselves.

By developing our natural divination skills, we find the core of truth in our relationships to Self, Nature, and Spirit. We learn to understand our path as mirrors. We know when we are reflecting the energies of others. We know when they are seeing themselves, even when they feel they are seeing us. We accept this shamanic gift by being an honest mirror, even when we reflect what others may not wish to see. We accept ourselves as channels for energies that help others find truth in their own lives.

In the East we learn to stay centered and clear, because we have a greater understanding and definition of our own path. The energies of the East often come to us wildly, like storms or gales. We learn to wait, at times, until the wind dies down. Riding the Wheel of the East gives us the serenity of clear vision and deep-level awareness.

The East section has been designed to give you exercises, images, and methods for developing your shamanic awareness. Oracle methods with traditional meanings and psychic methods with intuitive meanings are presented for you to blend into your personal forms of divination. It is for you to adapt these to meet your own needs. All of the images presented may also be used as journey methods for yourself and others. Most of these arose from my personal journeys and were adapted for clients and workshops. Feel free to adapt them for yourself on your path.

Divination is a sacred skill. Like other shamanic skills, it is ultimately a gift. Illumination flows through you, helping you to divine or read for yourself and others. Be ever aware that this comes to you from Source. Take time to center your energies. Learn to get out of the way as wisdom comes through. When this wisdom channels through, be gentle with how you direct its messages for yourself and for others.

The following exercises are designed to help you develop clarity of mind and receptivity to illuminating images.

Clear-Mind Awareness Exercise

Begin by taking a long, slow breath. Just take a few moments to be with your breathing. Be aware of your breath flowing in and out of your body. Feel how your body expands as you breathe in. Fill yourself with your breath and hold it gently. Release your breath slowly. Feel your body contract and relax as you breathe out.

Take as long as you need to focus on your breathing. As you breathe deeply, begin to stretch your body slowly and gently. Reach out your legs one at a time. Slowly stretch and tense the muscles in your legs. Relax.

Now reach out your arms one at a time. Reach and stretch. Relax.

Now yawn a really wide, luxurious yawn and slowly stretch your whole body. Feel each muscle flex and release as you ripple the stretch throughout your body. Breathe deeply and slowly through your nose. Release through your mouth. Sigh deeply.

Yawn and stretch again if you choose. Feel the quiet in your body. Feel the slower, more gentle rhythm of your breath. Let your breath breathe for you. Watch your breath find its own rhythm.

Become aware of where you are. Feel the position of your body. Slowly stretch and relax any parts of your body that are not comfortable. Feel the difference as you release the muscle.

Become aware of the temperature around you.

Feel the air move around you.

Now breathe deeply, and listen for the sounds around you.

Listen carefully for even the softest sounds. Listen for the sound of your breathing. Listen again for the sounds around you. Let each sound signal your body to become more and more relaxed.

Quietly listen for the sound of three breaths in and three breaths out.

One in . . . one out.

Two in . . . two out.

Three in . . . three out.

Imagine that your forehead is a blank screen ready to reflect your images. For a few moments simply let images flicker briefly across the screen, one after another as though they were advertisements, or previews of a coming attraction. Let each of these images slip past quickly, frame to frame.

Feel your body relax deeply as the screen becomes blank once more. No sounds, no sights. Just the feel of your body and the rhythm of your breath.

Breathe an especially long, slow breath and begin to expand the screen. Allow the screen to become larger and larger until you are only aware of the blankness and the quiet of the screen.

Enjoy the stillness of your body. Feel the quiet focus of your mind. If you are sitting, you may wish to rock slightly back and forth as you experience your image. In your mind's eye allow yourself to step into the blank screen. Feel the peacefulness.

Deep-Level Hypnotic Imaging Exercise

Become aware of all the noises around you. Perhaps you hear the sounds of someone breathing, or the sounds of conversation in another room. Take time to note these sounds now, and file them away in your mind.

When you are in a deeply relaxed state, you will be focusing only on your images. Sounds will not bother you. Indeed, you may not hear any sounds other than the sounds that you may hear in your image. If you do, let them signal you to relax.

Breathe deeply, and focus on yourself. Before you relax into a comfortable position, take time to stretch and breathe deeply. As you take a deep breath, hold it for a moment, then release it with a noisy sigh.

Now stretch out both arms and wave both hands. Wiggle all your fingers and imagine all your tension flying out from the ends of your fingers.

Once again take a deep breath . . . stretch your arms . . . wave your hands . . . wiggle your fingers . . . and relax. Now take another deep breath, and stretch out your right leg, then your left leg . . . roll your ankles . . . and wiggle your toes.

Allow any remaining tension to fly out of your fingers and your toes.

Now take an especially long, slow, deep breath. Stretch your entire body gently, tense all your muscles, and hold your breath and your muscles for just a moment.

Now breathe in a little deeper . . . hold it. Now throw out your breath and all your tensions. Relax your muscles.

Let's try that one more time.

Inhale . . . tense your muscles . . . hold it. This time *gently* release your breath and gently relax your muscles.

Release . . . relax.

Feel the difference in your vibration.

Now breathe deeply, and let your head roll very gently to the left . . . and around from the left to the right. Feel the muscles in your neck as they tense and relax while you roll your head from left to right.

Now breathe deeply again, and return your head to the center, balanced on your neck. Begin to roll your head once more, this time from the right all around to the left. Feel the muscles soften and relax as you roll your head gently on your shoulders. Now breathe deeply, and return your head to the center, once more balanced on your neck.

Breathe gently now; move your head from side to side and relax. Let your head rest.

Make yourself comfortable . . . legs and arms uncrossed . . . relaxed . . . quiet . . . serene.

In a moment, you will take a breath to the count of seven, hold it for the count of seven, and release it to the count of seven.

First count. Ready? Take a deep breath.

Inhale . . . two . . . three . . . four . . . five . . . six . . . seven.

Hold . . . two . . . three . . . four . . . five . . . six . . . seven.

Release . . . two . . . three . . . four . . . five . . . six . . . seven.

Do this two more times . . . and then you may establish your own pace of breathing.

Now, making no special effort, begin to watch your breath. Observe the pace of your breathing. Feel the rhythm as it flows in and out.

Let your breath breathe for you.

As you watch your breath, you may image it like waves flowing in and out. If you become distracted, just return the focus of your attention to the pace of your breathing and the rhythm of your breath.

Know that distractions sometimes arise when you are releasing tensions. Let these distractions be a signal to you that you are becoming more and more relaxed.

As you watch your breath, become aware also of the pauses between your breaths. There is a pause after you inhale; and a pause after you exhale. Notice the feel of the pauses. Pay close attention—these pauses can become an experience of timelessness. Some people experience a floating, a weightlessness in these pauses.

Breathe deeply and create an image of a bright light just above your head. Feel the warmth of the light spread down . . . around your head and neck . . . over your face . . . across your shoulders . . . down your back and chest . . . down your arms into your hands . . . and fingers . . . down over your hips and tummy . . . down your thighs and legs . . . into your ankles, feet, and toes.

Image yourself surrounded by a glow of warmth and light flowing through your body . . . deeply relaxing energy.

Breathe deeply. Relax your muscles even more.

Attune yourself to your deepest inner being. Now that you are deeply relaxed, feeling the flow of light and energy surrounding you, know that you are receptive to your inner being. Breathe gently.

Begin to allow images to emerge from your inner self.

Allow them to flow through you slowly and gently.

Take all the time you need for the images to flow.

One . . . let all the other images fade.

Two . . . let your special image take form.

Three . . . bring it into sharper focus.

Four . . . create your special image.

Take a few moments to be with your special image, and to get a sense of its meaning for you. You have all the time you need to enjoy your special image.

Breathe deeply once again.

Now, as I count from four to one, I want you to let that special image fade, and to begin to return to this time and place.

Four . . . breathe deeply and release the image.

Three . . . let it fade gently.

Two . . . breathe again, and watch the image drift away.

Know that you can recall your special image whenever you choose.

When you have awakened from your deeply relaxed state, you may wish to express your special image. You may do this by dancing the image, by drawing the image, or by describing the image in words either spoken or written. Or you may wish to let your image stay as an inner expression of yourself. The choice is yours.

And now . . .

One . . . your special image has faded away from view but not from memory.

Take a few moments to allow yourself to come back to this time and place. Become aware of yourself in the present moment.

Begin to wiggle your fingers . . . wave your hands . . . stretch out your arms. Take a deep breath and relax your arms.

Begin to wiggle your toes . . . roll your ankles . . . stretch out your legs . . . and relax. Feel yourself becoming alert and awake.

As the count goes from seven to one, you will become more alert, awake, and energized.

Seven . . . six . . . five . . . four . . . three . . . two . . . one.

Stretch once more. Come into the present moment, fully awake and alert.

Chapter 13

SACRED KEYS

Ancient wisdom and modern physics have come to a point of blending in the Aquarian Age. The Wyrd, or life weaving, described by magicians, shamans, mystics, and metaphysicians, has become recognized by the new physics as the "tissue of events" that connects us all. All worlds are part of a great fabric of energies. Sometimes we are able to glimpse the pattern of this fabric. The illumination we receive from divining this pattern comes to us from the highest aspects of Self, Nature, and Spirit. In the East we learn to recognize that we are all threads in this fabric, and that we are all weavers of this sacred energy we call life.

> We are the Flow
> We are the Ebb
> We are the Weaver
> We are the Web.
> —Neopagan Chant

Wise Weaver

You are floating in a small boat on a dark, still lake.

The boat drifts silently in the moonlight, carrying you toward an island in the middle of the lake.

Mists along the shoreline rise up to greet you. Breathe deeply, and feel the coolness of the evening refresh you. You step out of the boat, onto the sandy bottom, into the shallow water. Tie your boat to a low-hanging branch of an old cypress tree.

You climb a narrow path among rocks, to the top of a great windswept plain.

Just ahead, in the distance, there is a large round hill rising from the grassy plain.

The darkness of night clouds keeps the top of the hill hidden, even in the light of the moon. A knoll, a tor with a path spiraling upward.

You begin walking up the hill on the spiral path. Slowly, and carefully, you pick your way, as the path carries you around and around the hill, toward the top.

As you climb higher the air seems thinner, and the breeze takes your breath away. You begin to feel the energy of the place.

Breathe deeply, and slow your pace as you climb upward.

The path around the hill spirals more narrowly and you know you are close to the top.

A few final steps and you find yourself on smooth level ground, at the top of the hill. Dark clouds block the light. You can barely make out the circular shape of a structure just ahead of you. Breathe deeply, and ask the wind to help the clouds drift away a little faster, allowing you to see more clearly.

As the moon lights the structure, you see a series of concentric circles made of large stones set upon one another. The space between the stones is large enough so that you can see a small round building at the very center of all the walls.

There is a light in the window of the small round building, and though you cannot see inside from where you are, the light from the window illuminates the stone walls that encircle it.

You notice, in your image, that there are runic symbols painted on the stones of the outermost wall. Moving like the hands of a clock, sun-wise, begin to explore the outermost wall. Notice that these paintings reflect signs and symbols from all times and all places.

Notice that even the ones that you have not seen before seem strangely familiar to you now.

Take all the time you need to read the signs and symbols painted on this wall. Allow them to show you scenes and stories of your Self.

Now breathe deeply again, and listen for the sound of wind chimes blowing in the breeze. From where you are, you can see most of the path as it spirals down the tor. You turn to face the next wall, whose stones are set somewhat closer together. As you squeeze between the stones and step into the circle, you notice that the light inside these walls seems to move, swirling around.

As you look closer, you notice there are mirrors on the stones in this wall. As you walk around, you gaze into each mirror. Each mirror reflects a different aspect of your Self. In your image, take your time, and look *lovingly* into each mirror. Do this with compassion for what you see, without judgement of what you may expect to see.

How many mirrors are there on this stone wall in your image? Take time to see the reflections of your Self.

Now breathe deeply, and release all the reflections that you have seen.

The next wall in is supported by four great stones encircled by a swirling band of lights and colors. This band of colors streams out from inside the small stone building at the center. Breathe deeply, and allow the threads of light and color to lead you into the building.

As you step inside, notice that you can *feel* the threads of light and color. Breathe deeply, take time to notice the many textures of the threads. Each texture represents an aspect of your Self, of your life.

Look again at the colors of the threads. Do certain colors have certain textures for you?

Know that these colors and these textures reflect the threads that are you.

Hot colors—reds, oranges, yellows.

Cool colors—greens, blues, violets.

Silver—gold—platinum—crystal clear—black—and white.

Some rough . . . some soft . . . some silken.

All of these are merging together in the center of the room. The colors dance and reflect in the crystals embedded in the wall of the room.

It is difficult, at first, to tell where the threads arise from. Breathe deeply, for balance amidst this chaos of lights and colors.

Listen carefully, and you will hear the steady rhythm of a great loom. Breathe deeply, and *feel* the sound of the loom.

As you move closer to the sound, this swirling mass of colors and threads steadies. This allows you to see a figure, draped in heavy robes, sitting at the loom, guiding the threads as they come in.

The figure sits forming patterns . . . textures . . . tones.

This is the Weaver of the Wyrd, who takes the threads of experience and weaves the web of the fabric of your life.

As you move closer, you notice that something about the figure seems most familiar to you now. Breathe deeply, and recognize that the weaver is you. This is an image of your higher Self, your Wise Weaver.

Take all the time you need to become reacquainted with this, the highest aspect of yourself, your image of your higher Self.

Listen to the rhythm of the loom, and become that rhythm.

Follow the rhythm as you weave the fabric of your Self.

Take a deep breath and ask the Wise Weaver to show you the threads that are being woven now. What is the pattern of this weaving? Why are these threads being used now? Do you choose to change the pattern, to change the thread?

Perhaps you do not know what you want to change, or how to choose a new pattern. Take a few moments to create a pattern that better reflects what you choose, or what you want.

Perhaps you do not choose to change the pattern of the weaving at this time. Perhaps you choose to accept the wisdom of the Weaver, the wisdom of your higher Self.

Even as you choose, or do not choose, the weaving continues.

The fabric, the web of life, spills out of the loom, cascades around the Wise Weaver, and slowly flows out of the small round room . . . into the mirrors of the middle wall.

There, the web breaks up into a myriad of colors, lights, and textures. These reflect out of the mirrors, returning as threads once again, purer, finer, more resonant and resilient.

Breathe deeply.

Know that you are the web and the Weaver.

Change and grow. Trust the pattern of your weaving.

Step inside, closer to the loom. In your image, put your hands on the loom and feel confident in your ability to weave a fine pattern.

Affirm that you are at one with yourself, and with your higher Self, your Wise Weaver.

Allow all the threads of color and light to spiral around you. Breathe deeply.

Knowing that you may return to this place any time you choose, slowly begin to release the image.

You may wish to return by retracing your steps down the spiral path on the the hill, the tor. Or you may wish to allow the threads of light and color, of your life, to weave themselves around you.

Breathe deeply.

Be centered within your Self.

Return to this time and place, refreshed and energized. Return alert and be peaceful.

The process of divination is best strengthened by learning to stimulate our communication with the highest aspects of ourselves— the Wise Weavers of our lives, of all life. Down through the ages, countless systems have been developed to help us make this connection. Systems of divination designed with specific meanings or keys to help us interpret what we receive are called oracles. Many traditions hold that oracle systems are the primary way to read or divine the energies of life. In this age of blended wisdom, it seems most appropriate to use oracle systems as a foundation to work from.

The increased capacities of our highly evolved brains allow us all to be channels for illuminating wisdom. In ages past, very few had, or utilized, these abilities. These people were often called oracles, or sybils. Today, to give strength and support to our own psychic and intuitive abilities, we can use the ancient wisdom and methods of divination they developed.

It would take volumes to describe all of the many and varied oracle forms. This chapter provides a select few I use and that have been time-tested. Like any time-honored tradition, they connect us to deep roots of wisdom and guide us on our journey on the path of the shaman.

Stone Oracle

This system is based on the concept that your connection with a particular stone or metal at times during your life reflects your need for its specific energy on the direction of your path.

Ancient diviners had splendid collections of stones and metals that they had the querist (the person questing for information) choose from. Today we may make our own collections, using samples found on our journey. It is not necessary to have fabulous, expensive stones and metal samples—rough, uncut forms work quite effectively. It is also possible to simply list the stones and metals. You may have the querist select three or four in order of preference, or just one to use for a specific question.

After a stone (or metal) has been selected, I ask the querist why that one seemed attractive in regard to the issue being discussed. I do this before I interpret. It is amazing how many times the querist already "knows" the property of the stone and has chosen the exact one most needed at that time. I also advise the querist to obtain a similar stone for use as a totem.

Traditional Meanings of Stones and Metals

Stones

Amethyst	Rich stone of love, good fortune, and positive spiritual magick. Can indicate a new spiritual awakening.
Coral	Strong protection against all kinds of personal misfortunes. Can indicate deep emotional turbulence.
Diamond	Strong attraction to power, luxury, and wealth; also attracts friendships. Can indicate a relationship strengthening.
Emerald	Powerful stone for one's present inner vision and psychic abilities. Can indicate negativity being averted.
Garnet	Stone of honesty, truth, purity, and compassionate benevolence. Can indicate overactive selflessness.
Jade	Sacred balancing stone for overall harmony and personal power. Can indicate a need for spiritual serenity.
Lapis Lazuli	Stone of connection to the spiritual realms between the worlds. Can indicate strong spirit guides are present.
Moonstone	Stone of gentle passions and faithful, supportive love. Can indicate a need for greater receptivity.
Opal	Somewhat tricky stone of mystical attunement and perceptive gifts. Can indicate superstitious beliefs.

Ruby	Regal stone of one's present loyalty, faith, and powerful courage. Can indicate the quest of a spiritual warrior.
Sapphire	Powerful stone of synthesis, peace, harmony, and healing. Can indicate a need for magical studies.
Topaz	Active stone of protection, focus, and achievement of goals. Can indicate a need for self-confidence.
Turquoise	Soothing stone of personal peace, Nature wisdom, ideals. Can indicate scattered energies.

Metals

Aluminum	Ingenuity, perception, creativity, and practical materialism. Can indicate a career change.
Copper	Self-healing abilities, inspirational gifts, friendly nature. Can indicate a need for flexibility.
Gold	Active leadership, power in relationships and career. Can indicate too many goals present.
Iron	Protective nature, strong supportive tendencies, willfulness. Can indicate possessiveness and pride.
Lead	Mystical tasks to be achieved, karmic debts to be balanced. Can indicate piety and martyrdom.
Silver	Receptivity, emotionality, psychic gifts, projecting power. Can indicate a secretive nature.
Tin	Friendliness, expansiveness, joyful tasks present, positive outlook. Can indicate an overactive ego.

Tarot

Although it is not known to be a fact, legend holds that the tarot was originally created by a group of magicians who foresaw the dark times of magical suppression. The symbols on the original decks are keys to intricate systems of knowledge and sacred wisdom. Today, many tarot decks have moved away from the ancient symbols to develop interesting blends for a new age.

Whatever tarot deck you choose, be sure that it has a balanced system representing a full scale of magical vibrations. A guide to the deck you have chosen should be as well thought out as the cards themselves. Most esoteric bookstores have decks open to let you get a feel for the cards. If you can't do this at a store, ask for the book that best represents that particular tarot deck, or ask for a deck based on the most traditional tarot systems. There are plenty of books written on the older decks, and these provide a good place to start.

One of the easiest ways to divine with tarot cards is to simply use the major arcana, or the trump cards. Have the querist choose several in order of preference, or one in connection with a specific question. Traditionally, these cards are dealt (in a variety of ways) by the diviner. I feel it is useful at times to let the querist pick cards from a face-up spread. This is especially effective with people who are not familiar with tarot, and helps them develop their own divination skills.

The Major Arcana

0. The Fool — Choice, willingness to learn, flexibility, right decisions made. Can indicate gifts not being used.

1. The Magician — Innovations, experimental attitude, success and expansion. Can indicate scientific detachment.

2. The Priestess — Experiences of great wisdom, intuitive gifts earned. Can indicate spiritual struggles.

3. The Empress — Harmonious life after much hard work and success. Can indicate a need to live in the moment.

4. The Emperor — Strength, leadership, power, bravery, courage, will-power. Can indicate strong career developments.

5. The High Priest — Inspiration, illumination, growth through luck and fate. Can indicate risks taken.

6. The Lovers — Fortunate in love and other relationships, union of mind and spirit. Can indicate an unusual attraction.

7. The Chariot — Positive outcomes in the midst of difficulties, obstacles surmounted. Can indicate a need for self-healing.

8. Justice — Tricks of fate, karma chosen at very high levels of self, adversity. Can indicate negative influences from others.

9. The Hermit — Misunderstood intentions, good motives, unwise actions. Can indicate a need for restraint.

10. The Wheel of Fortune — Chaotic forces from a variety of life experiences. Can indicate karmic choices activating.

11. Strength — Goals met with self-determination, fortunate outcomes despite unfavorable odds. Can indicate unrealistic self-expectations.

12. The Hanged Man — The wisdom of spiritual choices, self-acceptance and flexibility. Can indicate a desire to be unique.

13. Death — Transformation, renewal, change of present path and lifestyle. Can indicate an attraction to crisis.

14. Temperance — Fertility through careful planning, priorities, orderly progress on the path. Can indicate a need for organization.

15. The Devil — Self-criticism, spiritual challenges to self-determination. Can indicate temptations to excesses.

16. The Tower — Unseen forces, supernatural events, rapid purifications. Can indicate a need for a positive philosophy.

17. The Star — Harmony, inspiration, sharing, love, joy, renewal. Can indicate a need to teach or serve.

18. The Moon — Emotional conflicts, lack of real-world connections, illusions. Can indicate an escapist personality.

19. The Sun — Achievements, tasks, practical applied wisdoms bringing success. Can indicate an overactive work ethic.

20. Judgement — Avoidance, resignation to fate, indecision, superstition. Can indicate negative self-expectations.

21. The World — Fortune, satisfaction, abundance, gain balancing loss, hopefulness. Can indicate a windfall or unexpected bonus.

Seneca Cycles of Truth

This ancient Native American system of divining your personal path, or Earth Walk, is far too intricate to discuss in the scope of this book. However, I do want to share a few of the basics, to give you a special method to use and share with others. This system was updated for our use in modern society by Wolf Clan mothers. It relates the gifts and tasks of Truth according to the month of your birth.

It has long been understood by magicians, mystics, and medicine people that the time of your birth has a strong influence on your Earth journey. This system, although it overlaps with astrology in some ways, does not attune to the astral aspects. This system is "not about the stars—but about our earth walk and earth connections."

Here is one wheel of the Seneca Truth cycle.

Draw a wheel with twelve points, like a clock. Beginning with January, at one o'clock, move clockwise around the wheel until you reach the point opposite January—this is July.

A person born in January comes into the Earth Walk with the task of learning Truth. This is accomplished by using one's spiritual gift of birth. For the January person, this gift is the attribute or skill of kinship. So, through kinship with others, with Self, and with Nature and Spirit, a January person may learn Truth. However, the higher task for this individual is to "travel" across to July and assume the task of July, which is to love Truth. Therefore, the January person may, through kinship, learn Truth and love the Truth that is learned.

For a July person, the tasks are reversed. This individual may, through the attribute of love, love Truth and then learn Truth.

Here are the Seneca Truth months and attributes. This is but a fraction of the intricate system developed by the Seneca. I hope it will encourage you to seek more.

January—Learn Truth
with kinship

July—Love Truth
with love

February—Honor Truth
with knowledge

August—Serve Truth
with intuition

March—Accept Truth
with self-determination

September—Live Truth
with will

April—See Truth
with prophecy

October—Work Truth
with creativity

May—Hear Truth
    with harmony

November—Walk Truth
    with magnetism

June—Speak Truth
    with faith

December—Thank Truth
    with healing

You can get a glimpse of the wisdom of this system just by noticing how well the opposites balance one another and serve as supports on both ends of the Earth Walk.

There are many systems that you can explore to divine the energies and to find your way on any magical or shamanic path. Each system represents wisdom that has been collected and preserved to share and to be a key for future wisdom. Regardless of our feelings about the validity or reliability of any given system, it is good to honor the intentions and the efforts of those who worked to construct it, sometimes at great risk. Explore and experience many systems — then construct your own.

Chapter 14

SACRED SYMBOLS

The images we receive in inner visions and shamanic journeys can provide us with a wealth of information to determine and illuminate our progress on our path. This is particularly true of the personal myth or archetypal images of ourselves. These reflect our higher Self and our spiritual connections to past, present, and future. Whether we consider these images to arise from reincarnation memories or from manifestations of our connection to universal thought-forms, they are significant to our Earth Walk.

To divine with these images, we learn to stimulate the flow of visions that give us a sense of another time or place. We learn to recognize that these images are internal to self, rather than external from self. We learn to acquaint ourselves with the many images of our higher Self. When we are continuously aware of our own images, we are better able to help others tap into theirs. We are also better able to recognize whether images that emerge are for us to dance with or for the querist we are "reading" for.

Sometimes these images tap into strong energy patterns that we share with many others. These are the gods, elemental spirits, and devas of Nature, whose patterns are often strong enough to have universal archetypal meanings. Still, it is our personal connection to these that we must interpret to divine their significance in our lives. These are our symbols, regardless of how universally they are recognized.

Some traditions hold that our symbolic images, emerging archetypes, or past-life memories are strictly related to our physical genetic codes. My sense is that we are more likely to have all of the universal

257

codes in our genetic makeup as human beings. We just haven't evolved quite enough to access them freely most of the time.

I do feel that we can use our familiar genetic codes to unlock doors to deeper symbolic realms that we all share. From there we can divine patterns of universal significance. We can begin by allowing these symbolic images of Self to come into our consciousness. When we do, we can relate these therapeutically to persons, relationships, and situations on our present Earth Walk. This is high-level divination that allows us to glimpse the sacred connections we come into this life with. When we learn to view these images with compassion and positive regard, we are able to use them for self-healing, as well as for illumination.

Spiral Connection Image

Breathe deeply, and begin to connect all the parts of your self together. You may wish to stretch out your arms to pull in all parts of your being.

Breathe deeply, and slowly allow all the parts of your self to begin resonating at the same vibrational level, to the same rhythm.

Gently let the rhythm of your self match the rhythm of your heartbeat. Now, breathe an especially long, slow breath and slow your rhythm.

You may wish to hum, deeply and slowly, in order to pace your own rhythm.

Aum . . . aum . . . aum . . . mmm . . . mmm . . . mmm.

Now give yourself permission to go deeper than before—more relaxed, more open, more receptive to your self.

Open all the channels of your senses.

Breathe deeply, and come into the present moment of awareness with your senses.

Allow yourself to hear more distinctly, see more clearly, touch, taste, and smell more sensitively.

Breathe deeply and consider, for just a moment, each of your senses.

Take all the time you need, then let it go.

It is time to step into an image of going to the movies.

This time the movies are somewhat different. Even more than 3-D, these movies are experiential.

You will experience these movies, yet always with the same detachment you have while watching a movie in a theater.

Breathe deeply, and settle yourself in to enjoy your movies.

Know that this is your image, your movie.

You are, at the same time, both connected to and detached from what you image in your movie.

It is a personal reflection of your life drama.

It is a drama played out on the screen of your own mind, a screen with no boundaries of time and space.

A few of your movies may seem to reflect another time or space— some that you have experienced in your personal consciousness; some at another deeper level of consciousness, another life.

Breathe deeply, and know that however these images may come to you, they have significance for you now—whether they are in this life or another.

Breathe gently . . . detach, and observe the movies of your lives.

Begin by creating an image of a life of high resonance and power.

Take all the time you need to let the images of this life emerge.

Open all your senses to experience this life of power.

Breathe deeply, and know that you may come from this place of power within yourself when you need this power.

Acknowledge your right to this life of power and high resonance.

Feel the depth of this life of power *well used,* the partner of high resonance. Feel the energy of this high vibration.

Feel the energy of the power of your Self.

Breathe deeply. Take all the time you need to experience this life of power.

Then let it go.

Now, having energized your self and your image with a life of high resonance and power, begin to let images of other lives emerge.

Breathe slowly and gently.

Let the images come and go as they will.

Allow the images of other lives to flow through you onto the screen of your mind.

Detach and observe the changing images on the screen.

As you watch the changing images, notice that you may experience parts of them with detachment.

Breathe deeply and observe your images.

As the images change, lives change in image.

Experience the changing images of your lives. Experience that some are lives of less struggle. Some lives are whimsical and joy-filled. Some flooded with sadness.

Breathe deeply and let them flow through you so that you may observe them, connected yet detached.

Begin to notice patterns of similarity in your images. Do some of your movies seem like remakes of others? Are some of your movies sequels to each other?

Breathe gently and notice the thread of challenge running through these images.

Notice times, places, styles, and types of people in your images.

Know that whatever emerges for you has significance for you now.

Now I want you to take another especially long, slow breath.

Slow the pace of your images and slow the pace of your personal rhythm.

Allow yourself to go deeper into your own personal life image, your magick movie.

Regardless of the time and place that may emerge, this life has meaning for you at this time.

Breathe deeply, and allow an image of your Self to emerge.

Take all the time you need to experience this image fully.

Then ask yourself, Why has this image appeared now? What does it have to do with my present life at this time? Slow your pace to receive an answer.

Perhaps you will observe another image that connects with this life.

Perhaps you will get a sense of your life's message to your self.

Are you listening to your life's message?

Are you listening to your Self?

Breathe deeply and observe an image of your life now.

You may "rewind" to observe your past.

You may wish to watch your present-life movie.

You may even wish to fast-forward to a future life.

Time is an eternal present, some say. The now.

Detach and observe the images of your life without the boundaries of time and space.

Breathe deeply. Spend a few more moments letting images flow and project them onto your mind screen.

Now slowly breathe again.

Let the images on your screen fade gradually, leaving just the emptiness of the screen. Know that you may choose what to project next onto your screen.

Be open to your choices.

Allow the experience of other-life images to reveal your choices to you now.

Breathe deeply and begin to write a movie about your self.

Know that when you are ready, you will project your own movie, your own image, your own choices.

Where will the setting of your new movie be?

Who will be the cast?

What will be the lessons?

Allow these questions to move to the back of your mind, to guide you in your own higher choice.

Know that you may return to observe your movies, be they movies of the past, the present, or the future.

These are your personal creations, your personal myths.

Breathe deeply. Knowing that you may observe these images whenever you need to, slowly allow all the images to fade.

Return to your present time and place, renewed and energized.

Come into the moment and be peaceful.

Bringing our divination work somewhat closer to our Earth Walk is useful for daily awareness and divination. Our totem helpers and our shamanic activities can provide us with an ongoing attunement to the flow and patterns of energies around us. We can do this by paying close attention to the patterns of new totems appearing or reappearing in our lives.

A kettle (or flock) of hawks flew in formation, two by two, over a house we had just moved into. I puzzled over this for a long time until I realized this signified the beginning of a very specific part of my shamanic journey. It marked the time that I began to sharpen my aim to focus on creating this book, though I didn't know it at the time.

A long-time relationship had to change significantly in order for us both to grow. I placed a bloodstone that signified my friend in my garden, at the base of an ivy-covered wall. When the ivy died I was horrified, for my intention had not been negative. I knew that ivy signified friendship, so I was concerned that the relationship would not survive.

I remembered that death is transformation and took heart from that. When I looked for the bloodstone to cleanse and recharge it, it was nowhere to be found. Almost a year later, as I prepared to move to my home state, I found the bloodstone again, just where I had left it originally. This told me that transformation can bring renewal and redefinitions to our life dances.

My owls, which had become quite tired from extensive academic work, reappeared just before I began intensive work with a Native American medicine teacher whose traditions hold owls as negative symbols. My owls kept me clear in my own philosophy as I shared wisdom with another. They taught me to hold what is sacred to me, regardless of another's opinions.

Two owls appeared one afternoon on the roof of my house just as major hurricane was forming in the Gulf of Mexico. They circled the house, flying over the tops of certain trees, and then flew off in the direction of a nearby town. My sense was that the storm would come but would not damage us severely. Three days later, the eye of the hurricane passed over the town that the owls had flown toward, not far at all from our house. Each of the trees the owls had flown over was clipped at the top by a tornado that jumped from the hurricane and circled our house.

A large piece of green quartz developed a brown line directly across its center as I worked on my graduate school project. My project represented a break with strict academic traditions to do my heartfelt work. I saw this line as a symbol of growth, much like the rings of bark on a tree.

Several of my crystal clusters and points split just as I was breaking from a group whose work I admired but whose hierarchical organization and methods I opposed. After several journeys, I saw these splits as symbolic of the changes and the energy release we must undergo in order to find personal synthesis.

When I was finally coming to terms with the Red Ray energies of my makeup, a red candle my healing catalyst friend and I had lit burned with a flame eight to ten inches straight in the air. As I reached out carefully to get a feel for the height, the flame shot up toward my hand. This symbolized to me the validity of my connection to the Red energies.

At a time when I needed to focus on my mind and body energies, I was completely unable to get a lavender or purple (spiritual energy) candle to light.

A small white candle I had lit for an extremely ill friend produced black rolling clouds of smoke the entire time it burned. Not wanting to put negative energies to the situation, I sent healing energies to my friend. Still, when my friend crossed over into Spirit, I was grateful that I had been given the sign that helped me prepare for the loss.

A candle lit when a friend far away was giving birth, in conditions that concerned us all, flamed and torched brightly for several minutes. Later we discovered that this was the exact time of the birth. Still later, a photograph taken of my friend and her new daughter showed a distinct column of white light shining down on them both in the hospital bed.

During the time I was considering the wisdom of returning to my home state of Georgia, a fox in an heirloom painting "jumped" as I walked by. Since the fox was my first totem animal as a child, I knew to begin preparing for the emotional good-byes of a move. Since I have been in Georgia, fox totems have presented themselves to me continuously. They have come welcoming me and helping me reconnect to my deepest Nature roots. A tiny figure of a red fox, smiling and looking upward with great expectation and joy, sat on my desk during the final preparations of this book.

A very bedraggled, tired hawk feather showed up in a box of my books, giving me the strength of humor in a time of great transition. Worn, bedraggled or not—it was still a hawk. It symbolized the supporting energies of my totem on my path.

Hematite began to show up from all directions at a time when I was anemic, but didn't know it. The properties of hematite encouraged me to divine the need for more iron in my diet, as well as to pull from my Earth connections.

A tiny baby rabbit dropped by an owl in my back yard symbolized my need to feed or balance my many predatory totem animal energies.

A deep purple flower's appearance out of season signaled a time of deepening spirituality. After that flower appeared, I found I was once again able to light purple spiritual candles.

The shaman walks connected to the earth, always aware of the messages in the environment. I shared a number of my personal symbolic messages so that you can become more aware of your own. We often think of totems as just being supporting energies reflective of our strengths. Totems can be great diviners and illuminators. To use them for this, you must combine their traditional or oracle meanings with your own intuitive connections to them.

Divination is an ongoing process for the shaman, as well as a set, ceremonial journey. Here are a few forms of divination that are easily adapted for your use.

Sand Symbols

Take a wooden tray, a rectangular plastic storing container, or a baking pan. Fill with about two inches of sand (or salt, if need be). You will need a long pencil or wooden stick. (I use a chopstick.) Seat yourself, with writing tool poised and ready. If you can't resist looking at the sand, tie a bandana around your eyes. Concentrate on your question, or the querist's issue, and focus your energies. When you feel the need to write, let the tool make free marks in the sand.

When you feel you are finished, look carefully at what has been drawn or written. You may find that letters have formed, giving you clues to names or places in regard to the question. Generally, this is an intuitive exercise that opens you to illumination in inner vision. However, some marks have traditional meanings that can be guidelines:

A circle indicates union, completions, renewal, and growth.

A long line indicates travel or journey, either physical or spiritual.

A triangle indicates strength in practical matters, such as career.

A cross indicates a trial or obstacle to overcome.

An X indicates a love relationship; clear crosses show happy outcomes.

Time can be gauged by the position of the mark, symbol, or letter. By counting from left to right, you can divide the tray into twelve months at the most, and days at the least. I find this method very useful as a timetable divination.

Sand divination is wonderful when done at the beach, where the negative ions give a restful, clear-minded awareness. As always, the querist's connection to whatever marks are made takes priority over all other meanings.

Scribble Symbols

This form of divination is similar to automatic writing techniques, but is less linear and more conducive to free-flowing images.

Take large sheets of paper, such as newsprint or freezer paper. Select crayons, pastel chalks, markers in the eight "primary school" colors: red, yellow, blue, green, orange, purple, brown, and black. I prefer crayons or chalk to markers, because they show differences in the pressure used in drawing, and because they show blends better. Use what you like best.

Jumble the colors. Darken the room and close your eyes, or blindfold yourself. Sit in front of the paper and concentrate on your issue or question. When you are ready, grab a color (unknown to you—on this level) and draw. Keep changing colors and drawing until you feel you are done. Pay attention to images that flow through your inner vision, but don't focus on these. Focus on the experience of drawing. Feel the flow of energies move through you onto the paper.

When you feel finished, take time to remind yourself of the original question or issue. Sometimes illuminative energies sweep things out of our heads. Then take the drawing to a place with good light and study it carefully. It's often helpful to tape your thoughts or make notes of your reactions to the patterns and the colors you chose unseen. This divination method is amazingly effective for bringing up subconscious issues and information for your journey. It also releases many creative inhibitions and psychic blocks.

This may be adapted for use with people you are working with. However, I do advise that you darken the room instead of asking them to wear blindfolds. Using divination methods to work with people should create trust—not challenge it.

Water Symbols

Another effective divination method is to drip small amounts of liquid paints or food colorings (messy—be careful) into a bowl of water. The patterns formed can give clues to illuminate you. The blend of colors can represent the blending of Ray energies and their attributes in your life. If the colors seem static to you, stir very gently with a toothpick or pencil point and study what changes.

Hot candle wax dripped in a bowl of quite cold water can create amazingly symbolic shapes.

Years ago I did this for a woman I barely knew. An unmistakable figure of a baby formed immediately. The woman was very hesitant to discuss this, as her "question" concerned a career change.

We dropped wax in the water again, and it formed a shape somewhere between a heart and an egg. I suggested that she was not ready for a decision and that she needed to spend time finding out what she really wanted.

A few days later, she called to tell me that she had reached a decision. She apologized for not being open enough to tell me what her real question was—a common occurrence in divination. She was pregnant and had been considering an abortion or adoption. After the figure of the baby and the heart-shaped egg appeared, she felt strongly that this baby was meant to be hers. It was!

When people scoff at "silly" divination methods, I often share that story. It usually shuts them up.

Another method, which is simple and appeals to the somewhat less convinced, linear types, is divination with dice. This honestly makes me see spots; however, many I've done this with swear by it.

Dice Divination

You will need three dice. Some people throw these all at once; some individually. I like to throw them together. Then I read the meaning of the numerical total, and then each die individually. It's also useful to see if the dice fall close together or far apart. This can indicate a length of time or a strength of energy connection to the meanings.

1   The current situation of the reader
2   Slight influence of others
3   Surprising developments

4   Obstacles or unfavorable events
5   A time to make magical requests
6   Transformtion and change
7   A need for caution in your career
8   Major influence of others
9   A union or relationship
10   Renewal or rebirth, beginnings
11   A relationship drifting apart
12   Messages of joy or success
13   Karmic trials to endure
14   Support from friends or family
15   Stay centered and protected at this time
16   A pleasant journey, either physical or spiritual
17   Fate changes your plans, higher choice
18   Success in your life can be expected

Divination methods are useful ways to strengthen your connection to the energies around us all. It's best to try many to find the right fit. The best ingredients to use for divination are intuition, inner vision, self-acceptance, compassion, and *humor*.

Sometimes all divination methods seem to bog down in communication. In that case, just throw your fate to the winds and flip a coin—or maybe two out of three, three out of five? Sometimes we just have to wait things out a bit and try later.

Chapter 15

SHAMANIC MAPS

Divination is a multi-sensory, multi-leveled function. When we attempt to divine the energies around us, we use the sharpest aspects of our perceptive skills in a focused combination. This combined effort, or gestalt, of our abilities is often called our sixth sense. Many times we want to jump right in to activate our sixth sense without spending time on our basic physical five. If we do take the time to stimulate all our senses, our divination skills increase beyond measure.

Many systems of divination are based on ancient symbols. Each of these symbols is a map in concentrated form. To read such maps, we must be open to receive input from all of our sensory channels. Some people consider the channels we use for divination to be extrasensory or outside of ourselves somehow. I prefer to define extrasensory as *more* sensory, as using the deeper aspects of our abilities. If we start to consider abilities as being external to us, we may block the connections we have. Divination and illumination happen at the Source level, where we are all connected. All keys in divination, whether universally symbolic or personally talismanic, are there to help us reach that level of Source that is shared by all.

Here is an image which may help you find and develop your sensory keys to illumination and intuition.

Talisman of Knowing

Imagine yourself in the midst of a great storm.

Feel the energy of the storm flowing through you.

Take a deep breath, and allow the storm energy to clear away mists and fog in your mind. Allow the storm to sweep away those things that prevent clear knowing and clear seeing.

Breathe deeply and absorb the full energy of the storm. Feel how it refreshes you, recharges you, replenishes you, and stimulates every cell of your being.

Allow the storm energy to open new pathways through your self.

Let the energy of the storm soften. Breathe deeply as the storm becomes gentle healing rain. Experience the rain as it replenishes your spirit. Let the freshness of the rain bring you focus. Breathe deeply and become aware of the now.

Come into the present moment.

Be the rain.

Be the gentle manifestation of storm energy.

Breathe deeply and listen for the sound of the rain as it falls on the earth. Follow the rain into the ground.

Feel the changes as you become aware of being beneath the ground. Listen to the muffled sounds above you. Notice the quiet around you.

Feel yourself moving slowly in the darkness and warmth beneath the earth. Notice how the earth supports you, making you feel comfortable and secure.

Breathe deeply. In your image, notice the roots of a great magical tree, ageless and wise.

Feel the energy of the roots.

Feel the connection of the earth to the roots, of the earth to the tree. Reach out and touch the roots and experience their energy.

Breathe deeply and absorb the nurturing energy around you.

In your image, begin to move hand over hand up the roots. Notice how the roots gradually become larger, stronger, with more power.

Feel the energy change as you move up the roots, closer to the center.

Notice a dark, warm, active energy emerge.

Feel the richness and the smell of the earth. Move again up the roots. Continue hand over hand until at last you find the place where two giant roots originate in the trunk of the tree. Breathe deeply and feel the energy of this place.

Look carefully where the two roots meet. As your eyes become accustomed to the dimness of the light, you notice a small wooden door just between the roots of the tree. Breathe deeply to energize your image. Make it real.

Look carefully at the door. You can see symbols carved in the wood of the door. Some of these symbols are mysterious. Some of them are familiar. Move closer to the door. Notice a small silver plaque in the middle of the door. Engraved on the plaque are large letters that read CHOOSE TO KNOW; and smaller letters that read CHOOSE A SYMBOL.

Breathe deeply and take time to examine all the symbols on the door. Reach out and touch the shape of the carvings if you choose to. Which of these symbols speaks most clearly to you? Which symbol stimulates you most deeply at this time? Take all the time you need and choose your one personal symbol.

When you have chosen one symbol, breathe deeply and focus on the image. Reach out in your image and touch your chosen symbol as you find it on the door.

Touch it, feel its shape with your fingers. Connect with your symbol, make it your own.

Place the palm of your hand on your chosen symbol.

Feel the energy of the symbol move from the door into the palm of your hand. Move your hand away and notice that the symbol has disappeared from the door.

Look at the palm of your hand and find that the symbol has reappeared there, perfect, highly charged, visible only to you.

Your chosen symbol has become your Talisman of Knowing.

Breathe deeply and absorb all the energy you need for this image.

Notice energy begin to pulsate throughout your body. Be with it.

Let it heal you and replenish you.

Place the palm of your hand with the symbol in the center of your chest. Allow the symbol to connect with your heart. With compassion, love, and trust, open your heart to your self and others.

Allow your connection with your heart to help you meet your inner self. This is your guide through feeling. Feel trust in your self to learn without judgement, but with compassion.

Celebrate inner knowing. Feel how it empowers and energizes you. Trust your Self. Celebrate this trust.

Breathe deeply and move your palm slowly upward over your chest . . . your neck . . . your chin . . . and your face. Let it come to rest on the middle of your forehead.

Breathe deeply and connect with the energy of your mind.

Connect with this center of intuition. This is your point of synthesis; this is the mystical third eye.

Note the energy difference of this point of your mind. It is electric and rapid fire. Feel the knowledge of this center as it expands around you . . . out beyond time . . . beyond space.

Use the point of your mind to tap into Universal Consciousness.

Use the point of your heart to tap into Universal Love.

Use them together to be Universal Energy.

Be with this energy. Give yourself permission to be this energy.

Celebrate the connection with heart and mind. Know your heart. Know your mind. Breathe deeply to energize.

Refocus on your image. You are standing in front of the carved door between the two roots of the great magical tree. In the palm of your hand is the symbol that is your Talisman of Knowing. You have touched your palm to your chest and your forehead.

As you move your palm from your forehead, you notice the door begin to open slowly. As it opens it reveals a spiral staircase carved out inside of the tree. There are seven steps.

Each of the steps is a different color: Red—Orange—Yellow—Green—Blue—Violet—Indigo.

Look to the top of the stairs and find yet another door. Only one symbol is carved on this door at the top of the stairs. Breathe to focus. Discover that the one symbol on the door is your personal symbol, your Talisman of Knowing.

Breathe deeply and slowly climb the steps Red—Orange—Yellow. Step carefully onto the Green step and absorb this color of the heart.

Move up to the Blue and the Violet. Come to rest on the top step of this staircase. The color of the seventh step is deep Indigo, the color of synthesis. Feel the energy of All-Knowing. Breathe deeply and be Universal Energy.

Breathe to focus your image, and notice a small plaque on the door under the symbol. The plaque is engraved with the words SENSORY OPERATIONS.

Fit the symbol on the palm of your hand onto the symbol carved in the door above the plaque. Breathe deeply and feel the energies connect. Point to point, fitted like a key in a lock.

The door swings open slowly to reveal a large circular room.

As you stand at the door looking into the room, you can see five large control panels. Each control panel has a viewing screen.

Looking down, you can see a pattern painted on the floor of the room. You can see that it is a five-pointed star closely surrounded by a circle that touches each point of the star.

A control panel and screen is located at each point of the star.

Breathe deeply and step into the room. Feel the energy moving around you. Go ahead and step into the center of the star . . . into the center of the circle.

From here you can see that a word is written inside each point of the star. The words are SEE, HEAR, TOUCH, TASTE, SMELL.

Turn slowly from point to point. As you do so, you will notice there are words written on the circle around the star. These words are ALL SENSES, ALL KNOWING, ALL CARING.

Breathe deeply to energize. Image yourself in the center of intuition . . . of knowledge . . . of compassion.

As you stand there, centered in your knowing, begin to watch as each screen projects itself onto you . . . through you.

These are the screen projections of your own senses.

Through the use of these senses, you are able to be in the world . . . with the world . . . to be the world.

Give yourself permission to allow the projections of each of these senses to empower your ability to know, to stimulate your intuition.

Breathe deeply, and step into the point of the star marked with the word SEE.

As you move closer to the control panel, you will see a large magick button marked with your personal Talisman of Knowing.

Take a deep breath for power and fit the palm of your hand on that button. As you press this button, a myriad of lights and patterns dance across the screen, projecting power into your sense of sight.

Give yourself permission to accept a better sense of knowing and intuition through *seeing*.

Affirm the clarity of your new vision, unlimited by judgement, supported by your heart.

Taking your time, create your own images. Move from panel to panel, in whatever order you choose . . . until you have been at each of the five panels and screens of sight, hearing, taste, touch, and smell.

As you move from point to point, give yourself permission to accept a greater skill in each of these senses.

Affirm and celebrate that these senses are supported by the trust that you have in your own inner knowing.

Trust in your self to be open and accepting of the knowledge that you receive through your senses.

Be intuitive, without judgement, with compassion.

Breathe deeply and take time to be with each of your five primary senses.

Know that each time you press the magick button on the panel, you will deepen your skill and ability in that sense.

As you finish moving from point to point, sense to sense, know that whenever you need more information, more intuition about a person or a situation in your life, all you need to do is project the image of that person or that situation onto the sensory screen of your choice, or onto all the screens together.

Breathe again very deeply, and step into the center of the star.

Step into the center of the circle.

Take all the time you need to turn about slowly in a complete circle. As you turn, breathe deeply and pull in the energy of each of the five senses.

Now continue to turn slowly; feel the energy change as all of the senses circle together.

Their dance lights up all of the screens at once.

Notice how the lights and energy swirl around you, blending and growing. Feel the power of all your senses working together.

This is the Spirit of Intuition, the All-Knowing. This is what is sometimes called the sixth sense.

Allow the energy to move through you and around you. Let the energy build into a great storm of activity and energy.

Breathe deeply and look at the symbol in the palm of your hand. This is your Talisman of Knowing. It will remain with you as long as you want it to.

Place the palm of your hand on your chest and on your forehead once more. Affirm the unity of heart and mind in knowing.

Breathe deeply to energize your image. Allow the storm of energy with which you began to swirl around you. Feel yourself lifted gently up from the star in the circle and out of the room. Up and out through the trunk of the tree . . . onto the limbs . . . find yourself resting in the branches.

Feel yourself gently rocked by the wind as you rest in the cradle of the branches.

When you are ready, breathe deeply and release yourself upwards to the sky. Be the sky . . . be the energy . . . be the knowing . . . be the storm.

Take all the time you need and absorb what you need from the storm of energy and knowing. When you are ready, let the storm subside.

As the storm subsides, the rains begin.

Be the rain, gentle, healing, renewing rain.

Be the rain and return to the earth.

Knowing that you may return to this image whenever you choose, return now to your present place and time.

Come into the moment. Be aware of yourself.

Be your own Talisman of Knowing.

Down through the ages, shamans have been mapmakers. The Navaho sand painters, the Nordic Runemals, and the sorcerers with their astrolabs all sought ways to chart the wheels of the universe. They developed systems using wisdoms and symbols that had become sacred to their peoples. Using these traditional symbols, the shamans were able to map energies, growth cycles, and patterns of life for themselves and the people they served. At the same time, the people of folk magick devised simple systems to examine the signs and journeys of their own lives.

Many of these systems, whether elaborate or simple forms, were based on using a circle or wheel to represent the universe and the cycles of life. The diviners often cast stones or markers with runic symbols on them into the circle. The pattern these stones formed and the position in which they landed gave symbolic and intuitive information to the diviner. Sometimes objects were spun in the circle to point out the answer to questions. Other diviners used pendulums made from small weights, needles, or crystals suspended by string or chains. These pendulums swung in different directions to indicate a response to the question. All of these methods, as with many others, were based on the concept that the answer, and the question, were part of a pattern set by the fates. Once in a while the fates would share a few illuminating clues to enable the querist to proceed a bit less blindly through life.

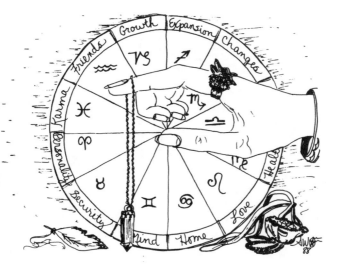

At this point in our evolution, we are somewhat more sophisticated about our relationship to the fates of our lives. We know that much of what we encounter on our path comes to us from aspects of our higher Self—*that we can reach and communicate with.*

Sometimes it seems that our life decisions are made at levels of Self we are not yet able to reach. Still, we never know what we can grasp if we don't reach out.

Today we can view divination as a sacred form of communication with our higher Self. We create pathways and channels to the levels of illumination within. Although we may not always reach the levels we seek, we map the way for our next attempts. Each journey we make to access wisdom from Source strengthens our abilities to reach higher and expand our vision. The growth we gain benefits and illuminates not only ourselves but others as well. The increased ability of one person increases the abilities of all by divining and opening still another channel to wisdom.

This chapter was designed to provide you with some methods to blend wisdoms and create your own shamanic maps. A few basic circles or wheels have been included along with suggestions on how to use them effectively. After you have worked with these wheels and divination systems, you may be encouraged to map a few of your own.

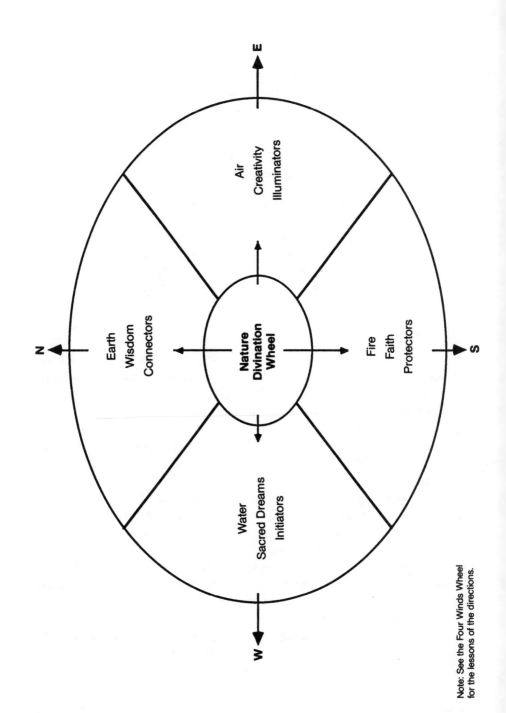

E

Air
Creativity
Illuminators

N ←

Earth
Wisdom
Connectors

**Nature
Divination
Wheel**

Fire
Faith
Protectors

→ S

Water
Sacred Dreams
Initiators

W

Note: See the Four Winds Wheel
for the lessons of the directions.

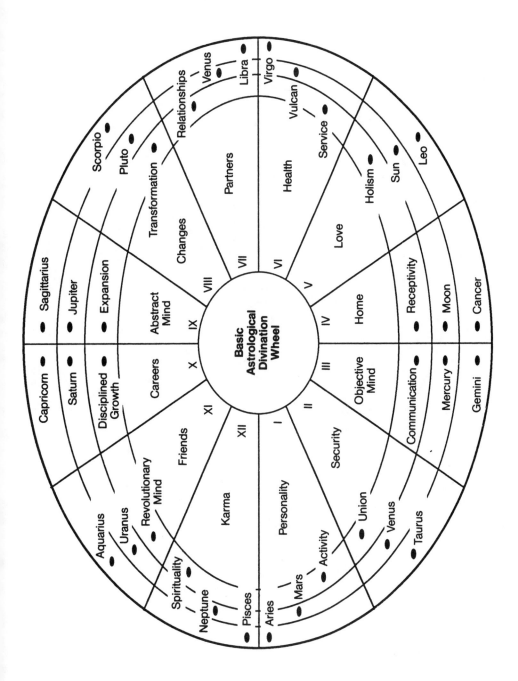

Basic Astrological Divination Wheel

Witches' Divination Wheel

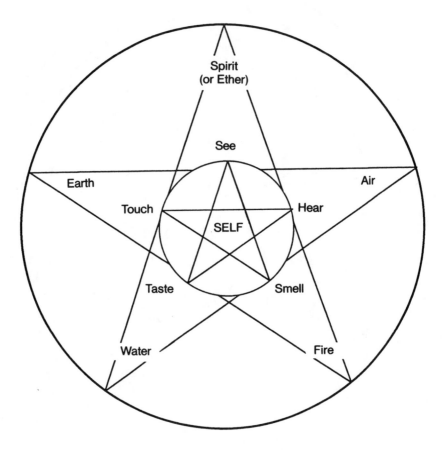

Note: Learn the elemental
attributes for divination.

Basic Wheels

Nature Wheel	Includes the four cardinal directions and their elements and attributes as they reflect in our lives
Astrological Wheel	Shows the primary attributes of the signs and the houses
Witches' Wheel	Presents the pentagram wheel with significant deity energies and the elements and aspects of Self

Here are some suggestions for divining with basic wheels such as those described.

1. Use a commercial set of runes, or runes you have painted on stones. Focus on the question. When you have focused clearly, cast the runes on your wheel. Read by combining the traditional runic meanings, your intuitive sense of the pattern, and their positions on the wheel.

2. Draw a basic wheel in the sand or on the ground. Use plain shells or stones to cast onto the wheel. Read by combining the positions in which they fall and your intuitive sense of the pattern they form.

3. Place three or four small feathers in the center of a wheel. Leave in a closed room overnight. In the morning, read the patterns they have formed. This is quite subtle, so draw a small wheel.

4. Spin a crystal point in the center of a wheel and know that the position pointed out has extra significance for you, as crystals are amplifiers.

5. Suspend a feather on a string above a circle. Tie in place or hold. (I advise you to tie it first.) Watch for feather movements in response to your questions.

6. Suspend a crystal (double-terminated crystals have extra connections here) by a thread or a thin silver chain. Hold over your

wheel and watch for movements that indicate direction.

7. Roll dream stones, such as Herkimer diamonds and fluorites, onto a wheel. Use the pattern, the positions, and the vibrations of the stones to divine the answers.

8. Tie mandrake root to a string and use for a pendulum. It's fairly magnetic and responds to energy vibrations very well.

9. Mugwort in a tiny pouch is a good pendulum.

10. Lodestone is also a good magnetic tool for a pendulum.

11. Silver chains thrown onto a circle can be read by examining their pattern and their connection to other aspects on the wheel. Silver is very receptive to spiritual questions. I use a woven silver chain as a circle in which to cast.

12. Gold rings are excellent to use either suspended as a pendulum or spun in the center of the circle. The active nature of gold lends itself to questions about our Earth Walk activities and relationships.

If you really wish to cast on a wheel effectively, I suggest that you make your own set of casting stones. The basis for this set may come from any system you feel comfortable with; your stones may represent any symbols or energy connections you choose. These stones can be cast on a specific wheel, on a plain circle, or just scattered on the ground.

Diviners who are extremely experienced use little more than a circle or a cloth marked with the cardinal points and a center. Their familiarity with their own systems allows them to rely on a practical combination of traditional meanings and intuitive illumination.

I still like to cast my stones on a well-worn wheel that has many aspects and attributes clearly marked. I find that it supports my intuitive hunches and provides a foundation from which to start the reading. Also, this keeps me sharp for the time I cast with no charts or "props." When I am casting for someone else, I find that the chart provides a great communication tool for the reading. It's a kind of cosmic conversation piece!

The system I used to create my casting stones is based on Western astrological wisdom. My stones have planetary, elemental, and psycho-philosophical attributes assigned to them. Whenever possible, I use a stone, shell, root, or small talismanic symbol or fetish that best reflects the aspect I intend.

I have cast my stones on many different wheels, with interestingly similar results. I began with the basic astrological wheel, which is still my admitted favorite. It's good to have your casting stones and your wheels be fairly compatible. Still, it's difficult to go wrong with a basic Nature wheel.

As a psychotherapist, I naturally have an abundance of psychological and philosophical attributes represented in my casting stones. It's an occupational hazard of ours to split hairs from time to time. I advise you to begin with a very basic set of stones. As you work with this system, you will almost certainly want to add little extras to make this your personal casting set. Tiny figures and objects from Nature also make good casting "stones," but let's start with just the stones themselves.

Here is a traditional casting stone set to get you started. These are just suggestions. After this, I will tell you about my own set to give you some further ideas.

Casting Stones • Traditional Set and Meanings

Planets

Sun	Success, fame, luck, monetary gain, health, self-confidence.
	Stones used: topaz, amber, tiger-eye, sunstone, diamond.
Moon	Fertility, receptivity, home, children, psychic powers, intuition.
	Stones used: pearl, mother-of-pearl, abalone, moonstone, opal, crystals.
Mars	Victory, energy, ambition, goals, upheaval, strife, arguments.
	Stones used: jasper, ruby, garnet.
Mercury	Intellect, communications, business awareness, messages, perception.
	Stones used: agates, onyx, carnelian, citrine, fluorite, selenite.

Jupiter	Health, love, expansion, success, money, business growth, fame.
	Stones used: lapis lazuli, amethyst, turquoise, sapphire, azurite.
Venus	Friendship, unions, beauty, sensuality, artistic creations.
	Stones used: malachite, jade, peridot, aventurine, emerald.
Saturn	Karmic debts, magical knowledge, self-discipline, sacred wisdom.
	Stones used: obsidian, agates, onyx, lodestone, hematite, jet.
Neptune	Psychic communication, imagery, journeys into inner vision, illusion.
	Stones used: coral, shells, pearls, amber, beach stones.
Uranus	Deep shamanic journeys, magick, mental expansion.
	Stones used: blue lace agate, amethyst, royal azule, alexandrite.
Pluto	Sensuality, lust, deep karmic personal journeys, transformation.
	Stones used: black jade, obsidian, lava (and the metals pyrite and gold).

Elements

Air	East, beginnings, illumination, creativity, intellectual growth.
	Stones used: crystals, yellow fluorite, amethyst, alexandrite, yellow or blue stones, rainbow stones.
Fire	South, nurturance, protection, purification, vitality, self-knowledge, power.

Stones used: carnelian, jasper, ruby, rhodo-chrosite, agates, lava.

| Water | West, self-healing, inner vision, security, emotions, journeys. |

Stones used: blue topaz, aquamarine, blue fluorite, lapis, sodalite.

| Earth | North, strength, practical wisdom, stability, magick, symbols, teaching. |

Stones used: azurite, amethyst, royal azule, tourmaline, rutile or tourmalinated quartz.

Attributes

Love	Ruby, carnelian, rhodonite
Health	Selenite, quartz crystal, chalcedony
Home	Moonstone, granite, marble
Goals	Jasper, citrine, crystal points
Magick	Amethyst, Herkimer diamond
Obstacles	Coral, lava, flint, gravel, onyx

Also, a stone is used to represent the querist or the question itself. I keep a jar of tumbled agates for this purpose. I give the querist the "question stone" so that he can use it as a personal totem and further divine his own answers.

When the stones are cast, pay attention to the overall pattern. And examine this from several points of view. Next, consider the density of the group of stones. They can indicate blocks or slow progress. Stones that are too scattered can indicate a lack of personal balance. The stones that fall closest to the center indicate a more immediate effect and personal connection. Stones that fall out of the circle are not relevant to the issue. Stones on the edge may just be coming into play, or leaving.

Here is a description of my stones, which may help you put together a collection of your own:

Planets

| Sun | Orange carnelian |

Moon	Moonstone and a black jade crescent
Mars	Red jasper
Mercury	Yellow-banded agate
Jupiter	Green chalcedony
Venus	Pink agate
Saturn	Brown-banded agate
Neptune	Lapis lazuli with a lot of white
Uranus	Lavender amethyst
Pluto	Black jade with white triangle
Earth	Blue-green amazonite

Elements

Air	Quartz crystal
Fire	Orange-banded agate
Water	Sodalite
Earth	Azurite with malachite inclusions

Attributes

Passion	Heart-shaped jasper
Happiness	Clear orange agate
Metaphysics	Dark amethyst
Healing	Green agate
Hidden Fire	Rough opal
Inner Vision	Blue fluorite
Money	Aventurine
Wealth	Rough emerald
Spells, Magick	Rough moonstone
Power	Six-sided crystal point
Health	White chalcedony

Serenity	Lapis lazuli
Enthusiasm	Turquoise
Obstacles	A rock
Banishing	Hematite with a point
Limitations	Cube-shaped jet

Fetish Extras

Helping Spirit	Tiny coral owl
Trickster	Tiny clay laughing head
Spiritual/Psychic	Tiny double-terminated crystal
Connections	Short length of chain made of silver links
Illusions	Red artificial ruby
Mirror	Convex silver charm
Visions	Blue cat's-eye marble
Nature Wisom	Mandrake root
Oriental Wisdom	Small Buddha
Western Wisdom	Small scarab
Eastern Wisdom	Tiny brass bell
Goddess	Small nautilus-like shell
God/Consort	Tiny bit of horn

As you work with casting stones, you may be surprised to find that they become more like totems. This marks a deeper level of connection for you to channel through energies of illumination and divination. Making a collection of casting stones requires the same skills and attitude with which you make your many other medicines.

Chapter 16

SHAMANIC SENSING

I cannot sleep. The combination of too much sun and too much humidity makes it impossible for me to get comfortable. The air conditioner struggles valiantly, but it is overwhelmed by a Texas August.

I remember that a friend of mine swears by smooth, tumbled amethyst rubbed gently on the face to relieve headache and sinus pressure. I decide to try it for this late-summer malaise and insomnia.

I get an image in my inner vision of one particularly nice piece of tumbled amethyst that I bought in Colorado. If nothing else, just the image of those cool Rocky Mountains will help. I am not patient with insomnia.

I move quietly in the darkness so as not to wake my husband. He's fairly open to what I do, all in all. Yet, he isn't likely to be pleased at being awakened at three in the morning by my looking for a rock to rub on my face.

I find the narrow wooden tray on the windowsill and run my fingers over the compartments until I find the last one on the right—tumbled and rough amethyst. Silently applauding my great filing system, I climb back into bed, stone in hand.

I relax myself as much as possible. I gently place the stone where I need it most—in the middle of my forehead, on my third eye. I breathe deeply and try to focus on snowy peaks and wildflowers in mountain meadows. Colorado is so healing. The images are slow in coming, so I decide to stop visualizing and simply focus on the feel of the stone.

Suddenly, a flash of heat races up my spine. Light seems to burst out through my forehead. My mind races with images of ancient, multi-armed Hindu deities. I smell the heaviness of centuries of incenses. I hear the sound of a slow, deep hum and chant. I feel the stone's vibration moving through all the levels of my being.

I pull the stone off my head and sit up quickly. I'm still rocking from the intensity of the experience. When I recover myself, I take the stone and slip into the bathroom, where I can turn on the light.

When I do so, I see that the stone is not the one from Colorado. This I had suspected almost right away. It is a very similarly shaped tumbled amethyst. I had given it to a friend on the spur of the moment to carry for me when I found out she was going to India.

It had been many months later before we connected again. When she had given the stone back to me, she had said, "I took this stone to all of the sacred places I went. I took it into the temples and held it to the altars to receive that energy."

I am up for several more hours. When I finally do sleep, I dream that George Harrison is playing a sitar on the edge of the bed. Mandalas float in my inner vision for days. This stone packs a wallop.

I try the stone again about a week later. I know that expectation will have some effect. I am, eternally, a scientist—an experiential scientist. When I focus on the stone, I have no images or sensations at all. I fall into the dark rich color of the stone immediately and drift into the void. I still do—every time.

It is an interesting paradox that some of the deepest connections to energies come when we are not expecting them. I read a stone for a Wolf Clan brother once—psychically, not according to any traditional system. He had found it near a sacred spot on Seneca land and had worn it around his neck on a leather thong ever since. I expected to get illuminative information about him more than anything else. When I placed the stone on my forehead, I fell into a completely different time and place.

From the stone's point of view, I could see a ragged group of prehistoric people huddled around a meager fire. I seemed to be held by an ancient woman speaking in words I could not understand at all. The sense I got was that I was an extremely sacred stone and was to be a gift to the fire!

Perhaps there had been a severe winter and these people wished to appease the "spirits of warmth and light." I felt extreme cold all around me. I was passed into another person's hands. This time a young man held me tightly for a few moments. Then he opened his hand and approached the fire.

When he did that, I jumped out of my image and slammed the stone back on the table—much to the surprise of my Wolf Clan brother. Naturally, he wanted more information about the stone in regard to the little journey it had just taken me on. I decided to "freeze-frame" the image and go back for more detail. I spent some time in the image, pointing out details about the people and getting a feel for that time and place. But I refused to proceed through the fire!

I had learned long ago that sensations received in a manner such as this did—literally—move through my being. Many years before, when I was still a teenager, I had encountered a young man with powerful magical skills. Unfortunately, his use of these skills was distinctly on the dark side of the line. Once, when he was "teaching" me to read the vibrations of objects, he gave me a bracelet that he said had belonged to someone he knew. He told me to let him know if I picked up anything from it.

With all the cockiness of a teen, and the receptivity of a child, I opened my channels to the energies in that bracelet. What I received was an experience of such pain and horror that I will not share it here—or ever. It seems that the bracelet had belonged to a girl who had died of a drug overdose.

I can still hear his laughter at my distress and shock. Despite all his black, twisted motives, he taught me a valuable lesson about the deepest levels of divination. It was many, many years before I allowed myself to tap those levels again. And then only when I had learned to veil myself as much as possible and knew how to detach from the energies I was receiving. I pass this rather unpleasant lesson on in hopes that you will learn the skills of detachment first—not the hard way.

Since I tapped those channels with that poor girl's bracelet, I have had to deal with similar energies from time to time. I never go looking for them. When I know that I must dance with those energies, I always call on my highest spiritual helpers to stand beside me. Even in the simplest forms of divination, we can tap very strong energies. We need never do it alone—that is the way of the ego, not the way of the shaman.

I mentioned before that there are some who divide shamans and people of wisdom into two distinct categories: healers and diviners. In my experience, though the energies of the two are somewhat different, they are far more the same. Divination can be as dramatic and as transformative as any healing activity. Because of this, we must be prepared to do divination in a serious, sacred manner. If we don't, we may as well go back to using divination as a parlor game or rainy-day form of amusement.

Here are a few guidelines to use when divining for anyone, including yourself.

1. Be compassionate and be sure that you mean it.

2. Be honest about what you do not know. Too many diviners would rather appear mysterious than learn to say some of the most magick of all words—*I don't know.*

3. Be considerate of another's privacy. A divination that is invasive will not accomplish anything and may result in some of your channels being shut down. After all, your higher Self knows what is right behavior in divination.

4. Check any advice you feel you must give through yourself first. It may really be for you anyway.

5. Encourage your querist to divine for himself. If you make someone dependent on you, there will be a lot of regrets later.

6. Keep yourself centered and clear. If you are scattered, say so.

People often make very serious decisions based on what a diviner says. Do you want the responsibility of having influenced a situation with static rather than with illuminative truth?

7. Meditate a great deal more than you would if you were not divining for yourself or others. Time "in" the divinatory channels requires much more time "out" to rest.

8. Never, never read another person's sacred totems or ritual objects. The same applies to crystals and most of the higher-vibration gemstones that attune to the psychic and mental levels. This type of divination is far too invasive to be considered, except in times of extreme crisis.

    Examples of this would be if the person has lost contact with reality, is being overtaken by the energies of another, is deeply depressed or ill for a reason you cannot determine in any other way. If you ever have to do this, be absolutely sure you do it in your most sacred ritual circle. Call on your council and the council of the person being read for. Then, ask permission. If you still feel more than just an ethical hesitance—STOP. This is not for you to deal with. Release any energies you may have gathered from the other person and walk away.

9. Always be willing to ask for help from all levels and sources. Help has a way of showing up. Let it in.

When we move full circle on our path, we find that our journey leads us back to the deepest aspects of our Self. From these aspects, we gain the faith to trust our intuitive gifts, the clarity of our self-healing experiences, the strength of symbolic wisdom, and the creativity to use illumination in our lives.

Ultimately, the shamanic path calls us to connect directly to the energies we work with in divination. We have learned that symbols and traditional methods are keys that unlock doors to our deepest self-wisdom. No system can substitute for our shamanic abilities to read energies purely. Regardless of the divination tools we use, we must rely on the gift of shamanic sensing to give us that special channel to illumination. Shamanic sensing arises from our deepest center.

The relationship of shamanic sensing to traditional divination systems is like the relationship of luck to skill. We work to sharpen and utilize our skills (and systems) to the fullest. Still, there comes a point when that added edge (which we sometimes call luck) opens our channels fully to let us divine through shamanic sensing.

Shamanic sensing is most directly related to psychometry. A psychometric diviner traditionally divines by reading the energies of an object that belongs to someone, and channeling those energies. It is a very pure and shamanic form of divination. It requires the diviner to receive energies quite personally and purely from the person through the object. Needless to say, the psychometric diviner must be prepared to deal with what comes through. All of us are familiar with the investigative diviners who use psychometric techniques to solve the mysteries of missing persons. Sometimes these mysteries are solved with joyful results—sometimes not. We can only marvel at the honor of that sacred gift and be grateful that there are those among us who can handle energies of that kind.

Most of us will probably never be called on to use our gifts of divination in quite so difficult or dramatic a way. However, as we deepen our shamanic sensing abilities, we must be prepared for whatever comes through.

As we deepen our divination skills, we find that we become able to read the energies around us with greater intuitive insight. We come to rely less and less on systems of divination. Instead, we opt for developing an ongoing illuminative awareness that gives us a continuous flow of information with which to divine the direction of our path and that of others. We learn to trust that little voice, that unique kinesthetic prickle, and the images that arise in our inner vision. We find that our shamanic consciousness is constantly at work divining the energies. We learn to tap that consciousness directly, with or without a formal system to help us.

One of the most constant methods of divination that we all do, mostly without realizing it, is the reading of auras. Reading auras is a direct way of connecting to the energy patterns in our Self and in others. Auras are the energies we emit. They reflect the state of our mental, physical, and spiritual makeup at any given time.

Although we speak of "seeing" auras, it is more accurate to say that we sense them. Auras are the "vibes" we get from people, animals, stones, and even plants. All things have vibrations; therefore all things have auras. Some are more subtle than others, yet present just the same.

Some traditions have very specific meanings for all auric patterns and colors. I feel that auras are far too individual to have iron-clad patterns. They do seem to have some commonalities that we can use as a foundation for our more intuitive interpretations and methods of divination. These commonalities are related to the basic Ray energies, which both influence and reflect the weavings of our lives.

Here is an imagery exercise that is designed to help you connect with and interpret the basic energies reflected in auras.

Aura-cle

Breathe deeply and tense all of the muscles in your body—hold it.

Now release your breath and relax your muscles.

Do this again—this time slowly inhale and slowly tighten your muscles. Hold it gently for just a few moments . . . then release gently.

Breathe deeply once again, and give yourself permission to be more and more relaxed. Be open to your self.

Trust your ability to know.

Trust knowing. Trust your intuition.

Trust your inner teacher.

Breathe deeply and deepen your rhythm.

Image yourself standing in the middle of a large five-pointed star surrounded by a circle.

In the center of the circle you are in the center of your self.

In the center of your own power . . . and your own knowing.

It is time to renew your acquaintance with each of your five senses: seeing—hearing—touching—tasting—smelling. Allow yourself to open the channels of these five senses wider than before.

Stimulate the pathways in your brain that bring the messages of each of your senses.

Stimulate new pathways to intuition.

Stimulate the partnership of heart and mind in knowing.

Allow an image to emerge for you of a personal symbol or Talisman of Knowing. Touch your forehead and your chest.

Affirm the connection of heart and mind in self-knowing. In intuition.

Look in your image to the top point of the star. Notice the word SEEING written inside the point.

It is traditional to say that auras are seen. Yet auras are more than that. Auras are received through all of your senses.

Allow yourself permission to learn to sense auras—yours and those around you.

Breathe deeply, and in your image turn point to point around the five-point star.

Affirm seeing ... affirm hearing ... affirm touching ... tasting ... smelling.

Affirm your ability to receive information from all of these five senses together.

Affirm the sixth sense—the synthesis of all your intuition.

Breathe deeply again and create an image of a control panel with many buttons of many colors, many hues, many shades, and many intensities.

The instructions on the control panel read PUSH TO RECEIVE.

Select a button of your favorite color and push it. When you do, the color leaps out of the control panel and swirls around you until everything has the vibration of that color.

Take time to receive that color from every sense: see it, listen for the sound of that color, taste the flavor of your favorite color, touch it, and catch the fragrance it gives.

Allow yourself to capture the sense of that color for your self.

Take all the time you need in your image to push a few more buttons and open your senses to receive the meanings of these colors for you.

Take time and note the colors that you choose, for these have significance for you. Indeed, these may be colors from your own aura. Enjoy the experience.

Now breathe deeply, and listen to some information about auras.

Auras are a reflection of energy.

Auras are a forcefield, some say, electromagnetic in nature, which surrounds and energizes.

Auras are like a little magick circle of your self, reflecting and emanating from inside your being.

Visible and apparent only to those who are open to knowing.

Allow yourself to be open to self-knowing.

Aura colors have traditional meanings that may be used as a guideline for your learning.

Breathe deeply, and file these meanings if you choose to.

Allow each color to appear in your image and notice the "sense" it has for you.

Breathe deeply, and listen for the traditional meanings of some aura colors. Know that if your intuition disagrees with the meanings given, you may disagree also.

You may create your own program of meanings—work with your intuition, your inner teacher.

Let us begin by imaging Red. This is the traditional color of energy, strength, and courage.

The brighter reds are more physical. A brownish red often indicates anger. A deep red shows sensuality. Crimson is loyalty. Scarlet is confidence.

Breathe deeply again and take all the time you need to get the sense of Red.

Now image Pink, the color of love and optimism.

Next image Rose, which is sometimes the color of self-love and self-appreciation. A rosy glow of confidence is another way to describe an aura reading that has a lot of Rose Pink.

Be open to what your senses can say to you.

Orange is the color of joy and vitality. The balance of the physical, fiery energy of Red and the mental, airy energy of Yellow.

Feel the vibration and pace of Orange.

Now breathe deeply and image Yellow, the color of wisdom and mental creativity. If the Yellow in an aura is dull, then it may symbolize thoughts clouded with worry or fear.

These things you will learn to recognize.

Now image Green, the color of compassion, the heart, healing, growth, and ingenuity. A person with much Green in his aura is often loving and expansive.

Do you sense the Green in your aura?

If the Green is pale, it is the Green of a healing person. Pale Green is the blending of the White of Spirit with the Green of heartfelt compassion.

Breathe deeply, and receive the vibrations of healing Green in your aura.

If Green appears dull, it is the color of pessimism, jealousy, or envy . . . a shadow of love.

You will learn to notice the play of colors, and the tones will take on meaning for you, increasing your knowing.

Next image Blue, the color of idealism, spirituality, and imagination. If dull, then Blue indicates depression. Haven't we all had the blues at times?

If Blue is hot and bright this is the color of intellectual quests and idealistic spiritualism. Turquoise and Ultramarine are these types.

Ultraviolet Blue often flows through the auras of spiritual leaders, be they leaders of themselves or leaders of a group.

Breathe and allow the image of Violet to emerge. This is the color of a more purely spiritual power of deep philosophical strengths.

The deeper violets indicate a level of majesty or royalty of spirit.

The lighter tones of Lavender represent a high level of self-healing energies and spirituality. These are the blend of the White of Spirit and the Violet of power.

Now image the purity of the color White. This White is the combination of all vibrations and colors in balance. It is the color of pure spirituality. It is the White Light we hear about and send to those we love. And which we surround ourselves with to find this self-healing balance.

You can create White Light in your aura.

Breathe deeply, and receive White Light in all your senses.

Rare to see, or sense, is the presence of Black in an aura.

Black can mean a person seeking Light, or Black can show a great depth of depression. Sometimes an aura with Black in it may be cleansed with love and White Light. Allow White Light to flow through you at the first thread of Black you may see—it chases away shadows.

To read Black in an aura, look at it in relationship to other colors.

Let the image of Black fade, and create an image of rich, earthy Brown. This is the color of connection with the earth's energy. Dull browns are low energy, listless and tired. Rich browns are enthusiastic and friendly.

Now let the image of Grey emerge. Grey is a veil in auras. Grey is a tricky color, often used to mask or suppress the vibration of another color, another aspect of the self. Notice, whenever Grey appears, which colors it surrounds or masks. What do you think that masking means? These are questions to stimulate your learning. Ask yourself questions all the time. Your intuition will give you answers, or at least a few hints.

Breathe deeply again, and allow the colors of higher vibration to emerge.

Gold, the active, universal color of high mindfulness and spirit.

Allow Gold to appear in your aura and feel the active power of its vibration.

Next image Silver, the receptive meditative color of psychic vibration.

Silver is traditionally an indication of openness to wisdom and intuition.

Let Silver flow through your aura.

Finally image golden light flowing down from above your head.

Breathe deeply and blend all the colors together until you have surrounded yourself with glowing White Light. Follow with Silver and Gold.

Know that the colors may be used, as well as read, in order to heal and balance.

As you practice you will find your own ways to work with colors, to work with the aura-cle who is in your self.

Now breathe deeply and allow yourself to create one more image.

Image yourself in a dark theater; the only light is a spotlight on the stage. Take a seat and watch the stage.

In your image allow a person you know to step into the spotligt on the stage.

Know that this is a very special spotlight. The spotlight of your intuition.

As this person moves about in the spotlight, perhaps silent, maybe speaking, notice the trail of colors in that person's aura.

Take all the time you need to "read" the aura of that person.

Perhaps the next time you see that person outside of this image, you will sense the presence of the same colors and vibrations.

Take all the time you need to explore the image.

Now breathe deeply and carefully, and let your self step into the spotlight on the stage. Create an image of your self and observe the aura of your self.

If this is difficult, you may wish to image your self as you do when looking into a mirror.

Take all the time you wish to pick up colors and vibrations in your own aura. This is the mark of an aura-cle . . . self-knowing.

Perhaps you can let colors emerge into your image and surround your self.

Remember, the colors you choose are most often the colors you reflect.

Take all the time you need for self-knowing in sensing your aura.

Know that you may return to this image whenever you choose to practice your skills as an aura-cle.

Return replenished. Come into the moment.

Divination is another of the sacred gifts of the shaman. If it is done without a judgmental attitude and with very few expectations, it can become one of the strongest tools of the shamanic path. Along with the gift of divination comes the gift of perspective. If you can pass this on to people you read for, you will have shared a truly special gift. Teach yourself, and others by your example, to regard divination as a special gathering of the energies that spin at the center of the shaman's path. Teach yourself and others how to divine. Let the energies through.

Afterword

I used to think that I had to work *on* a situation. I structured the entire process—perfectly, of course. Then I began to feel that I needed to work *with* a situation. So I only structured it to meet my needs. More and more, I began to *observe* the situations doing their own work.

Then I *experienced* that I was working, too—on myself. That frightened me at first. So I decided not to involve myself with any situations at all for a time—other than what I considered to be my own.

After a time, I *released* the need to even do work on my Self—at least for a while. I would just be. And I noticed an interesting thing: when I would just be, others would just be.

And the strangest thing happened. All around me people I was just being with began to have all kinds of self-healing and self-transformation in their lives. And so did I—without structuring anything.

Now, when I work with myself or others, I still take along lots of wonderful tools and totems. But I have learned that the time comes when I must get out of the way and *let the energies flow naturally.* Only in this way can I channel the energies of Source and catalyst those channels in another. Only in this way can I fan the flames created by the divine spark in us all.

Appendix A

Appendix A

Empowerment Image • Circle of Self

Breathe deeply and allow yourself to go deeper than before. Give yourself permission to connect all the parts of your Being. Experience synthesis. Be at one with the universe. Step into the circle of life. Step into the circle of yourself.

Imagine yourself in a place of Nature all your own. Breathe deeply to energize the image. Notice the sights and sounds of this place. Breathe in the fragrances and flavors of this place. Feel the climate of all that is around you. Be at one with this place. Be with the energy of this place. Know that you are a manifestation of this energy. Use this energy and begin to construct your own universe. Breathe to empower yourself. This is your place in Nature. Alone with the earth and sky. Alone with yourself. Attuned.

In your Nature image, turn to the East and face the rising sun. This is daily a new source of energy. This is the element of Air, the element of spirit and philosophy for yourself. This is the soul of your Being. Look to the East for illumination and renewal. Breathe deeply and experience the energy of the East. Allow it to flow through you. Let it go.

In your image turn right to face the South. This is the element of Fire, the spark that stimulates action. This gives you the strength of your energy. Look to the South for the dynamic energy of relationships— person to person, Self to self. Breathe deeply and experience the energy of the South. Allow it to flow through you. Let it go.

Turn right again to the West. This is the element of Water. This is the source of your compassion. From this flows your emotions. Welcome your emotions. Allow them to float freely by. Look to the West for introspection. Breathe deeply and experience the energy of the West. Allow it to flow through you. Let it go.

Turn right again to the North. This is the element of Earth. This is your reason and your logic. This grounds you. This is the magnetic point of connection. Look to the North for wisdom. Breathe deeply and experience the energy of the North. Allow it to flow through you. Let it go.

Turn right again to the East. Complete the circle. Breathe deeply, and center in your place in Nature. Center yourself in your image.

Now cast a circle of light around yourself. Allow it to focus energy and power. Cast the circle of yourself. Breathe to energize your image.

Imagine a situation in your life that you wish to change in some way. Remember that you are in your special place in Nature. You are, at the same time, alone and at one with all the elements of your Being. This is your image. This is your universe. Knowing that you have complete control in this image to say or do as you choose, ask the question, make the request for change. Then release it to the higher elements of your Being. Give it to your higher Self and let it go.

Breathe a long, slow breath. Now become fully aware and prepared to receive a clarification. Open all your senses. You may receive directions, you may receive answers. Breathe deeply to energize your image.

Perhaps you will find another way to deal with this situation. Another idea, an alternate plan. Perhaps you will find a clearer path. Take all the time you need. Be open to your Self. Allow yourself to be open to changing your mind.

Know that you have received the images that you need. You have the clarity you need for action. Know that you can create your own images, your own universe. With intentions of goodwill, for the good of all, begin to create the situation you want. Image the desire. Create what you want. Project this in front of you. Complete. Ask yourself, "Is this what I want?" As far as you can see, is it for the good of all? Is it for the good of yourself?

Breathe energy into your image. Make adjustments. Change your mind as you choose. Breathe life into your image. Affirm it. Now carefully, gently, step into your image. Be one with it. Affirm it. Know it. Integrate it. Make it a part of yourself. Spend a few more moments making this real. Celebrate the completion.

Know that you may affirm this at any time by creating the image and breathing life into it. Know that as much as you need is within you.

Breathe deeply and find yourself once again in yourself in your special place in Nature. Face the rising sun. Notice that the sun is brighter and warmer, higher on the horizon. Allow the warmth and light of the sun to energize you. Let it heal and replenish you. Be at peace with yourself. You can create the life that you want. Take time to heal, and be at peace with yourself.

Make the circle once again. Turning each time to the right, breathe and absorb the energy of each direction. Take all the time you need. East—South—West—North.

Complete the circle of yourself. Celebrate all the elements of your Being. Celebrate your oneness with Nature. Celebrate your oneness with all things.

Know that you may always return to your place in Nature. This is your choice. Begin to come back to your present awareness. Return fully alert. Be aware of your body. Wiggle your toes. Wiggle your fingers. Stretch your body. Clap your hands. Be here now.

Appendix B

Four Winds Wheel

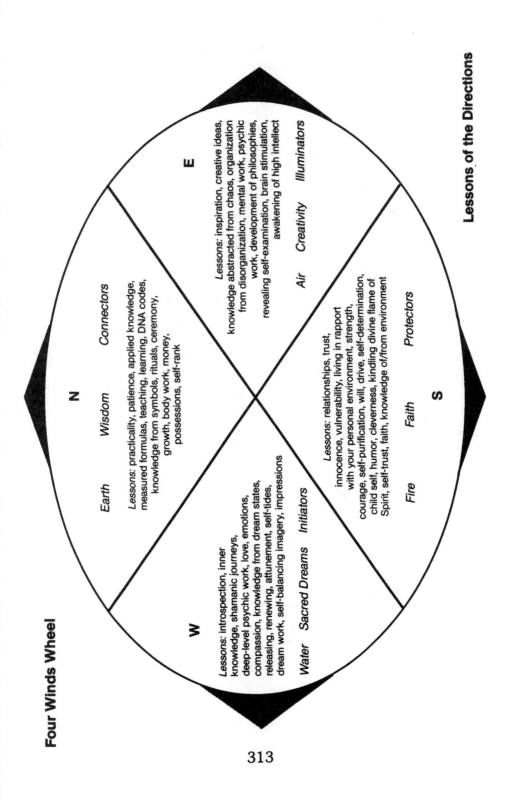

N

Earth   Wisdom   Connectors

Lessons: practicality, patience, applied knowledge, measured formulas, teaching, learning, DNA codes, knowledge from symbols, rituals, ceremony, growth, body work, money, possessions, self-rank

E

Air   Creativity   Illuminators

Lessons: inspiration, creative ideas, knowledge abstracted from chaos, organization from disorganization, mental work, psychic work, development of philosophies, revealing self-examination, brain stimulation, awakening of high intellect

W

Water   Sacred Dreams   Initiators

Lessons: introspection, inner knowledge, shamanic journeys, deep-level psychic work, love, emotions, compassion, knowledge from dream states, releasing, renewing, attunement, self-tides, dream work, self-balancing imagery, impressions

S

Fire   Faith   Protectors

Lessons: relationships, trust, innocence, vulnerability, living in rapport with your personal environment, strength, courage, self-purification, will, drive, self-determination, child self, humor, cleverness, kindling divine flame of Spirit, self-trust, faith, knowledge of/from environment

Lessons of the Directions

313

Mineral World Totems

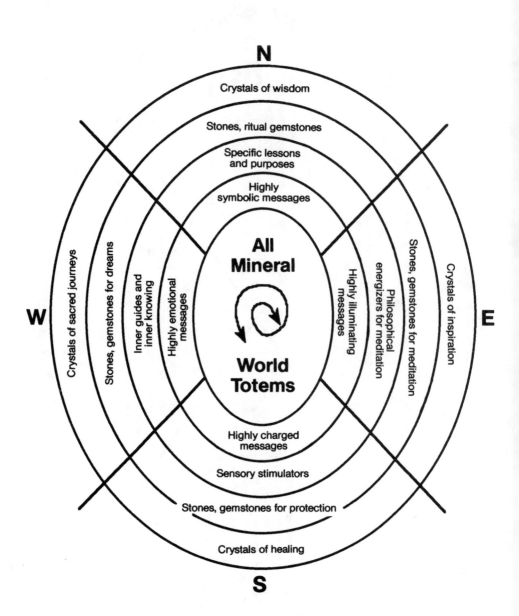

Animal World Totems

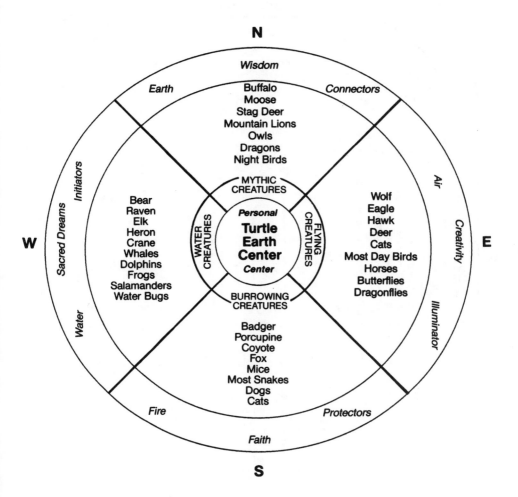

Plant World Totems

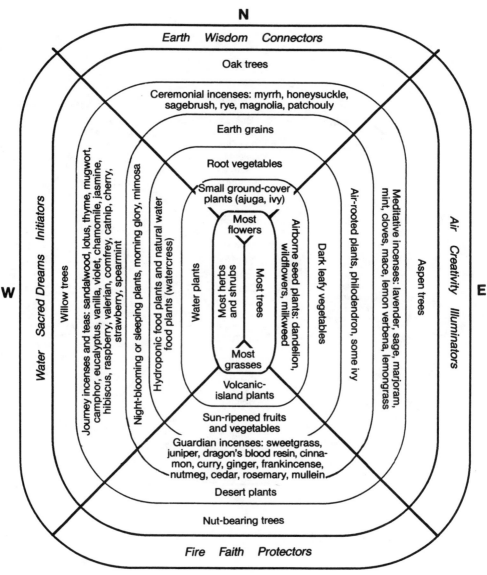

Human World Totems

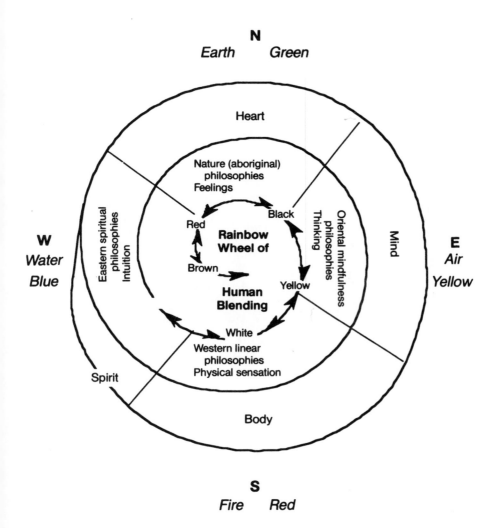

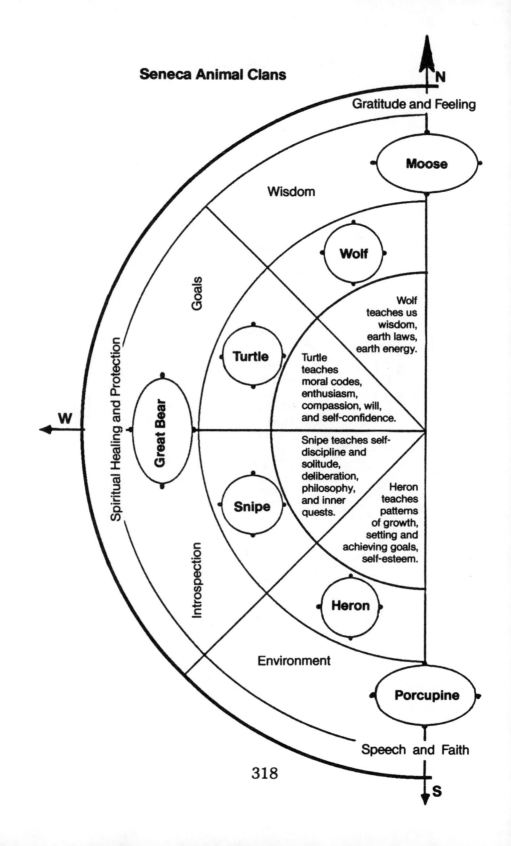

Seneca Animal Clans

Gratitude and Feeling

Moose

Wisdom

Wolf

Goals

Wolf teaches us wisdom, earth laws, earth energy.

Turtle

Turtle teaches moral codes, enthusiasm, compassion, will, and self-confidence.

Spiritual Healing and Protection

Great Bear

W

Snipe teaches self-discipline and solitude, deliberation, philosophy, and inner quests.

Snipe

Heron teaches patterns of growth, setting and achieving goals, self-esteem.

Introspection

Environment

Heron

Porcupine

Speech and Faith

N

S

318

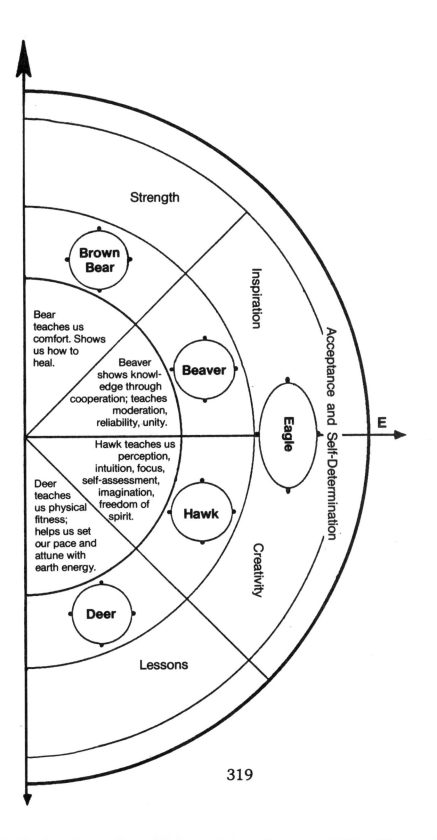

Strength

Brown
Bear

Bear
teaches us
comfort. Shows
us how to
heal.

Beaver
shows knowl-
edge through
cooperation; teaches
moderation,
reliability, unity.

Beaver

Inspiration

Eagle

Acceptance and Self-Determination

E

Hawk teaches us
perception,
intuition, focus,
self-assessment,
imagination,
freedom of
spirit.

Deer
teaches
us physical
fitness;
helps us set
our pace and
attune with
earth energy.

Hawk

Creativity

Deer

Lessons

319

Chart of Trees

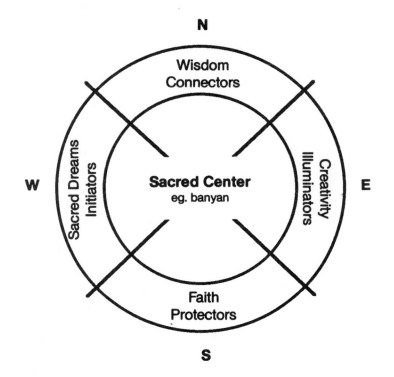

N

Wisdom
Connectors

W   E

Sacred Dreams
Initiators

Creativity
Illuminators

Sacred Center
eg. banyan

Faith
Protectors

S

Note to Reader:
This particular wheel represents a place in my life. As my life changes, so does the wheel change. As you choose different trees to be your helpers, watch for patterns that are maps for you.

Example:
You may interpret the wheel in this way: With luck (banyan) rooted at my center, I am able to reverence the creativity that comes to me with the help of my illuminator tree (ash). The protector (maple) inspires enthusiasm and faith in the kinship I have in my relationships. The emotionality (pine) I experience in my dreams and journeys initiates me along the path. The wisdom of the great oak provides a magical Earth connection.

320

Apple	**Birch**	**Palm**
The apple is a tree of honor. It is a working tree, useful in matters of love, healing, and faith, and is sacred to the Goddess.	The birch is a powerful tree for protection and purification. It is a working tree that helps by giving gentle yet firm maternal support and care.	(Date or Coconut) The palm is a working tree for abundance and fertility. The full crops represent renewal of life's fruits under limited conditions.
Honor	*Support*	*Renewal*
Ash	**Hickory**	**Pecan**
The ash is a sacred tree of sensitivity and intuition. It is a deep medicine tree for reverence of life, focus, peace, and awareness.	The hickory is a sacred tree of endurance. It is beneficial to those who must be firm in their beliefs and courageous in their actions.	The pecan is a working tree for prosperity. The richness and the sweetness of the nutmeat represent luxury.
Reverence	*Endurance*	*Prosperity*
Banyan	**Maple**	**Pine**
The banyan is a sacred tree of continuing luck and good fortune. It earths the manna of heaven with its many roots.	The maple is a working tree that helps in matters of kinship and love. It fires the enthusiasm and giving energy of relationships.	The pine is a sacred tree of spiritual and emotional expression. Its evergreen leaves and tapering, reaching branches direct spiritual growth through emotionality.
Luck	*Kinship*	*Emotionality*
Beech	**Oak**	**Redwood**
The beech is a very physical working tree. It helps by giving one steadfastness in organizing and achieving goals and wishes.	The oak is a sacred tree of earth magick and spiritual strength. It represents the highest dimensions of awareness and philosophical ideals.	The redwood is a sacred elder tree of truth. It is a strong tree for people involved in intellectual pursuits along the path of truth.
Steadfastness	*Magick*	*Truth*

Willow	The willow is a working tree, most healing by its gentle flexibility and loving nature. It is a tree of great strength and grace.	*Grace*

Astrological Elements

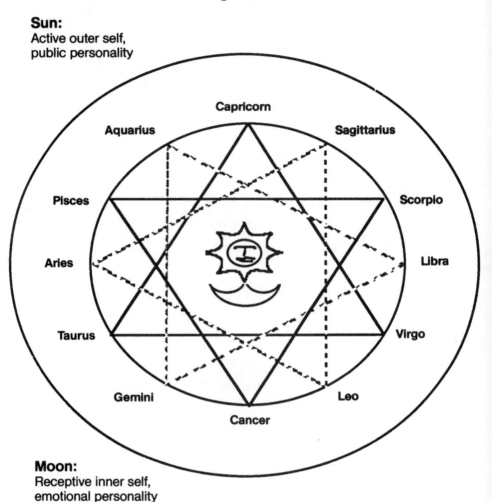

Sun:
Active outer self,
public personality

Moon:
Receptive inner self,
emotional personality

Elemental Triplicities

Aries, Sagittarius, Leo	△ Fire	Protectors, relationships, ideas
Pisces, Scorpio, Cancer	▽ Water	Initiators, inner knowing, emotions
Capricorn, Virgo, Taurus	⩡ Earth	Connectors, wisdom, behaviors
Libra, Gemini, Aquarius	⩘ Air	Illuminators, creativity, philosophies

Basic Personality Attributes

Fire signs: Energetic, creative / intense, impulsive

Water signs: Receptive, compassionate / oversensitive, dependent

Air signs: Communicative, philosophical / overbearing, spacey

Earth signs: Practical, organized / stubborn, obsessive

Sample Combinations for Elements and Possible Effects

Fire
+ Water = Squelched, dampened, calms, steams
+ Air = Fueled Fire, creative Fire, burnout, hysteria
+ Earth = Banked Fire, smouldering, repression
+ Fire = Consumes or expands Fire (tricky)

Water
+ Earth = An anchor point or "muddy waters," confusion, stagnation
+ Air = Enthusiasm, effervescence, "bubbles" joy
+ Fire = Squelches Fire, creates steam, heat
+ Water = Increased flow, rainout, flooding, catharsis

Earth
+ Air = Erosion, either slow or fast, overwhelms, irritates, motivates
+ Fire = Can be a catalyst, can soothe
+ Water = Dampened ground, increased sensitivity, emotionality, depression
+ Earth = Supportive for strength or too fixed, solidified

Air
+ Fire = Can heighten Fire, creativity, activator, or use up Air
+ Water = Soothes pace, increases sensitivity, oppression, density
+ Earth = Grounds, stabilizes, impedes, suffocates
+ Air = Increased intellect, spirituality, flighty, self-consuming

Totem Care Schedules

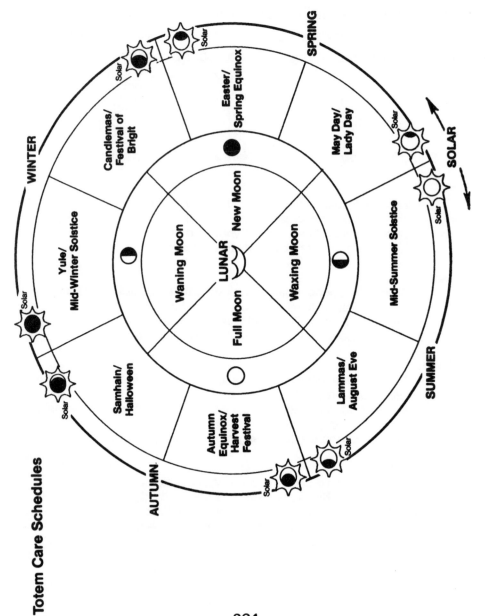

LUNAR WHEEL

Waning Moon

Take time to rest self and totems. Cleanse totems of any negative residue from work. Do deepest cleansings or purgings at dark of the moon.

New Moon

Begin to charge new totems. Renew relationships with old totems. Awaken spirit of totems. Instruct and listen.

Waxing Moon

Deepen spiritual and emotional connections with totems. Allow totems to work and teach; continue to energize.

Full Moon

Celebrate the connections between self and totems. Charge totems in full moon. Draw in energy to self and to totems.

SOLAR WHEEL

Yule / Mid-Winter Solstice

Celebrate the light and spirit that connects all life and Nature. Share energy with totems. Take time to give "gifts" and thanks.

Mid-Summer Solstice

Nurture totems, receive energy through totems, and send energy through self to totems. Take time to work for deep empowerment. Exercise totems. Allow for summer healing, summer growth.

Candlemas / Festival of Brigit

Take time to kindle the fires of inspiration. Learn to communicate with totems. Listen for inner wisdom. Allow time for rest and reflect on self as totem. Know and dance totems.

Lammas / August Eve

Begin to use totems more often, for work and growth. Do ceremony for removing obstacles from self-path; awaken totems as protectors and guides. Release totems that need to go. Renew with the totems that stay.

Easter / Spring Equinox

Gently awaken spirit in totems. Take totems out into mild sunlight. Bring gifts of buds, new growth; renew relationships with totems, with self, with Nature. Balance totems with self-energies.

Autumn Equinox / Harvest Festival

Celebrate the harvest of Spirit that your connection to totems gives you. Do ceremony to plan for future work with totems. Discard totems that are no longer yours. Share totems with others. Time for group work with totems. Balance energies of totems and self.

May Day / Lady Day

Time for deep bonding with totem objects; focus active energy on totems for future work and growth. Play with totems and begin deep empowerment of totems.

Samhain / Halloween

Remove all barriers between Spirit and self using totems. Time for deep shamanic journeys. Summon guides and helpers from Spirit. Open veils to let Spirit flow into and through totems and self. Celebrate harvest of self.

Totem Medicine • South

Physical pacing, rest, renewal, self-healing, relationships, physical and personal vulnerability, stress, elusiveness, protection, courage, love

Gold, Red, or Orange Items
Fire-forged items, red feathers (esp. courage)

Animal World
Bear: physical self-healing
Deer: self-pacing
Tigers, lions: stress, courage
Porcupine, badger, hedgehog: protection, defense
Bobcat: elusiveness, courage
Foxes, coyotes, squirrels: vulnerability and elusiveness, relationships (tricky)
Mouse, rabbit, possum: renewal, self-healing
Snakes: protection

Human World
Western body awareness philosophies and therapies
Counselor guides and spirit vibrations

Mineral World
Smoky crystals, esp. citrines
Gemstones of warm hues
Lava formations, beach sands
Gold, copper, steel, pyrite
Textured or patterned stones
(Use for all South aspects.)

Plant World
Maple tree
Nuts, seeds, pods: relationships
Nut trees: love
Cactuses, thorn bushes, spiney plants: protection
Guardian incenses: sweetgrass, juniper, cedar, frankincense

326

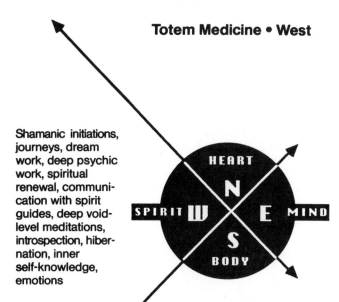

Shamanic initiations, journeys, dream work, deep psychic work, spiritual renewal, communication with spirit guides, deep void-level meditations, introspection, hibernation, inner self-knowledge, emotions

Blue, Black, or Silver Items
Water treasures, seaweeds,
roots, dark feathers,
void meditation

Animal World
Bear: spiritual healing and renewal
Dolphin: deep psychic work
Raven: spirit communication
Heron: inner self-knowledge
Jaguar: self-initiations
Panther: introspection
Night creatures: journeys
Water creatures: dream work

Human World
Some Eastern transpersonal philosophies
Deeply personal helping spirits and
guides

Mineral World
Gemstones of water hues
Water-colored crystals
Rainbow crystals
Translucent, crystalline stones
River or ocean rocks
Mercury, silver, platinum
Coral, shells
(Use for all West aspects.)

Plant World
Willow: journeys, magick
Pine trees: emotions
Magnolia: dream work
Gardenia: spirit guides, love
Lavender: summoning spirits
Journey incenses: violet, myrrh,
sandalwood
Soothing teas: chamomile, raspberry,
jasmine, catnip
Jasmine flowers: shamanic intuition
Water plants: dreams

327

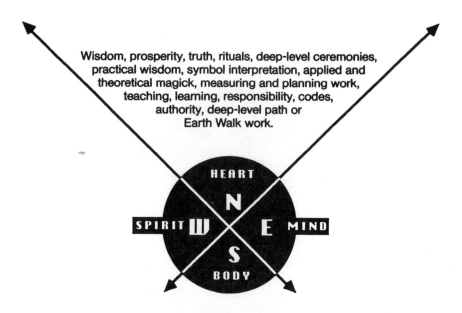

Wisdom, prosperity, truth, rituals, deep-level ceremonies, practical wisdom, symbol interpretation, applied and theoretical magick, measuring and planning work, teaching, learning, responsibility, codes, authority, deep-level path or Earth Walk work.

Purple, Gold, Green, or Black Items
Shadow plants, violets, night treasures, owl feathers, night birds

Animal World
Buffalo, moose: practical wisdom
Wolf: earth wisdom, magick learning, teaching
Dragon: ritual, magick
Mythic animals: symbols, codes, magick
Heron: applied, measured wisdom
Stag deer: authority, magick
Mountain cats: Earth Walk teachers
Owl: wisdom, clarity, purpose

Human World
Nature or aboriginal philosophies
Medicine helpers, Wiccan guides

Mineral World
Crystal formations: energy gathering
Dark crystals and gemstones
Geometrically shaped stones
Ores, earthy rocks
Salt, soil
(Use for all North aspects.)

Plant World
Oak trees: magick
Redwood: wisdom, truth
Banyan: luck, prosperity
Evergreens: ritual
Ceremonial incenses: mugwort, magnolia, roots

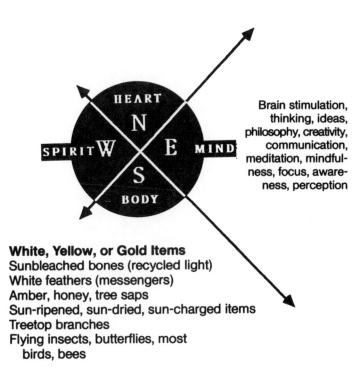

Brain stimulation, thinking, ideas, philosophy, creativity, communication, meditation, mindfulness, focus, awareness, perception

White, Yellow, or Gold Items
Sunbleached bones (recycled light)
White feathers (messengers)
Amber, honey, tree saps
Sun-ripened, sun-dried, sun-charged items
Treetop branches
Flying insects, butterflies, most
  birds, bees

Animal World
Racoon: thinking
Parrot: communication
Hawk: focus
Eagle: philosophy
Wolf: communication
Cats (domestic and predatory)
Foxes: awareness
Deer: perception
Turtle: creativity

Human World
Oriental mindfulness,
  awareness philosophies
Buddha spirit vibrations and
  guides

Mineral World
Very clear crystals
Gemstones of exceptional clarity
Smooth translucent stones
Silver: for receptivity
Smooth sand and salt
(Use for all East aspects.)

Plant World
Ash trees: peace of mind
Birch, aspen, beech, and palms:
  mental health
Meditation incenses: lemon balm,
  mint, sage, lavender for quieter
  spirits
Clover, wind weeds, wildflowers,
  air plants

Ray Energies

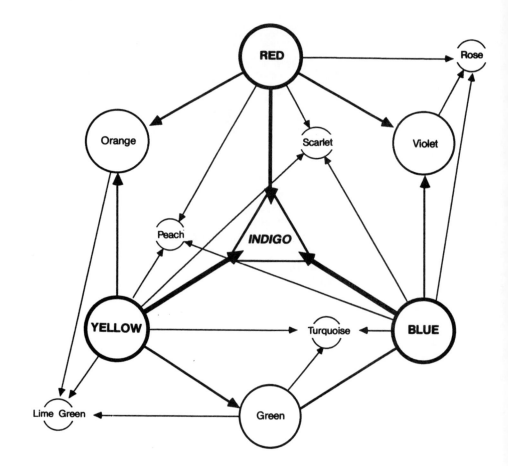

Primary Rays

| Red | *e* | (+) Freedom, honor, determination, strength |
| | | (−) Anger, lust, violence, impatience, rebellion |

| Yellow | *a* | (+) Joy, sincerity, mental discrimination, discipline, intelligence |
| | | (−) Contempt, selfish laziness, criticism, cowardice |

| Blue | *o* | (+) Love, wisdom, security, compassion, mercy |
| | | (−) Fear, isolation, worry, depression, anxiety |

Secondary or Two-Part Rays

Green   *a*

Equal parts Yellow and Blue
(+) Expansion, enthusiasm, harmony, hope, sharing
(−) Jealousy, greed, envy, disorder, resistance

Orange   *e*

Equal parts Red and Yellow
(+) Courage, action, creativity
(−) Cruelty, might, ignorance

Violet   *u*

Equal parts Blue and Red
(+) Self-motivation, devotion, idealism
(−) Obsession, agitation, martyrdom

Blended Rays of Three or More Parts

Scarlet   *i*

Primarily Red with Blue and some Yellow
(+) Communications, balance, yin-yang, relating, rapport
(−) Egocentricity, furry, extremes, boredom, noncommunication

Turquoise   *aw*

Primarily Blue with Green and some Yellow
(+) Zeal, service, cheer, dedication, determination
(−) Glamour, ego, anger, perfectionism, expectations

Lime Green   *i*

Primarily Green with Yellow and some Orange
(+) Blending, release, rejuvenation, freshness, openness
(−) Envy, delay, disassociation, confusion, regrets, delusion

Rose   *y*

Primarily Red with Violet and some Blue
(+) Serenity, maturity, endurance, temperance, compromise
(−) Intolerance, cynicism, gossip, moroseness

Peach   *a*

Primarily Yellow with Red and some Blue
(+) Peace, humor, openness, organization
(−) Strife, vanity, conflict, sadness

Synthesis Ray

Indigo   *om*
(*o*-physical/
m-spiritual)

Red, Yellow, and Blue in balance
(+) Synthesis, ceremony, ritual, unity, calm, magick, balance
(−) Separateness, pride, conceit, remorse, imbalance, chaos

Rainbow Stone Energies

(Note: When in doubt, use the primary color of the Mineral World totem as a determining factor for the Ray.)

Red Ray (includes Rose & Scarlet)
Jasper
Red Amber
Red Carnelian
Ruby
Garnet
Cinnabar
Some Coral (pink and red)
Some Marble
Some Shells
Rose Quartz
Kunzite (pink)
Rhodonite
Pink Tourmaline
Rhodochrosite
Dolomite

Orange Ray (includes Peach)
Orange Carnelian
Peach Carnelian
Rhodochrosite
Some Shells
Fire Agates
Fire Opals
Orange Opals
Orange Amber
Dolomite
Orange Jade
Orange Zircon (Jacinths)
Orange Citrine
Orange Topaz

Yellow Ray (includes Lime Green)
Cream Jade
Citrine
Most Topaz
Yellow Jade
Yellow Gold
Yellow Fluorite
Yellow Sapphire
Peridot
Some Marble
Yellow Amber
Yellow Zircon
Yellow Diamonds
Yellow Peridot
Some Shells
Tiger-Eye

Green Ray
Unikite
Greenish Fluorite
Epidot
Dioptase
Green Jade, Quartz, Moonstone, Turquoise
Emeralds
Green Tourmaline
Peridot
Serpentine
Aventurine
Malachite
Bloodstone

Blue Ray (includes Turquoise)
Blue Topaz
Amazonite
Aquamarine
Blue Lace Agate
Some Coral
Celestite
Blue Moonstone
Blue Fluorite
Chrysocolla
Light Sodalite
Light Lapis Lazuli
Light Sapphires
Turquoise
Some Granite

Indigo Ray
Dark Sapphires
Azurite
Blue Amber
Blue Tiger-Eye
Dark Lapis Lazuli
Dark Sodalite
Some Alexandrite
Some Fluorite
Star Sapphires

Violet Ray
Amethyst
Alexandrite
Lavender Jade
Some Violet Garnets
Some Fluorite
Sugalite (Royal Azule)
Dark Opals
Some Coral
Some Tourmaline

White Ray
Selenite
Mother-of-Pearl
White Coral
Some Opals
Pearls (white or cream)
White Moonstone
Chalcedony
Some Shells
Some Fluorite
Marble

Crystal Ray
Some Geodes
Clear Kunzite
Clear Topaz
Selenite
Rock Crystal*
Herkimer Diamonds
Zircon*
Diamonds*
Some Fluorite
Rutilated or Tourmalinated Quartz with few inclusions

*unless colored or rainbowed

Brown Ray
Mahogany Obsidian
Iron Ore
Cinnabar
Fossils
Bone
Clay
Soapstone
Sardonyx
Selenite
Some Jaspers, Agates, Marble, & Topaz
Smoky Quartz
Pipestone (Catlinite)
Petrified Wood
Sandstone
"Ruin Rocks"
Shells

Black Ray
Mica
Turitella
Black Jade
Jet
Onyx
Obsidian (Apache Tears)
Black Tourmaline
Dark Smoky Quartz
Dark Tiger-Eye
Some Granite and Marble
Lava
Black Sand
Some Shells

Grey Ray
Fossils
Hematite
Some Moonstone
Scarabs
Dark Pearls
Some Shells
Pewter
Some Celestite
Epidot
Some Serpentine
Granite and Marble Quartz

Rainbow Ray
Crystals with rainbow inclusions
Abalone
Mother-of-Pearl
Opals
Bournite (Peacock Ore)
Diamonds and Zircons with rainbow fire

Gold Ray
Heavily Rutilated Quartz
Purely Gold Citrine
Golden Topaz
Golden Amber
Pyrite
Gold
Copper
Some Herkimer Diamonds
Brass
Bronze

Silver Ray
Some Granite
Hematite
Mercury
Silver
Iron
Steel
Platinum
Aluminum and Tin
Silvery Moonstone
Some Turquoise (heavily grained with silver veins)

Combination Ray*
Salt
Sand
Soil
Some Composite Rocks
Some Geodes
Some Opals (tricky)

*(Use for all Mineral World Rays if need be.)

Sacred Symbols

Spiritual Symbols

	Pentagram (Traditional Celtic Witch's Foot)		Mithras (Persian Sun God)
	Pentagram (Neopagan)		Owl of Wisdom
	Star of David (Solomon's Seal)		Water
	Ankh		Air
	Scarab of Kyphi		Fire
	Christian Cross		Earth
	Celtic Cross		Spirit (Light)
	Phoenix (Thunderbird)		Moon Goddess (Athenesic, Native American)
	Bridget's Cross		Druidic Wheel (Eight-point Star of Regeneration)
	Eye of God (Ojo de Dios)		Egyptian Sacred Eye
	Crusaders Cross (Jerusalem Cross)		Odin's Cross
	Yin-Yang		Wolf's Cross
	Primitive Cross (Nature's Cross)		Manito (Great Spirit, Native American)

	Wiccan Symbols				
	Theban Alphabet	Runic Alphabet		Theban Alphabet	Runic Alphabet
A			N		
B			O		
C			P		
D			Q		
E			R		
F			S		
G			T		
H			U		
I			V		
J			W		
K			X		
L			Y		
M			Z		

Zodiacal Symbols

⊕	Earth	♈	Aries
☽	Moon	♉	Taurus
☉	Sun	♊	Gemini
♀	Venus	♋	Cancer
♂	Mars	♌	Leo
♃	Jupiter	♍	Virgo
☿	Mercury	♎	Libra
♄	Saturn	♏	Scorpio
♇	Pluto	♐	Sagittarius
♆	Neptune	♑	Capricorn
♅	Uranus	♒	Aquarius
♀	Vulcan	♓	Pisces

Shamanic Self-Healing Chart

Chakra	Disorders	Activate/Energize	Balance/ Soothe at all Locations
1ST ROOT	Anger, frustration, impatience, rage Depression, fatigue, anemia, nerve & skin disorders	Redirect flow of energy with Rose Energize with Rose, Red, & Scarlet (start slowly; move carefully to stimulate blood building)	Soothe with Blue, Green, and Indigo Counterbalance with Light Blue and Turquoise
2ND SACRAL	Repression, fear, inhibitions Digestive disorders, vitality drains, etheric body drains	Release inhibitions & open repressive channels with Peach and Orange Redirect energy flow & revitalize with Red, Orange, Peach	Soothe fears, etc., with Green for courage Soothe digestion with Blue and Green; move slowly into Indigo for completion
3RD SOLAR PLEXUS	Mental overload, brain drain Poor circulation, intestinal viruses, colds	Recharge mental capacities with Golden Yellow Surround the body in Sunny Yellow and Gold	Soothe overstimulation & overload with gentle Lavender, Indigo, & Violet Soothe tissues with Pale Yellow & Light Gold
4TH HEART	Jealousy, envy, greed, negativity, resistance Ulcers, flu, blood pressure, heart palpitations	Activate deep positive energy with Emerald Green Energize with clear healing Green, light to dark	Clear out all negativity with Gold Follow with Emerald Green and soothing Forest Green
5TH THROAT	Passivity, isolation, possessiveness Throat problems, respiratory infections, cramps	Activate positive energy flow with clear Orange Follow with Sky Blue and Turquoise; energize healing with rich Golden Amber	Soothe insecurities (which lead to isolation, etc.) with Baby Blue Soothe inflamed areas with cool, clear Blue
6TH BROW	Arrogance, irritability, conceit, totalitarianism Upper respiratory, nervous mental stress, headaches, sinus	Activate compassion and tolerance with Sunny Yellow-Orange and gentle spirit with soft Blue Soothe strains and constrictions with rich Royal Blue and Indigo; balance with Gold	Soothe overinflated ego with rich, earthy Gold and Brown Balance energy flow with pale Grey-Blue, deeper into Royal, then rich Indigo
7TH CROWN	Overexcitement, nerves, creative exhaustion, depression Overall lowered resistance, insomnia, bladder and kidney disorders, migraines	Activate natural creative flow with vibrant Violet and Gold Revitalize with Red-Purple, Blue-Violet; soothe with Violet and Lavender	Soothe exhausted capabilities with cool dark Violet; balance depression with pale healing Lavender Redirect proper flow of toxins with Gold and Violet

Human Totems	Animal Totems	Plant Totems	Mineral Totems
Movement—dance it out; act—express it Eastern void, deep meditative states; self-healing and renewal	Buffalo to see it all through Bear to heal hurts Cardinal to lift spirits	Willow for flexibility and to slow pace Oak for strength and endurance Dragon's blood resin	Rutile quartz to pull energy up, unblock anger Ruby, red amber, rose quartz, rhodochrosite to energize self and lift spirits
Act it out; journey into fear, etc., (make notes) Eastern void meditation for deep-level healing and renewal	Strong personal predator for protection Mythic animals such as dragons Doe to even pace Hawk to revitalize	Bright, blooming flowers (hibiscus) for courage, confidence Mints and fragrant teas (raspberry, strawberry) Orange for energy	Rhodochrosite, citrine, topaz, tiger-eye for confidence & expression Unikite, dolomite, and calcite for soothing Amber to revitalize
Physical exercise and baths to pull self out of mental into body Healing & stimulation of healing energy flow	Rabbit, mouse, kitten, chipmunk Small, playful, gentle animals with quick pace to energize and amuse	Magnolias and large tropical plants to slow pace Blooming tropicals for Sun-energy healing	Cool jade to soothe Amethyst for overloads Golden citrine, amber, topaz for golden healing
Nature walks and time to reconnect with gifts of Nature Solitude in a place of natural beauty—heal	Cougars, bobcats, & lynx for self-worth & confidence Owls for wisdom to see personal natural healing	Evergreens and nut-bearing trees to connect with the natural abundance of life	Emeralds, malachite, green fluorite, bloodstone, dioptase, green jade, green tourmaline, copper for warmth
Active group work to stimulate flow of energy; start small work up Talk, talk, talk—on tape if need be	Parrots, coyotes, squirrels, magpies, mynah birds Expressive animals and birds	Flowering and fruit trees Wildflowers that bloom in bunches, daisies, etc.	Golden and orange amber for healing warmth Blue topaz, celestite, aquamarine to soothe
Zen one-point awareness exercises; Nature festival celebrations Laughter, humor, art, dance; Oriental mindfulness	Gentle fawn, rabbits, dolphin for humor (& to show a superior mind) Whales for perspective Herons and doves for peace	Redwoods to give perspective Elm, ash, and oak for strength and real security (not false pride) Rose for peace	Jaspers and agates to earth energy Coral for energy flow Celestite, lapis, sodalite, aquamarine, sapphires, azurite for strength
High magick and ceremony to attune with high-vibration energy Eastern deep void meditation for deep healing earth magick	Eagles to replenish tired ideals Mythic animals to connect with energy through symbols Bear for nurturance and healing	Oak to ground tension and give deep-level support Evergreens for spiritual renewal Blossoming trees	Garnet, alexandrite, celestite, amethyst, purple fluorite, royal azule (sugalite) for accessing DNA codes and for proper energy flow

Sacred Wheels

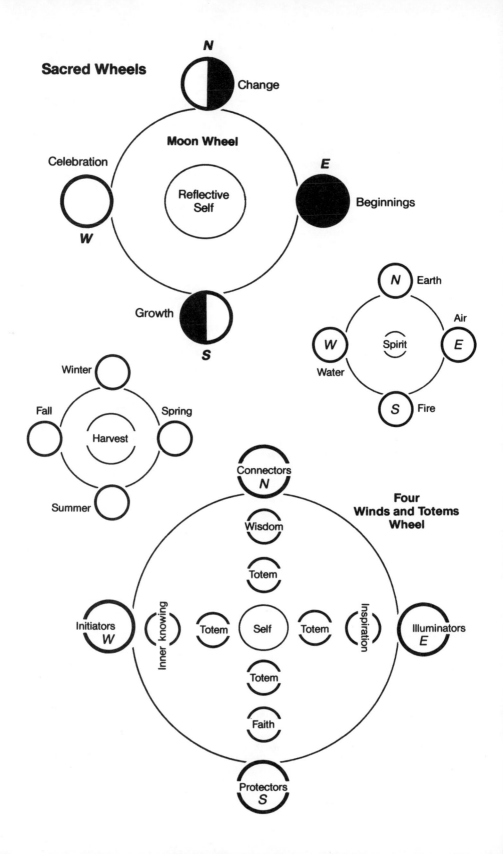

Moon Wheel

N — Change
E — Beginnings
W — Celebration
S — Growth
Reflective Self

N — Earth
E — Air
S — Fire
W — Water
Spirit

Winter
Spring
Summer
Fall
Harvest

Four Winds and Totems Wheel

Connectors N
Wisdom
Totem
Initiators W
Inner knowing
Totem
Self
Totem
Inspiration
Illuminators E
Totem
Faith
Protectors S

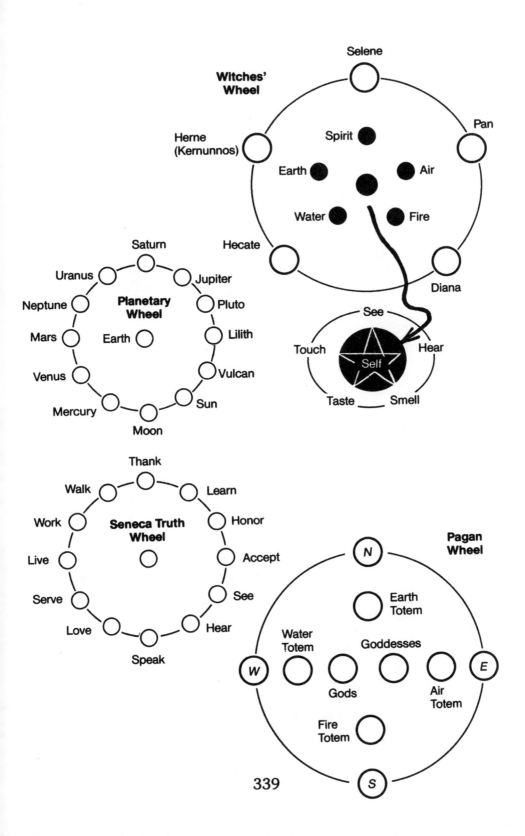

Witches' Wheel

Selene
Pan
Herne (Kernunnos)
Hecate
Diana

Spirit
Earth
Air
Water
Fire

See
Touch
Hear
Self
Taste
Smell

Planetary Wheel

Saturn
Uranus
Jupiter
Neptune
Pluto
Mars
Lilith
Venus
Vulcan
Mercury
Sun
Moon
Earth

Seneca Truth Wheel

Thank
Walk
Learn
Work
Honor
Live
Accept
Serve
See
Love
Hear
Speak

Pagan Wheel

N
Earth Totem
Water Totem
Goddesses
W
E
Gods
Air Totem
Fire Totem
S

339

Nature Cycles and Totems

Waning Moon *Plant:* mandrake, garlic, rue, frankincense, juniper, willow, sage, sweetgrass, cedar, night flowers. *Animal:* raven, wolf, bear, jaguar, panther, owl, nighthawks, mythic animals. *Human:* shamanic journeys, Eastern void meditations, deeply personal rituals and burnings, earthings, casting out ceremonies. *Mineral:* obsidian, jet, smoky quartz, black jade, dark amethyst, onyx, hematite, lava, soil.

Dark of the Moon Deeply personal protective totems and select familiar banishing totems.

New Moon *Plant:* any newly budding plant, or new growth from a plant, vanilla, cinnamon, mugwort, jasmine, myrrh, rosemary, mandrake. *Animal:* heron, cats, hawks, bear, fox, butterflies, doves, cardinals, wrens. *Human:* Zen one-point awareness, burnings, focus, exercises, art. *Mineral:* all crystals, lodestones, rose quartz, carnelian, amber, soil, peridot.

Waxing Moon *Plant:* pine, honeysuckle, sandalwood, holly, blooming flowers and plants. *Animal:* deer, working dogs, beavers, bobcats, large water birds, squirrels, chipmunks. *Human:* structured Nature rites and set rituals, "business update" and strategy management sessions with yourself. *Mineral:* carnelian, jasper, agates, malachite, chrysocolla, turquoise, citrine, dioptase, tourmaline, rutilated quartz.

Full Moon *Plant:* oak, ash, evergreen, roses, gardenias, lotus, full blossoms, palms, allspice, bayberry, almond. *Animal:* bear, white doe, mythic animals. *Human:* natural and expressive spirituality, dancing, singing, drawing, ceremony (freeform and set), ritual. *Mineral:* clear, bright gemstones and crystals, esp. emeralds and sapphires, amethysts, silver.

340

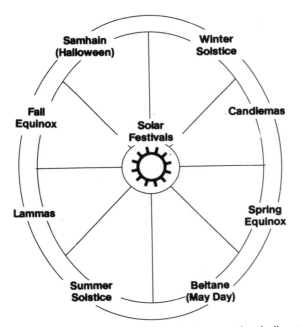

Winter Solstice *Plant:* All evergreens, pine, juniper, cedar, holly, mistletoe, oak, frankincense, myrrh, bayberry. *Animal:* horned goats, owls, stag deer, mythic animals, eagles. *Human:* healing, sharing circles and group journeys, vision quests. *Mineral:* gold, topaz, malachite, garnets.

Candlemas *Plant:* crocus, camellias, shamrocks. *Animal:* rabbit, owl, hibernating animals (esp. bears). *Human:* music, dance, writing, art, inner journeys, creative work. *Mineral:* copper, marble, river stones, lava, jasper, smoky quartz.

Spring Equinox *Plant:* spring flowers, new green leaves. *Animal:* all newborn, gentle animals, spring birds. *Human:* ceremonies and gentle festivals of gratitude. *Mineral:* rose quartz, carnelians, topaz, lavender amethyst, blue lace agate.

Beltane *Plant:* wildflowers, tuberoses, lilies, oak, ash, willow. *Animal:* hawks, stag deer, white doe, rabbits, rams, ewes. *Human:* weddings, celebrations of joy and fertility, dances, picnics, ceremonies of Nature. *Mineral:* malachite, agates, carnelian, ruby, silver.

Summer Solstice *Plant:* roses, jasmine, mimosa, hibiscus, blooming plants. *Animal:* peacock, peahen, white doe, jaguar, doves. *Human:* healing circles of all types, Nature ceremonies, shamanic journeys. *Mineral:* malachite, emeralds, sapphire, lapis lazuli, turquoise, amazonite, silver, moonstone.

Lammas *Plant:* corn, barley, wheat, fall leaves, sunflowers. *Animal:* stag deer, buffalo, bears, wolves, hawk, eagle. *Human:* spiritual house cleaning, organize mind, body, spirit. *Mineral:* carnelian, amber, tourmaline, malachite, soil, ores, marble, shells.

Fall Equinox *Plant:* maple, hickory, sage, sweetgrass, sandalwood. *Animal:* bighorn sheep, mountain goats, squirrels. *Human:* group and circle work for balancing healing energies. *Mineral:* gold, emeralds, jasper, agates, citrine.

Samhain *Plant:* lavender, ivy, harvest vegetables, leaves, roots. *Animal:* black cat, raven, panther, owl, shadowy animals. *Human:* shamanic journeys, seances, releasing, Nature rituals. *Mineral:* copper, gold, silver, amethyst, obsidian, soil, granite.

Talismanic Squares

(A talismanic square is like a computer code and taps into Universal Intelligence.)

4	9	2
3	5	7
8	1	6

Talisman of Saturn

(The number three is sacred to Saturn.)

Burn in the flame of a dark blue candle on a Saturday for concentration, endurance, and patience.

4	14	15	1
9	7	6	12
5	11	10	8
16	2	3	13

Talisman of Jupiter

(The number four is sacred to Jupiter.)

Burn in the flame of a dark green candle on a Thursday for success in business, finances, and social affairs.

11	24	7	20	3
4	12	25	8	16
17	5	13	21	9
10	18	1	14	22
23	6	19	2	15

Talisman of Mars

(The number five is sacred to Mars.)

Burn in the flame of a red candle on a Tuesday for leadership, strength, vitality, and power.

6	32	3	34	35	1
7	11	27	28	8	30
19	14	16	15	23	24
18	20	22	21	17	13
25	29	10	9	26	12
36	5	33	4	2	31

Talisman of the Sun

(The number six is sacred to the Sun.)

Burn in the flame of a gold candle on a Sunday for peace and universal love.

22	47	16	41	10	35	4
5	23	48	17	42	11	29
30	6	24	49	18	36	12
13	31	7	25	43	19	37
38	14	32	1	26	44	20
21	39	8	33	2	27	45
46	15	40	9	34	3	28

Talisman of Venus

(The number seven is sacred to Venus.)

Burn in the flame of a rose pink candle on a Friday for romance, love affairs, and beauty.

8	58	59	5	4	62	63	1
49	15	14	52	53	11	10	56
41	23	22	44	48	19	18	45
32	34	38	29	25	35	39	28
40	26	27	37	36	30	31	33
17	47	43	20	21	46	42	24
9	55	54	12	13	51	50	16
64	2	3	61	60	6	7	57

Talisman of Mercury

(The number eight is sacred to Mercury.)

Burn in the flame of a yellow candle on a Wednesday for knowledge, mental abilities, perception, and logic.

37	78	29	70	21	62	13	54	5
6	38	79	30	71	22	63	14	46
47	7	39	80	31	72	23	55	15
16	48	8	40	81	32	64	24	56
57	17	49	9	41	73	33	65	25
26	58	18	50	1	42	74	34	66
67	27	59	10	51	2	43	75	35
36	68	19	60	11	52	3	44	76
77	28	69	20	61	12	53	4	45

Talisman of the Moon

(The number nine is
sacred to the Moon.)

Burn in the flame of a
silver candle on a Monday
for strengthening your
psychic and intuitive abilities.

Celtic Runes

Attainment/Wholeness
Use for support of disciplined growth, rewards worked for, acceptance of success, responsible use of abundance, and for self-completion, holistic balance, harmony.

Warrior/Revolutionary
Use to signal philosophical ideals, spiritual strength, love of humanity. Strengthen creative genius, support reform, and acquire the strength and courage to make changes in your life.

Karma/Journey
Use to strengthen personal service to your path, to signal deepest psychic connections, highest magick, journey. Karma is choice: choose your journey.

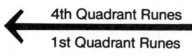

4th Quadrant Runes

1st Quadrant Runes

Self/Personality
Use for strength and courage to walk on your own, your personal path. Develop self-awareness, self-esteem. Knowledge is power: know your Self.

Security/Possessions
Use for material, financial, and emotional gain and satisfaction, for freedom from want or need.

Communication/Messages
Use to increase mental abilities, objectivity, and rapport with others. Sharpen clarity in speech, writing and listening.

Shaman Center
Self-Protection

Unknown Fates
Highest Self

Union/Partners
Use to strengthen love relationships, sex, marriage, and friendships. Support shared life journeys. Strengthen true partnership of self to Self.

Transformation/Initiation
Use to signal processes of deep personal intuition, renewal, regeneration, and spiritual awakening. Birth, death, transformation, rebirth.

Expansion/Breakthrough
Use for increased spiritual awareness; signal shift to higher aspirations, deeper psychic experience, shamanic dreams, wishes fulfilled, in the flow.

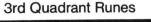

3rd Quadrant Runes
2nd Quadrant Runes

Inner Mind/Personal Psychic Work
Use to develop sensitivity and attunement to psychic self. Retreat for growth. Strengthen ties to home and family.

Love/Joy
Use to strengthen energy for physical relationships, kinships, artistic expression and creativity, pleasure.

Abundance/Health
Use to celebrate the harvest of self, holistic wellness. Strengthen relationships in work, family.

Divination Wheels

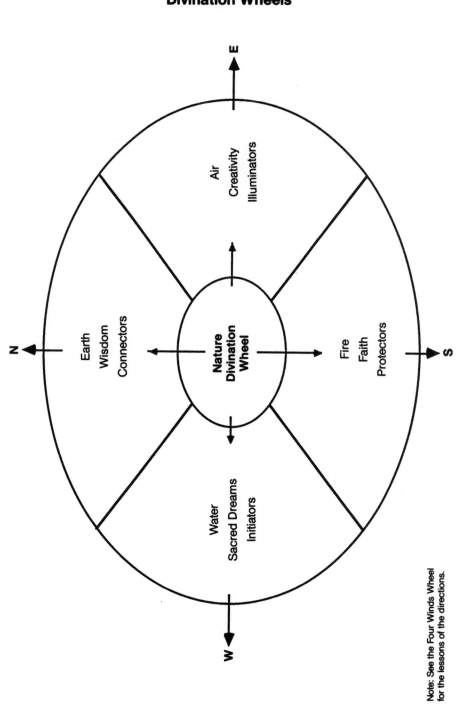

E

N

S

W

Air
Creativity
Illuminators

Earth
Wisdom
Connectors

**Nature
Divination
Wheel**

Fire
Faith
Protectors

Water
Sacred Dreams
Initiators

Note: See the Four Winds Wheel
for the lessons of the directions.

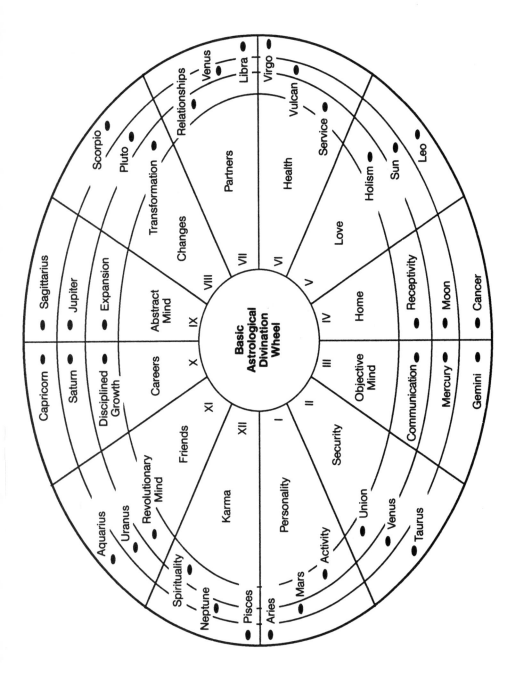

Basic Astrological Divination Wheel

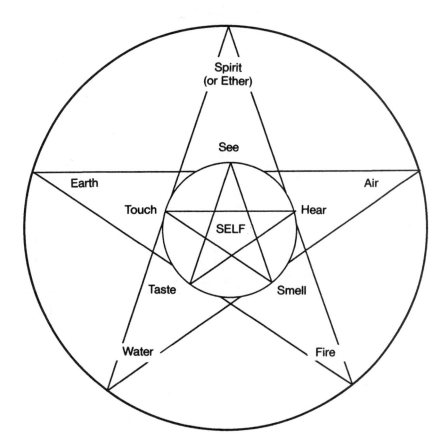

Witches' Divination Wheel

Note: Learn the elemental
attributes for divination.

Annotated Bibliography

It is not in the scope of this work to present all of the wonderful books that have contributed to my journey through the years. Instead of providing endless lists of reading resources, I have selected a few choice books and a few choice authors whose wisdom I have found tremendously valuable and supportive.

According to an ancient adage attributed to the Buddhist traditions, "When the student is ready, the teacher will appear." I have found this to be true of books as well. Books can be our dearest teachers, friends, and totems for self-growth and development.

Selected Authors

The authors I have selected have produced works of such value that I feel confident to preface each one by saying anything by this author can make a contribution to your journey on a magical or shamanic path.

Lynn Andrews, medicine teacher and shamanic counselor. Lynn Andrews describes her shamanic life journey with great courage and practical wisdom. Her books are especially useful for understanding the shamanic experience from a more feminine perspective than most shamanic writings. If you choose just one to start, I suggest *Flight of the Seventh Moon: Teaching the Shields,* Harper and Row, 1974.

Stephen Arroyo, psychologist and astrological counselor. Stephen Arroyo brings astrology to earth by emphasizing the interplay of the elements in our lives and our personalities. His books provide useful, understandable information we may apply for ourselves and in our work. To start, I suggest *Astrology, Psychology, and the Four Elements: An Energy Approach to Astrology and Its Use in the Counseling Arts,* CRCS Publication, 1975.

Joseph Campbell, mythologist and anthropologist. Joseph Campbell's in-depth exploration of myths and cultures is nothing short of amazing in its scope. His books present material that is impeccable in its academic quality yet fascinating in its wisdom. Although it is somewhat expensive, I suggest the very valuable resource *The Way of Animal Powers.*

Carlos Castenada, medicine teacher and shamanic anthropologist. Carlos Castenada has been chronicling his shamanic journey and sharing previously hidden wisdoms for many years now. His books provide useful, multileveled lessons taken from his own experiences on the path of the shaman. Of his many valuable works, I suggest *Journey to Ixtlan: The Lessons of Don Juan,* Simon and Schuster, 1972.

Scott Cunningham, master herbalist and teacher of earth magick. Scott Cunningham's work presents material that is useful for all followers of Nature, magical, or shamanic paths. His books are compendiums of research and information presented in a practical, friendly manner—much like having your own house wizard. I suggest that you collect his books as resources for your work. If you must choose only one to start, try *Earth Power,* Llewellyn Publications, 1985.

Ram Dass, psychologist and spiritual teacher. Ram Dass (Richard Alpert) has a message for us all in his works on spirituality, oneness, and service. His books provide a continuing source of inspiration and wisdom to help our souls' journey. To start, I suggest *Be Here Now,* Hanuman Foundation, 1978.

Dion Fortune, occultist, psychoanalyst, and co-founder of the Golden Dawn. Dion Fortune presents deeply esoteric information with clarity and practicality. Her books, fiction and nonfiction, help produce a workable, no-nonsense blend of therapeutic uses of ancient magical wisdoms for our own use on the path. As a foundation for any magical and shamanic work, I suggest *Psychic Self-Defence,* Samuel Weiser, 1984.

Jean Houston, psychologist and evocateur. Jean Houston's vision of the possible human as a multisensory, multimodal being is much in keeping with the ancient ways of training the shaman/ magician in ourselves as individuals. Her books are informative and instructive, as befits the writings of a founding member of the Human Potential Movement in psychology. As a manual for awakening your personal potential, I suggest *The Possible Human,* J. P. Tarcher, 1982.

Carl Jung, psychoanalyst and Western mystic. Carl Jung's exploration into the myths and makeup of mankind provides us with valuable insight into our own self-composition. His books reflect the wisdom and experience of a great mind and a great heart. For a personal sense of this man and his work, I suggest *Memories, Dreams, Reflections,* Random House, 1973.

Timothy Leary, psychologist and teacher of expanded potentials. Timothy Leary's works on the personal and social evolution of the human brain and mind are valuable insights into the patterns of our lives as individuals and as a society. His books present an intriguing set of ideas about the growth and direction of our intelligence and our positive potential as knowledgeable beings. I suggest *EXO-Psychology,* A Starseed/Peace Press, 1977.

Sybil Leek, witch and teacher of the Craft of the Wise. Sybil Leek may have paved the way for many of us in the varied works and public appearances she made during her lifetime. Her books are written with a gentle authority and a humorous wisdom that is rarely found. In some ways, she was much before her time, as is often the case with such teachers. Her books are difficult to locate, but well worth the effort. For a heartfelt balanced look at the Craft of the Wise, I suggest *The Complete Art of Witchcraft,* Signet, 1971.

Fritz Perls, psychiatrist and teacher of self-development. Fritz Perls is the father of Gestalt therapy, or personal, psychological synthesis methods. His works reflect the deep personal consciousness and self-awareness we need as followers of shamanic or magical paths. Additionally, Fritz Perls gives us insight and ideas that are foundations for our work with others. For a personal understanding of his concepts, I suggest *In and Out the Garbage Pail,* Bantam, 1977.

Marion Weinstein, witch and teacher of the Craft of the Wise. Marion
Weinstein's work presents historical, sociological, psychological,
and ritual information on earth magick in a warm, positive manner.
Her books are filled with practical information, as well as sacred
explorations of the ancient ways of Nature in relationship to the
Self. As a foundation for your own Nature wisdom and work, I
suggest *Positive Magic: Occult Self-Help,* Phoenix Publishing,
1981.

Selected Books

The works included here vary greatly in style and format. Yet
each one has been a keystone for many gates to spiritual growth, as
well as a useful resource of wisdom for me personally. Limiting these
to thirteen was a feat, accomplished in a few cases by that most
ancient system of divination—flipping a coin. These books were
selected to provide yet another tool for your journey on the path of
the shaman.

Achterberg, Jeanne. *Imagery in Healing: Shamanism and Modern
Medicine.* Boston: New Science Library, 1985.

Imagery in Healing provides an in-depth discussion of the
ancient and modern uses of shamanic images and visionary
healing. The history and evolution of ancient shamanic methods
into modern applications give support for our own shamanic
work.

Bates, Brian. *The Way of Wyrd: Tales of An Anglo/Saxon Sorcerer.*
San Francisco: Harper and Row, 1983.

The Way of Wyrd is a fascinating account in fiction form of a
shamanic journey and lessons in a Celtic tradition. For those
who enjoy exploring varied forms of shamanism, this book provides
information in an enjoyable manner.

Bonewits, P. E. I. *Real Magic.* Berkeley: Creative Arts Book Company,
1971.

Real Magic earned Bonewits a degree in thanaturgy (magick). It
presents magick, occultism, and metaphysics in a concise manner

with great wisdom and warm, personal understanding. It is a definitive work.

Chocron, Daya Sarai. *Healing with Crystals and Gemstones.* York Beach, Maine: Samuel Weiser, 1986.

Healing with Crystals and Gemstones is written with clarity and gentle spirituality. It provides a good foundation from which to explore the use of Mineral World totems for self-healing and personal growth.

Cornelia, Marie Williams. *Gemstones and Color.* West Hartford, Connecticut: Triad Publishing, 1985.

Gemstones and Color is designed to provide lots of information to help you use Mineral World totems and Ray energies for increased health, healing, and happiness. Its light format and friendly manner make it a very useful, readable book.

Drury, Nevill. *The Shaman and the Magician: Journeys Between the Worlds.* London: Routledge and Kegan Paul, 1982.

The Shaman and the Magician is an in-depth exploration and comparison of aspects of traditional shamanism and visionary magick in Western occultism. Though somewhat academic in nature, it is a valuable resource for those interested in shamanic or magical paths. It provides a bridge to both.

Gendler, J. Ruth. *The Book of Qualities.* Berkeley: Turquoise Mountain Publications, 1984.

The Book of Qualities at first appears to be a collection of images reflecting personality aspects. However, on further exploration this book provides a valuable tool for personal insight, and for viewing characteristics of the Human World in the animistic manner of shamanism.

Halifax, Joan. *Shaman, The Wounded Healer.* New York: Crossroad Publishing, 1982.

Shaman, The Wounded Healer is a multifaceted exploration of shamanism in many cultures. It provides many visual, as well as anthropological, resources to deepen the reader's knowledge of shamanism and the life quests of the shaman.

Harner, Michael. *The Way of the Shaman: A Guide to Power and Healing.* New York: Bantam, 1982.

The Way of the Shaman is designed to give the reader a map or manual for charting a shamanic path. For those who prefer a set method approach, this book is a very valuable resource. All followers of a shamanic path will enjoy the personal journey accounts and stories of shamanic explorations.

Knight, Gareth. *The Practice of Ritual Magic.* New York: Samuel Weiser, 1976.

The Practice of Ritual Magic is a primer designed to help familiarize those who are new to a magical path, as well as to support those who have studied for a long time. Its forthright and concise style makes it a useful tool to have.

Slater, Herman, ed. *A Book of Pagan Rituals.* York Beach, Maine: Samuel Weiser, 1982.

A Book of Pagan Rituals is a wonderful collection of information, rituals, ceremonies, and readings on the ancient Nature ways of the Craft of the Wise. It is presented as they are interpreted and practiced today. This book is designed to help the solitary Pagan as well as groups following Nature ways.

Starhawk. *The Spiral Dance: A Rebirth of the Ancient Religion of the Great Goddess.* San Francisco: Harper and Row, 1979.

The Spiral Dance is a collection of magical exercises, rituals, and poetic ceremonies designed to enhance the reemergence of the Goddess aspects within us all. Additionally, this book presents the Craft of the Wise in a clear, understandable format.

Walker, Barbara G. *The Woman's Encyclopedia of Myths and Secrets.* New York: Harper and Row, 1983.

The Woman's Encyclopedia of Myths and Secrets is an amazingly extensive collection of facts and information on magick, myth, mysticism, spirituality, and occultism. This is a valuable addition to anyone's library and provides a new look at some very ancient lore.

Note to the Reader

In order to help you map your journey on the shamanic path, as well as explore your relationships to the cycles of Nature and the moon, I suggest that you obtain *Llewellyn's Astrological Calendar* (yearly) and *Llewellyn's Moon Sign Book* (yearly). If you have an interest in astrology, I also suggest *Llewellyn's Sun Sign Book* (yearly) and *Llewellyn's Daily Planetary Guide* (yearly).

These calendars and guide books are a constant source of information and a valuable tool for any follower of Nature ways. They provide a clear, concise, and instructive resource to use as a support on your journey. Even after many years of using these, I continue to find new and illuminating insights. I suggest these to clients who are beginning to explore their dance with Nature, and to those who have walked in Nature ways for a long time.

If you must choose only one to start, I recommend *Llewellyn's Astrological Calendar*. This calendar is filled with useful information and guidance on how to interpret and map the ways of Nature in your life. Literally, the more you use it as a resource, the deeper your knowledge of Nature becomes.

STAY IN TOUCH

On the following pages you will find listed, with their current prices, some of the books and tapes now available on related subjects. Your book dealer stocks most of these, and will stock new titles in the Llewellyn series as they become available. We urge your patronage.

However, to obtain our full catalog, to keep informed of new titles as they are released and to benefit from informative articles and helpful news, you are invited to write for our bi-monthly news magazine/catalog. A sample copy is free, and it will continue coming to you at no cost as long as you are an active mail customer. Or you may keep it coming for a full year with a donation of just $5.00 in U.S.A. & Canada ($20.00 overseas, first class mail). Many bookstores also have *The Llewellyn New Times* available to their customers. Ask for it.

Stay in touch! In *The Llewellyn New Times'* pages you will find news and reviews of new books, tapes and services, announcements of meetings and seminars, articles helpful to our readers, news of authors, advertising of products and services, special money-making opportunities, and much more.

The Llewellyn New Times
P.O. Box 64383-Dept. 888, St. Paul, MN 55164-0383, U.S.A.
• • •

TO ORDER BOOKS AND TAPES

If your book dealer does not have the books and tapes described on the following pages readily available, you may order them direct from the publisher by sending full price in U.S. funds, plus $1.50 for postage and handling for orders *under* $10.00; $3.00 for orders *over* $10.00. There are no postage and handling charges for orders over $50. UPS Delivery: We ship UPS whenever possible. Delivery guaranteed. Provide your street address as UPS does not deliver to P.O. Boxes. UPS to Canada requires a $50 minimum order. Allow 4–6 weeks for delivery. Orders outside the U.S.A. and Canada: Airmail—add retail price of book; add $5 for each non-book item (tapes, etc.); add $1 per item for surface mail.

FOR GROUP STUDY AND PURCHASE

Because there is a great deal of interest in group discussion and study of the subject matter of this book, we feel that we should encourage the adoption and use of this particular book by such groups by offering a special "quantity" price to group leaders or "agents."

Our Special Quantity Price for a minimum order of five copies of *In the Shadow of the Shaman* is $38.85 cash-with-order. This price includes postage and handling within the United States. Minnesota residents must add 6% sales tax. For additional quantities, please order in multiples of five. For Canadian and foreign orders, add postage and handling charges as above. Credit card (VISA, Master Card, American Express) orders are accepted. Charge card orders only may be phoned free ($15.00 minimum order) within the U.S.A. or Canada by dialing 1-800-THE-MOON. Customer service calls dial 1-612-291-1970. Mail Orders to:

LLEWELLYN PUBLICATIONS
P.O. Box 64383-Dept. 888 / St. Paul, MN 55164-0383, U.S.A.

THE LLEWELLYN ANNUALS

Llewellyn's MOON SIGN BOOK: Approximately 400 pages of valuable information on gardening, fishing, weather, stock market forecasts, personal horoscopes, good planting dates, and general instructions for finding the best date to do just about anything! Article by prominent forecasters and writers in the fields of gardening, astrology, politics, economics and cycles. This special almanac, different from any other, has been published annually since 1906. It's fun, informative and has been a great help to millions in their daily planning.   **State year $4.95**

Llewellyn's SUN SIGN BOOK: Your personal horoscope for the entire year! All 12 signs are included in one handy book. Also included are forecasts, special feature articles, and an action guide for each sign. Monthly horoscopes are written by Gloria Star, author of *Optimum Child*, for your personal Sun Sign and there are articles on a variety of subjects written by well-known astrologers from around the country. Much more than just a horoscope guide! Entertaining and fun the year around.   **State year $4.95**

Llewellyn's DAILY PLANETARY GUIDE and ASTROLOGER'S DATEBOOK: Includes all of the major daily aspects plus their exact times in Eastern and Pacific time zones, lunar phases, signs and voids plus their times, planetary motion, a monthly ephemeris, sunrise and sunset tables, special articles on the planets, signs, aspects, a business guide, planetary hours, rulerships, and much more. Large 5 1/4 x 8 format for more writing space, spiral bound to lay flat, address and phone listings, time zone conversion chart and blank horoscope chart.   **State year $6.95**

Llewellyn's ASTROLOGICAL CALENDAR: Large wall calendar of 52 pages. Beautiful full color cover and color inside. Includes special feature articles by famous astrologers, introductory information on astrology. Lunar Gardening Guide, celestial phenomena, a blank horoscope chart for your own chart data, and monthly date pages which include aspects, lunar information, planetary motion, ephemeris, personal forecasts, lucky dates, planting and fishing dates, and more. 10 x 13 size. Set in Central time, with conversion table for other time zones worldwide.
          State year $9.95

Llewellyn's MAGICKAL ALMANAC
Edited by Ray Buckland
The Magickal Almanac examines some of the many forms that Magick can take, allowing the reader a peek behind a veil of secrecy into Egyptian, Shamanic,Wiccan and other traditions. The almanac pages for each month provide information important in the many aspects of working Magick: sunrise and sunset, phases and signs of the Moon, and festival dates, as well as the tarot card, herb, incense, color, and ingresses of the Sun and Moon associated with the particular day.

Articles addressing one form of Magick, with rituals the reader can easily follow, appear each month. An indispensable guide for all interested in the Magickal arts, *the Magickal Almanac* features writing by some of the most prominent authors in the field.the various fdorms of Magick provide rituals the reader can easily follow.
          State year $9.95

BIRTH OF A MODERN SHAMAN
by Cynthia Bend and Tayja Wiger

This is the amazing true story of Tayja Wiger. As a child she had been beaten and sexually abused. As an adult she was beaten and became a prostitute. To further her difficulties she was a member of a minority, a Native American Sioux, and was also legally blind.

Tayja's courage and will determined that she needed to make changes in her life. This book follows her physical and emotional healing through the use of Transactional Analysis and Re-Birthing, culminating in the healing of her blindness by the Spiritualistic Minister Marilyn Rossner, through the laying on-of-hands.

Astrology and graphology are used to show the changes in Tayja as her multiple personalities, another problem from which she suffered, were finally integrated into one. Tayja has become both a shaman and a healer.

In *Birth of a Modem Shaman* there are powerful skills anyone can develop by becoming a shaman, the least of which is becoming balanced, at peace with the world around you, productive and happy. By using the techniques in this book you will move tc\ward a magickal understanding of the universe that can help you achieve whatever you desire, and can help *you* to become a modern shaman.

0-87542-034-6, 272 pgs., 6 x 9, illus., softcover $9.95

THE MAGICAL HOUSEHOLD
by Scott Cunningham and David Harrington

Whether your home is a small apartment or a palatial mansion, you want it to be something special. Now it can be with The Magical Household. Learn how to make your home more than just a place to live. Turn it into a place of security, life, fun and magic. Here you will not find the complex magic of the ceremonial magician. Rather, you will learn simple, quick and effective magical spells that use nothing more than common items in your house: furniture, windows, doors, carpet, pets, etc. You will learn to take advantage of the intrinsic power and energy that is already in your home, waiting to be tapped. You will learn to make magic a part of your life. The result is a home that is safeguarded from harm and a place which will bring you happiness, health and more.

ISBN: 0–87542–124–5, 5¹/₄ x 8, illus., softcover $8.95

EARTH POWER: TECHNIQUES OF NATURAL MAGIC
by Scott Cunningham

Magick is the art of working with the forces of Nature to bring about necessary, and desired, changes. The forces of Nature—expressed through Earth, Air, Fire and Water—are our "spiritual ancestors" who paved the way for our emergence from the prehistoric seas of creation. Attuning to, and working with these energies in magick not only lends you the power to affect changes in your life, it also allows you to sense your own place in the larger scheme of Nature. Using the "Old Ways" enables you to live a better life, and to deepen your understanding of the world about you. The tools and powers of magick are around you, waiting to be grasped and utilized. This book gives you the means to put Magick into your life, shows you how to make and use the tools, and gives you spells for every purpose.

0–87542–121–0, 176 pgs., 5¹/₄ x 8, illus., softcover $8.95

WICCA: A Guide for the Solitary Practitioner
by Scott Cunningham

Wicca is a book of life, and how to live magically, spiritually, and wholly attuned with Nature. It is a book of sense and common sense, not only about Magick, but about religion and one of the most critical issues of today: how to achieve the much needed and wholesome relationship with our Earth. Cunningham presents Wicca as it is today—a gentle, Earth-oriented religion dedicated to the Goddess and God. This book fulfills a need for a practical guide to solitary Wicca—a need which no previous book has fulfilled.

Here is a positive, practical introduction to the religion of Wicca, designed so that any interested person can learn to practice the religion alone, anywhere in the world. It presents Wicca honestly and clearly, without the pseudo-history that permeates other books. It shows that Wicca is a vital, satisfying part of twentieth century life.

This book presents the theory and practice of Wicca from an individual's perspective. The section on the Standing Stones Book of Shadows contains solitary rituals for the Esbats and Sabbats. This book, based on the author's nearly two decades of Wiccan practice, presents an eclectic picture of various aspects of this religion. Exercises designed to develop magical proficiency, a self-dedication ritual, herb, crystal and rune magic, recipes for Sabbat feasts, are included in this excellent book.
0-87542-118-0, 240 pgs., softcover, 6 x 9, illus. **$9.95**

CHAKRA THERAPY
by Keith Sherwood

Keith Sherwood presents another excellent how-to book on healing. His previous book, *The Art of Spiritual Healing* has helped many people learn how to heal themselves and others.

Chakra Therapy follows in the same direction: Understand yourself, know how your body and mind function and learn how to overcome negative programming so that you can become a free, healthy, self-fulfilled human being.

This book fills in the missing pieces of the human anatomy system left out by orthodox psychological models. It serves as a superb workbook. Within its pages are exercises and techniques designed to increase your level of energy, to transmute unhealthy frequencies of energy into healthy ones, to bring you back into balance and harmony with your self, your loved ones and the multidimensional world you live in. Finally, it will help bring you back into union with the universal field of energy and consciousness.

Chakra Therapy will teach you how to heal yourself by healing your energy system because it is actually energy in its myriad forms which determines a person's physical health, emotional health, mental health and level of consciousness.
0-87542-721-9, 270 pgs., softcover, 5¼ x 8, illus. **$7.95**

THE WOMEN'S SPIRITUALITY BOOK
by Diane Stein

Diane Stein has become one of the most important voices in the women's spirituality movement, and this book has become a guiding light to many in that movement. It is composed of two major sections. In the first you will find out exactly what women's spirituality is. Then you will discover "herstory," the true record of events that male historians ignore or omit. You will find out about early (and modern) Goddess-oriented peoples and what happened to them when they were taken over by patriarchal societies. In studying creation myths and creation goddesses she enthusiastically informs you of the essence of women-centered Wicca using myths and legends drawn from a variety of world sources to bring this work to life. Non-patriarchal myths and tales intersperse the first half of the book, which leads the reader through the yearly progressions of rituals in some of the most complete descriptions of the Sabbats ever published.

The second half of the book is a valuable introduction to spirituality skills. Here you will learn the techniques of creative visualization, healing, the spiritual uses of crystals and gemstones, Tarot as a tool for transformation and a non-sexist view of the I Ching.

This book is filled with illustrations, both original and from ancient sculptures, or women and Goddess images. It is a tool for self-discovery and initiation into the Higher Self: a joyous reunion with the Goddess. This book gives you a background for approaching the world and a way of dealing with day-to-day situations, making this a beautiful source of spirituality for anyone.

0-87542-761-8, 296 pgs., softcover, 6 x 9, illus. **$9.95**

THE WOMEN'S BOOK OF HEALING
by Diane Stein

At the front of the women's spirituality movement with her previous books, Diane Stein now helps women (and men) reclaim their natural right to be healers. Included are exercises which can help YOU to become a healer! Learn about the uses of color, vibration, crystals and gems for healing. Learn about the auric energy field and the chakras.

The book teaches alternative healing theory and techniques and combines them with crystal and gemstone healing, laying on of stones, psychic healing, laying on of hands, chakra work and aura work, color therapy. It teaches beginning theory in the aura, chakras, colors, creative visualization, meditation, health theory and ethics with some quantum theory. 46 gemstones plus clear quartz crystals are discussed in detail, arranged by chakras and colors.

The Women's Book of Healing is a book designed to teach basic healing (Part I) and healing with crystals and gemstones (Part II). Part I discusses the aura and four bodies; the chakras; basic healing skills of creative visualization, meditation and color work; psychic healing; and laying on of hands. Part II begins with a chapter on clear quartz crystal, then enters gemstone work with introductory gemstone material. The remainder of the book discusses, in chakra by chakra format, specific gemstones for healing work, their properties and uses.

0-87542-759-6, 317 pgs., softcover, 6 x 9, color plates. **$12.95**

TAROT SPELLS
by Janina Renee
This book provides a means of recognizing and affirming one's own personal power through use of the Tarot. With the practical advice and beautiful illustrations in this book, the reader can perform spells for:

- Influencing dreams
- Better health
- Legal matters
- Better family relations
- Beating addiction
- Finding a job
- Better gardening

and more. Thirty-five areas of life are discussed, and spells are provided which address specific issues in these areas. The reader uses Tarot layouts in combination with affirmations and visualizations to obtain a desired result. Many spells can be used with color, gemstones or magical tools to assist the reader in focusing his or her desire.

Graced with beautiful card illustrations from the forthcoming *Robin Wood Tarot*, this book can be used immediately even by those who don't own a Tarot deck. No previous experience with the Tarot is necessary. Those familiar with the Tarot can gain new insights into the symbolism of their own particular deck.

0-87542-670-0, 6x9, 240 pp., illus.   **$12.95**

THE BOOK OF GODDESSES AND HEROINES
by Patricia Monaghan
Originally published in 1981, this groundbreaking book contained stories and information of 1,283 mythological and legendary female figures of all races and eras. It is the only complete, one-volume recitation of their legends in any available source bringing together images, stories and ritual details on goddesses from around the world.

This revised and updated printing contains an additional 250 goddesses, most of them from lesser-known cultures like the Baltic, Australian Aboriginal, Siberian/Korean, and Native American. In addition, color plates and photos of goddesses from around the world have been added.

Based on solid academic research, this book is both a valuable reference tool and a pleasurable book to read. The information on geographical and cultural origins, emblems, and iconography are written for the enjoyment of a wide audience.

0-87542-573-9, 6x9, 456 pgs., illus.   **$17.95**

CRYSTAL HEALING: The Next Step
by Phyllis Galde
Discover the further secrets of quartz crystal! Now modern research and use have shown that crystals have even more healing and therapeutic properties than has been realized. Learn why polished, smoothed crystal is better to use to heighten your intuition, improve creativity and for healing.

Learn to use crystals for reprogramming your subconscious to eliminate problems and negative attitudes that prevent success. Here are techniques that people have successfully used—not just theories.

This book reveals newly discovered abilities of crystal now accessible to all, and is a sensible approach to crystal use. *Crystal Healing* will be your guide to improve the quality of your life and expand your consciousness.
0-87542-246-2, 224 pgs., illus., mass market   **$3.95**

EARTH MOTHER ASTROLOGY
by Marcia Starck
Now, for the first time, a book that combines the science of astrology with current New Age interest in crystals, herbs, aromas, and holistic health. With this book and a copy of your astrological birth chart (readily available from sources listed in the book) you can use your horoscope to benefit your total being—body, mind and spirit. Learn, for example, what special nutrients you need during specific planetary cycles, or what sounds or colors will help you transform emotional states during certain times of the year.

This is a compendium of information for the New Age astrologer and healer. For the beginner, it explains all the astrological signs, planets and houses in a simple and yet new way, physiologically as well as symbolically.

This is a book of modern alchemy, showing the reader how to work with earth energies to achieve healing and transformation, thereby creating a sense of the cosmic unity of all Earth's elements.
0-87542-741-3, 294 pgs., 5¼ × 8   **$12.95**

THE GODDESS BOOK OF DAYS
by Diane Stein
Diane Stein has created this wonderful guide to the Goddesses and festivals for every day of the year! This beautifully illustrated perpetual datebook will give you a listing for every day of the special Goddesses associated with that date along with plenty of room for writing in your appointments. It is a hardbound book for longevity, and has over 100 illustrations of Goddesses from around the world and from every culture. This is sure to have a special place on your desk. None other like it!
0-87542-758-8, 300 pgs., hardbound, 5¼ x 8, illus.   **$12.95**